MICHAEL E. B

NONPROFIT FINANCE

THE FIELD GUIDE FOR FINANCIAL
OPERATIONS OF MINISTRIES, SCHOOLS,
AND OTHER PUBLIC CHARITIES

Copyright © 2021 Michael E. Batts.

All rights reserved.

No part of this book may be reproduced or transmitted in any form or by any means, electronic or mechanical, including photocopying, recording, or by any information storage and retrieval system, without permission in writing from the publisher.

Published by Christianity Today International
ChurchLawAndTax.com
ChurchLawAndTaxStore.com

Author: Michael E. Batts, CPA
Editors: Jim Bolton, Chris Lutes
Cover Design: Rick Szuecs
Interior Design: Michelle Dowell, Vasil Nazar

Unless otherwise noted, Scripture quotations are taken from HOLY BIBLE: NEW INTERNATIONAL VERSION®. © 1973, 1978, 1984, 2011 by International Bible Society. All rights reserved. Used with permission.

978-1-61407-244-7
24 23 22 21   1 2 3 4

Printed in the United States of America.

Dedication

I would like to dedicate this book with deepest appreciation to my wife, Karen, without whose steadfast love, patience, and encouragement my work would merely be as sounding brass or a tinkling cymbal. My work would not be possible without my wife's enduring support beginning from college days.

Acknowledgements

I would also like to thank my colleagues, Mike Lee, Kim Morrison, Dale Houser, and Danny Johnson, for their excellent work in preparing and reviewing the sample GAAP financial statements provided in Chapter 2 of this book.

I would like to thank my colleagues, Mike Lee and Michele Wales, for their excellent technical review of various components of this book.

Finally, I am extremely grateful for the assistance of my communications team, particularly Monica Brescia and Sarah Mattingly, for their excellent editing and proofing of the book content

Mike Batts

CONTENTS

Introduction xi

CHAPTER 1
MISSION, PURPOSE, AND BUDGETING 1
    It All Starts with Mission and Purpose 1
    Zero-Based Budgeting 2
    Makers of Excellence: What Constitutes
      Excellence in a Program, Activity, or Initiative? 3
    Spending Philosophy 4
    Compensation Philosophy 4
    Budgeting As a Strategy to Improve Liquidity and Financial Position 7
    Accounting Methods Applied in Budgeting 8
    Types of Budgets 10
    Budgeting for Revenue-Generating Activities 11
    Budgeting for Use of Donor-Restricted Funds 11
    Budgeting As an Expense Control Mechanism 14
    Alternatives to the Annual Budgets 18
    Identifying Expense Reductions 20

CHAPTER 2
ACCOUNTING AND FINANCIAL REPORTING 27
    General Definitions 27
    Internal Financial Reporting 28
    Nonprofit Accounting Definitions 34
    Nonprofit Accounting Methods 38
    External Financial Reporting 43
    Nonprofit Accounting Software 45
    Outsourcing Accounting and Financial Reporting 50
    Retention of Nonprofit Records 51
    Record Retention Schedule 53
    Sample GAAP-Basis Financial Statements 59

CHAPTER 3
INCOME—CONTRIBUTIONS 69
    Contributions Revenue 69
    Planned and Deferred Giving 77

Clawbacks of Charitable Contributions—a Continuing Challenge 88
Sample Gift Acceptance Policy 89

CHAPTER 4
OTHER REVENUE SOURCES 93
Alternative Source Revenue 93
Issues to Consider: Mission and Purpose 96
Issues to Consider: Legal 98
Tax Considerations: Unrelated Business Income 98
Specific Exclusions from Unrelated Business Income 103
Debt-Financed Income 109
Federal and State Filing Requirements 117
Implications for State and Local Taxes Other Than Income Taxes 124

CHAPTER 5
COMPENSATION 125
Compensation Is More Than a Number in the Budget 125
Compensation Philosophy 126
Planning and Setting Compensation 127
Benefits 127
Setting Compensation for the Nonprofit's Top Leaders 132
Managing Compensation Expense 135

CHAPTER 6
MANAGING LIQUIDITY AND FINANCIAL POSITION 139
Philosophy of Liquidity and Financial Position 139
Philosophy of Debt 140
Philosophy of Cash Flow Surpluses 140
Targeting and Achieving Desired Financial Position 143
Recommended Liquidity and Financial Position Objectives 144
Investment Management 148
The Uniform Prudent Management of Institutional Funds Act 148
Investment Philosophy 150
Investment Policy 150
Asset Management 151
Use and Management of Debt 152
Mortgage Debt Options and Terms 159
Tax-Exempt Financing 167
Bond Financing 167
10 Rules for Financial Health in a Nonprofit Private School 168

CHAPTER 7
MAINTAINING SOUND INTERNAL CONTROL ... 177
- A Biblical Example of Internal Control ... 177
- The Concept of Internal Control ... 177
- Practical Applicability of Internal Control for Nonprofits ... 178
- "Tone at the Top" ... 179
- Adequate Staffing and Financial Expertise: An Important Priority ... 179
- Screening Finance and Accounting Employees ... 180
- Insurance Coverage For Employee Dishonesty ... 181
- Protecting Cash Transactions ... 182
- Key Principles of Internal Control for Cash Transactions ... 184
- Specific Internal Controls Over Cash Transactions ... 188
- Safeguarding of Assets Other Than Cash ... 198
- Relevant and Timely Financial Reporting ... 199
- Compliance with Applicable Laws and Regulations ... 200

CHAPTER 8
AUDITS AND OTHER FINANCIAL ACCOUNTABILITY ACTIVITIES ... 201
- Financial Accountability ... 201
- Independent Accreditation—a Verifiable Demonstration of Accountability ... 201
- Audit ... 203
- Review ... 205
- Compilation ... 206
- Outsourced Accounting Services (With or Without Compilation) ... 207
- Agreed-Upon Procedures ... 208
- Advisory Services ... 211
- Internal Audits ... 212

CHAPTER 9
TAX COMPLIANCE ... 217
- What Tax Compliance Matters Should Be on the Radar of Nonprofit Leaders? ... 218
- Federal Tax Exemption Recognition for Nonprofits ... 219
- Organization ... 219
- Operations ... 219
- Private Inurement, Excess Benefit Transactions, and Private Benefit ... 220
- Political Campaign Intervention ... 226
- Lobbying ... 227
- Violation of Public Policy ... 228
- Unrelated Business Income ... 229
- Payroll Taxes ... 230

    Form 990 232
    IRS Examinations 236
    State Income Tax Exemption 237
    State and Local Sales and Use Tax 238
    State and Local Property Tax 239

CHAPTER 10
GOVERNANCE AND POLICIES 241
    Sources for Sample Policies 247
    Policies that Every Nonprofit Should Probably Have 248
    Policies that Nonprofits Should Have If Certain Factors Are Present 253

CHAPTER 11
RISK MANAGEMENT 255
    A Collaborative Approach Involving Both the Board and Staff 255
    All Risks Are Financial Risks 255
    Practical Application of Risk Management Steps 256
    Preventive Action Is the First Step—Insurance Is Secondary 258
    Risk Management Is an Ongoing, Recurring Process 259
    Areas of Risk to Consider 259
    Additional Resources 265

APPENDIX A
SAMPLE CONFLICTS-OF-INTEREST POLICY 267

APPENDIX B
SAMPLE EXECUTIVE COMPENSATION-SETTING POLICY 273

APPENDIX C
SAMPLE POLICY ON DISHONESTY, FRAUD, AND WHISTLEBLOWER PROTECTION 277

INTRODUCTION

Operating a nonprofit while treating financial administration as a nuisance is like building your home on a landfill. Financial administration is a critically important and foundational element of a sound and healthy nonprofit. Done well, financial administration helps the nonprofit establish its solid foundation. When financial administration is done poorly, every day can bring a new emergency or crisis, which can impair the credibility of the organization's message or otherwise impede its ability to carry out its mission effectively. And, while sound financial administration is critical to a nonprofit's health, we must remember that financial administration is a supporting role to the nonprofit's true purpose. Financial administration is not the "main thing" and should never become the "tail that wags the dog."

In some ways, financial administration is like the marker lines, guard rails, and signs on an interstate highway—with messages like "Caution," "Rough Shoulder," "Steep Grade Ahead," and "Speed Limit." The driver on the highway has a mission—to get to his destination. The signs, markings, and guard rails on the highway let him know what to watch out for along the way…and help him get to his destination safely. The signs and markings are not obstacles or impediments to the journey—they are aids. Those of us who serve in the arena of financial administration must keep that in mind. Our role is to aid the nonprofit's leaders in the journey and help them arrive safely at their destination. Of course, a fundamental premise in this metaphor is that the nonprofit leaders themselves (the drivers) are safety-minded…that they share the desire to arrive at the destination safely. When those dynamics exist together, the nonprofit can be incredibly effective.

An important aspect of financial administration is the principle of financial integrity. If a nonprofit organization cannot and will not stand for integrity in its finances—at least two very serious questions arise:

- How can any other aspect of its operations be trusted?
- What kind of message does that convey about the character and integrity of its leaders?

We start from the premise in this book that the nonprofit organization's leaders desire to operate with financial integrity—indeed, to be "above reproach." A major aim of this book is to make it practical and useful on a daily operational basis for people serving in financial leadership in nonprofits across the country. I hope you find it to be just that.

The topic of nonprofit finance can seem daunting—even overwhelming at times. With so many laws, rules, best practices, and other considerations that can apply to the financial administration of a nonprofit, even the best financial and administrative leaders need help from time to time in addressing particular issues. It is my privilege to work on this project. I sincerely hope that this book will serve as a helpful resource to those who are serving the nonprofit sector. Your work has a significant impact. May God bless you in it.

Mike Batts

CHAPTER 1

Mission, Purpose, and Budgeting

IT ALL STARTS WITH MISSION AND PURPOSE

Addressing nonprofit budgets starts with understanding the broader context of a nonprofit's mission and purpose. If a budget represents the financial blueprint for carrying out a nonprofit's strategic plan for a particular period of time, then logic would dictate that such a blueprint and its related strategic plan should be a function—a derivative—of the nonprofit's mission and purpose. Many times, however, nonprofits engage in elaborate budget development processes without first evaluating whether their activities are in alignment with their mission and purpose. In some cases, nonprofits operate without a well-defined expression of their mission and purpose. Ensuring that the nonprofit's budget is a function of its mission and purpose will help nonprofit leaders avoid putting the cart before the horse, or for that matter, having the cart *detached from* the horse.

No, your mission and purpose are not obvious

It may be tempting to assume that the mission and purpose of a nonprofit with a particular area of focus (e.g., a K-12 school) are obvious. An assumption like that can cause an organization's leaders to reason that there is little value for their organization to take the time to clearly express its mission and purpose. Such an assumption would be misguided, however, since each nonprofit is as unique as the individuals who comprise it—the mere fact that a nonprofit happens to have a particular area of focus does not make its mission and purpose obvious.

Let's consider an example of a nonprofit K-12 school. What is the specific calling of the school? Is it to prepare students for admission to rigorous, selective-admission colleges? Is it to provide students with a path for vocational training? Is it to offer an array of athletic and non-athletic extracurricular activities? Does the school plan to have specific admissions standards? What are they? Why? Is the school called to educate students in matters of faith? To what degree? Are families whose children enroll in the school expected to adhere to a particular faith? If so, why? What degree of quality does the school envision employing in its classroom and extracurricular activities? Are faculty members expected to have advanced degrees? Does the school envision attaining certain observable targets for the academic success of its students? What are those standards? What is the governance model for the school? Are parents involved in electing the governing body? Why or why not? From this limited list of questions alone, it should be clear that school leaders cannot reasonably take the position that their school's mission and purpose are obvious based simply on the fact that the organization is a school. To take such a position is to have no clear sense of specific direction and no underpinning rubric for developing a budget or a financial plan.

In addressing and expressing its own mission and purpose, a nonprofit must evaluate its own identity—its own calling. Nonprofit leaders should ask the following questions:

> For what *specific* purposes does our nonprofit exist?

> What are the *specific* objectives our nonprofit is called to accomplish or carry out?

Are we on mission?

Once a nonprofit has identified and clearly articulated its mission and purpose, it must identify the *specific* programs, activities, and initiatives that it intends to employ in order to accomplish its mission and purpose. In performing this step, the nonprofit should evaluate all of its *existing* programs, activities, and initiatives to determine whether they *significantly* assist the nonprofit in effectively accomplishing its mission and purpose. This step of the introspection process presents a great opportunity for nonprofits to critically evaluate the effectiveness of each of their programs, activities, and initiatives. The nonprofit is also able to make wise stewardship decisions by eliminating programs, activities, and initiatives that are not on mission or do not significantly carry out the nonprofit's mission and purpose.

> **The nonprofit should evaluate all of its *existing* programs, activities, and initiatives to determine whether they *significantly* assist the nonprofit in effectively accomplishing its mission and purpose.**

ZERO-BASED BUDGETING

The concept of critically evaluating the nonprofit's programs, activities, and initiatives is highly compatible with the use of "zero-based budgeting." Zero-based budgeting is the practice of deciding what specific activities should be conducted in order to carry out the nonprofit's mission and what those activities will cost.

Zero-based budgeting does not involve increasing or decreasing the prior year budget, a practice commonly referred to as "incremental budgeting." Rather, it starts with a blank sheet and asks the director of foster care services, for example, to list each activity or initiative he or she believes should be conducted within the foster care program and to apply a cost to each activity or initiative. Accordingly, when adjustments are made, they are not in the form of "10 percent across the board." Rather, they are in the form of "let's reduce the number of trips to theme parks for foster families this year." Applied across the entire nonprofit to every department, a genuine use of zero-based budgeting has an amazing knack for ferreting out waste and nonessential activity. It also allows nonprofit leaders to make specific priority decisions on an activity-by-activity or program-by-program basis, rather than in simple percentages or dollar amounts. It facilitates surgery with a scalpel as opposed to an ax.

MAKERS OF EXCELLENCE: WHAT CONSTITUTES EXCELLENCE IN A PROGRAM, ACTIVITY, OR INITIATIVE?

Once the nonprofit has identified the programs, activities, and initiatives that it believes will help the nonprofit effectively carry out its particular mission and purpose, nonprofit leaders should take the appropriate next step, which is to identify the attributes of each program, activity, and initiative that represent excellence. In other words, nonprofit leaders should ask the following question with respect to each program, activity, or initiative in which the nonprofit plans to engage:

What attributes of this program, activity, or initiative would constitute excellence?

Or, stated another way:

Markers of excellence are the identifiable, observable, and often measurable attributes that define whether a particular program, activity, or initiative is conducted with excellence (the inputs are excellent) and/or has excellent results (the outputs are excellent).

How will we need to conduct this program, activity, or initiative in order for it to be carried out in an excellent manner?

My term for the answers to this question with respect to any program, activity, or initiative is: **Markers of Excellence.**

Markers of excellence are the identifiable, observable, and often measurable attributes that define whether a particular program, activity, or initiative is conducted with excellence (the inputs are excellent) and/or has excellent results (the outputs are excellent).

Once nonprofit leaders have determined the answers to this question, they will have a much clearer ability to identify the costs associated with a particular program, activity, or initiative.

EXAMPLE Food Service Program in a Nonprofit School — Markers of Excellence
Assume that ABC School plans to operate a food service program to serve lunches to students attending the school. The leaders of the ABC School identify the "markers of excellence" for their food service program. The markers of excellence might include:

- Offering high quality, nutritious, and appealing food to students, faculty, and employees.
- Providing gluten-free, vegetarian, and vegan options.
- Polling students and parents periodically about food allergies, with staff adapting accordingly as potential risks are identified.
- Serving food and beverages cafeteria-style, with a very high quality presentation.
- Training servers to be very positive, friendly, and professional.
- Upholding the highest standards for sanitation practices.
- Using quality reusable dinnerware and flatware (not disposable), and ensuring it is thoroughly cleaned and dried.
- Creating an attractive environment, including the use of tables and chairs that are of high quality in function and appearance.
- Limiting costs to a certain amount per meal.

SPENDING PHILOSOPHY

Every nonprofit has a spending philosophy, whether it realizes it or not. In fact, nonprofits rarely articulate their particular spending philosophy. But a visitor can walk into a nonprofit's facilities and quickly observe the nonprofit's spending philosophy. A nonprofit headquarters with ornate architecture, travertine floors, dramatic lighting, marble columns, and manicured grounds clearly communicates a specific spending philosophy. On the other hand, a humble nonprofit building with worn carpet, exposed wiring, a patchwork of architecture, faded paint, and basic fixtures clearly communicates a different spending philosophy.

In the budgeting process, it is helpful for a nonprofit to define its spending philosophy. Such an expression provides useful parameters for spending prioritization decisions, which is immensely helpful when a nonprofit is considering construction or renovation of its facilities or the operation of its programs.

COMPENSATION PHILOSOPHY

Compensation often represents the largest single category of expense for nonprofits, and typically comprises a very large percentage (if not the majority) of a nonprofit's operating budget.

Before a nonprofit can begin making appropriate decisions about the compensation of its staff, the nonprofit must determine its compensation philosophy. Specifically, the nonprofit should decide how the compensation of its staff should compare with the compensation of other comparable nonprofits. In determining how a nonprofit's compensation of its employees compares with that of similar nonprofits, the nonprofit should look to nonprofit salary data. Compensation data for nonprofits is available from a variety of sources. Some data is specific to particular categories of nonprofits (e.g., foundations) and some data is more general. Some of the more general data (e.g., that which is available from GuideStar.org) can be parsed and stratified to identify data for particular segments of the nonprofit sector. In addition to GuideStar.org, other widely referenced sources for general nonprofit compensation data include The Nonprofit Times, The Chronicle of Philanthropy, and Association Trends. The National Council of Nonprofits is also a good source for information about region-specific nonprofit compensation data. Nonprofits that operate in subsectors served by associations in which they are members (e.g., hospitals, schools, religious organizations, etc.) should inquire of the associations of which they are members about the availability of subsector-specific compensation data. In some cases, it may be appropriate for a nonprofit to use compensation data from the for-profit sector for comparability—especially with respect to positions for which there are for-profit counterparts (e.g., physicians and nurses in for-profit hospitals, finance professionals, etc.)

Determining how a nonprofit's staff compensation compares to that of its peers is only part of the process. A nonprofit's compensation philosophy dictates *how* that particular nonprofit *intends* for its staff compensation to compare to its peer group. Some nonprofits express their compensation philosophy in terms of a *percentile* of their peer group. For example, a nonprofit may decide that it generally intends for its staff compensation to be in about the 75th percentile of its peer group. Alternatively, a nonprofit may express its compensation philosophy in terms of a relationship to the *average* (e.g., above average, average, and so on). Whichever way the nonprofit chooses to express its compensation philosophy, it is important and helpful for the nonprofit to do so, and for the nonprofit to express the basis for its particular philosophy.

In doing so, the nonprofit should also take into consideration the demographics of its donors and constituents, who may have certain expectations regarding the organization's compensation practices.

A nonprofit's staff compensation philosophy generally may be described by one of the following classifications:

- Well above average
- Above average
- Average
- Modest
- Vow of poverty

Consider individuality

While a compensation philosophy will guide the nonprofit broadly in its compensation planning, the nonprofit must take into consideration the individual skills, performance, abilities, and contribution of each employee in setting compensation. As a result, the compensation of individual employees may vary somewhat (within reason) from the norm established by the nonprofit's compensation philosophy. Of course, the nonprofit should document its basis for deciding to compensate an individual at a level that exceeds the amount supported by comparability data and the nonprofit's general compensation philosophy.

The need to document the nonprofit's basis for an individual compensation decision is particularly important when establishing compensation for the nonprofit's top leaders. As is described in more detail in Chapter 5, federal tax laws provide parameters for determining the reasonableness of the compensation of the top leaders of a 501(c)(3) nonprofit organization. Failure to comply with federal tax law in this area can subject the nonprofit's leaders to potential personal financial penalties and can, in extreme cases, jeopardize the nonprofit's federal tax-exempt status.

Don't forget benefits

When establishing compensation for the nonprofit's staff, nonprofit leaders not only must consider the regular salary or wages paid to each person, but also the benefits provided. The benefits package provided to a nonprofit's employees is just as relevant as salary or wages when it comes to performing any analysis of comparability. Accordingly, when a nonprofit compares the compensation of its staff to that of various peer groups by using salary survey data or other similar information, the nonprofit must be careful to ensure that benefits are not neglected in the analysis.

Additionally, under federal tax law, when determining whether a nonprofit leader's compensation is reasonable, all forms of compensation (including benefits) are taken into consideration—both taxable and nontaxable.

BUDGETING AS A STRATEGY TO IMPROVE LIQUIDITY AND FINANCIAL POSITION

A nonprofit's budgeting process should be much more strategic than simply estimating revenues and expenses. The budgeting process for a nonprofit is a pivotal moment in time in which the nonprofit has a unique opportunity to implement and follow a strategic financial plan.

This chapter on the topic of "Mission, Purpose, and Budgeting" should be read jointly with Chapter 6, on the topic of "Managing Liquidity and Financial Position," as these two topics go hand-in-glove. As described in more detail in Chapter 6, a nonprofit should set specific, targeted objectives for achieving a desired financial position as well as a timeframe for doing so. The combination of a specific, targeted financial position and a timeframe provides a roadmap for nonprofit leaders in their planning and budgeting.

How does the budget fit into the nonprofit's overall financial plan and how does it help the nonprofit achieve its financial objectives?

Before a nonprofit can answer that question, it must assess whether it has a financial plan and financial objectives. A financial plan and financial objectives include such elements as:

> **The budgeting process for a nonprofit is a pivotal moment in time in which the nonprofit has a unique opportunity to implement and follow a strategic financial plan.**

- Establishing cash operating reserves or debt service reserves of $ (amount) within a stated period of time.
- Reducing debt by $ (amount) within a stated period of time.
- Building a maintenance and replacement fund of $ (amount) within a stated period of time.

The false comfort of a "balanced budget"

In order to ensure that the nonprofit has adequate financial capacity to carry out its programs, activities, and initiatives, its leaders must ensure that the nonprofit's financial plan is sound. Sound financial management includes development and approval of a responsible operating budget. Many nonprofits operate under the belief that there is something improper about generating a positive bottom line—that is, a surplus of revenues over expenses. In fact, in many nonprofits, a desirable budget is a "balanced budget." While operating a balanced budget may seem like an admirable goal, it simply means that the nonprofit expects to incur expenses equal to its revenues. The term "balanced budget" sounds attractive because the term has a positive connotation (what's the alternative—an *"unbalanced* budget"? That doesn't sound like a good thing!). But, if the nonprofit's budget is prepared on a cash basis and the nonprofit has a "balanced budget," the nonprofit is essentially saying that it plans to spend every nickel of revenue that it brings in, with little or no room for error. An unexpected dip in revenues in an organization that follows such a practice can cause immediate financial stress for the nonprofit and its leaders. That is no way to manage a nonprofit's financial position.

A better approach to budgeting involves determining the nonprofit's desired or targeted financial position (liquidity, reserves, debt levels, and so on) and the desired timetable for achieving it. With a long-term plan for improving financial position, the nonprofit can develop operating budgets that not only provide for carrying out its mission and purpose, but also can contemplate using reasonable surpluses to contribute toward the targeted financial position.

Improving a nonprofit's liquidity and financial position requires intentional effort as an essential part of the planning and budgeting process. That effort must include planning to spend less than what the nonprofit receives in cash revenues. For a nonprofit that has been following the habit of spending all of its cash receipts annually, the transition can be challenging. If the nonprofit's revenues are growing, the nonprofit may be able to make progress in this area by slowing or stopping spending increases as revenues rise. For nonprofits whose revenues are not growing significantly, the transition will require the nonprofit to pursue additional revenue (through additional contributions from donors or from alternative revenue sources—see Chapters 3 and 4 for more information on these topics), apply expense reductions, or apply a combination of the two.

> **With a long-term plan for improving financial position, the nonprofit can develop operating budgets that not only provide for carrying out its mission and purpose, but also can contemplate using reasonable surpluses to contribute toward the targeted financial position.**

ACCOUNTING METHODS APPLIED IN BUDGETING

Nonprofits often prepare their operating budgets using the cash basis of accounting. Budgets prepared in this manner are, essentially, cash flow budgets. A primary weakness of cash basis budgets is the fact that they exclude depreciation expense. As is more fully described in Chapter 2, depreciation is a noncash expense that represents the "using up" or deterioration of a long-lived asset. Property and equipment other than land generally deteriorate over time and typically must be either repaired, refurbished, or replaced in the future. Nonprofits often overlook this very real economic expense that occurs continuously as assets deteriorate or are used up. Failure to recognize depreciation expense in the budgeting process creates an inadequate representation of the nonprofit's total expenses and can make it difficult for a nonprofit to achieve its targets for liquidity and financial position.

> **EXAMPLE** A nonprofit prepares its operating budgets using the cash basis of accounting. Depreciation expense is not recognized. The operating budget reflects estimated revenues for the year of $2.5 million and estimated cash operating expenses of an equal amount. The nonprofit considers this a "balanced budget," and follows this practice every year. If it were recognized, depreciation expense related to the deterioration of the nonprofit's property and equipment would amount to $400,000 annually. In reality, this nonprofit's operating budget is planning for a $400,000 deficit for the year because the very real economic expense of depreciation is not being recognized in its cash flow budget. At some point in the future, the nonprofit will be required to deal with the deterioration of its assets. The fact that the nonprofit has operated with no cash flow surpluses in prior years will not help the nonprofit build reserves to address its future property and equipment needs.

Funding depreciation

The practice of including depreciation expense in a nonprofit's operating budget, while still maintaining a bottom line that is either break-even ("balanced") or better, is sometimes referred to as "funding depreciation."

The practice of funding depreciation in an operating budget can be a big and challenging step for a nonprofit that has never done it, as implementing such a change could significantly affect other areas of the operating budget. As a result, nonprofit leaders may be reluctant to implement such a change. In such cases, the nonprofit should implement the practice of funding depreciation over a period of time, rather than all at once. Nonprofits should recognize depreciation expense in their operating budgets regardless of whether the depreciation is fully funded. This practice may result in an operating budget that reflects a deficit, but the more accurate the budget picture, the better the chances nonprofit leaders and those responsible for the nonprofit's financial oversight will realize the effects of depreciation on the nonprofit's overall economics. This picture may serve as an impetus to make funding depreciation a priority and a regular practice for the nonprofit's budget, even if it takes a period of time for the nonprofit to fully do so.

The accounting method used for budgeting should align with the accounting method used for internal financial reporting

Chapter 2 describes, in detail, the accounting methods used by nonprofits for internal financial reporting purposes. Whatever the method of accounting used by a nonprofit's leaders to monitor the nonprofit's ongoing financial activities, the same method of accounting should be used in developing the nonprofit's operating budget.

Use of the same accounting method for budgeting and internal financial reporting purposes makes it possible to effectively monitor and evaluate the nonprofit's actual operating results compared to its budget. Such a comparison is difficult, if not impossible, when the accounting methods used for budgeting and internal financial reporting are different. That fact notwithstanding, many nonprofits employ accounting methods for budgeting that differ from those used for the nonprofit's internal financial reporting—an unsound and even dangerous practice.

TYPES OF BUDGETS

A nonprofit operating budget should reflect the nonprofit's estimated revenues and expenses. Two significant elements of a nonprofit's cash disbursements do not constitute expenses—capital expenditures and debt principal reduction. Rather, a capital expenditure represents the purchase of, or improvement to, one or more assets. A debt

---

EXAMPLE ABC Nonprofit developed the following capital expenditures and debt principal reduction budgets for the year 20XX:

CAPITAL EXPENDITURES BUDGET

Roof replacement—headquarters	$ 40,000
New carpet—satellite office	$ 20,000
New computers	$ 12,000
Total capital expenditures	**$ 72,000**

Sources of funds	
Special gifts	$ 10,000
Operating surplus	$ 62,000
Total sources of funds	**$ 72,000**

DEBT PRINCIPAL REDUCTION BUDGET

Required principal reduction per terms of note	$ 64,300
Additional planned principal reduction	$ 35,700
Total debt principal reduction	**$ 100,000**

Sources of funds	
Operating surplus	$ 100,000
Total sources of funds	**$ 100,000**

principal reduction expenditure results in a decrease of one or more of the nonprofit's liabilities.

Accordingly, a nonprofit should prepare both an *operating budget* and a *capital expenditures budget* for the applicable period. If the nonprofit has outstanding debt, it should also prepare a *debt principal reduction budget*.

For a capital expenditures budget or a debt principal reduction budget, it is essential for the nonprofit to identify the sources of funds that will be used to make the capital or debt principal reduction expenditures. The sources of funds may be a surplus from the operating budget, cash reserves, special gifts expected to be raised for the particular purpose, or other sources.

BUDGETING FOR REVENUE-GENERATING ACTIVITIES

Some nonprofits do not include in their operating budgets the revenues and expenses related to auxiliary activities—particularly those that are self-supporting or that generate revenues from fees or other charges. For auxiliary activities that are partially self-supporting, nonprofits sometimes include in their operating budget an estimate for the "subsidy" that the nonprofit intends to provide from general funds to support the auxiliary activity. Examples of auxiliary activities for which nonprofits sometimes fail to fully budget include, but are not limited to, food service operations, special educational or missional group trips, and educational programs for which fees are charged. For a variety of reasons, it is a best practice for a nonprofit to budget the entire amount of revenues and expenses for its auxiliary activities. One significant reason to follow such a practice is that the operating budget serves as an internal control mechanism; comparing actual results to budgeted results can help identify aberrations or anomalies in revenues or expenses that require further attention. Additionally, failure to budget for the details of auxiliary activities often goes hand-in-hand with a failure to monitor financial reports for such activities—which is definitely a dangerous practice.

BUDGETING FOR USE OF DONOR-RESTRICTED FUNDS

Interestingly, nonprofits rarely have a formal policy that addresses who among the organization's leadership has the authority to release donor-restricted funds and to make specific decisions as to how such funds are to be spent. Additionally, nonprofits rarely budget for the specific use of donor-restricted funds other than building funds. For example, many nonprofits maintain donor-restricted funds to support building projects for new or improved facilities. As money accumulates in the nonprofit's building fund, decisions are made regarding expenditures made from the building fund. But who makes those decisions? And by what authority do they make those decisions? Does the nonprofit's governing board make the decisions? Is the nonprofit's staff leadership authorized to make such decisions? Are the expenditures budgeted? This area is often a "twilight zone" for nonprofits. Frequently, nonprofits simply follow a pattern of practices that they have developed over the years—and no one questions those practices—at least not until a misunderstanding or disagreement erupts.

Lack of a clear policy and board-approved practices for the expenditure of donor-restricted funds has been a source of numerous conflicts—some of them very serious—in nonprofits across America. Such conflicts have, in some cases, resulted in allegations of misappropriation and terminations of top nonprofit executives.

EXAMPLE Gertrude Johnson left a bequest in her will for ABC Nonprofit in the amount of $1,000,000 with a stipulation that the gift is to be used by the nonprofit to support its literacy program. The nonprofit received the bequest in 20X1. The nonprofit's CFO decided to apply $200,000 from Gertrude's bequest toward regular literacy program activities in each of the years 20X1 through 20X5, thereby reducing the amount that the nonprofit would ordinarily budget and spend from its general fund on its literacy program expenses. The CFO's decision to apply Gertrude's bequest in this manner was not clearly communicated to the nonprofit's governing board. Additionally, the nonprofit had no policy addressing who among the nonprofit's leaders has the authority to make spending decisions with respect to donor-restricted gifts, and the nonprofit's budgets do not address the use of donor-restricted gifts.

> **Lack of a clear policy and board-approved practices for the expenditure of donor-restricted funds has been a source of numerous conflicts—some of them very serious—in nonprofits across America**

In the year 20X6, the nonprofit began to explore constructing a new building to be dedicated to the organization's literacy program. Members of the nonprofit's board thought that it would be wise and appropriate to use Gertrude's bequest for the construction of the new building. Members of the nonprofit board were shocked to learn that Gertrude's bequest had already been fully expended on the regular operations of the nonprofit's literacy program under the direction of the CFO. Allegations of misappropriation and impropriety began to swirl. Allegations were also made by members of Gertrude's family that using Gertrude's restricted gift funds to replace regularly budgeted literacy program expenses was unethical and was inconsistent with Gertrude's expectations.

The organization's board members were livid over the CFO's decision to expend the funds. The CFO, however, argued that historically the CFO has made decisions regarding the expenditure of donor-restricted funds, and that the use of Gertrude's funds aligned with the stipulation in her bequest. Gertrude's family members shared their grievances and concerns with the media and in social media, creating a significant public relations challenge for the organization. Three of the nonprofit's board members resigned. The CFO was terminated. And the new literacy program building was never built.

This tragic example is an all-too-real scenario in the nonprofit sector.

Is it ethical to use donor-restricted funds to replace regularly budgeted expenses?

A frequent question among nonprofits is whether it is ethical for a nonprofit to use donor-restricted funds to replace regularly budgeted program expenses. For example, assume that a nonprofit regularly budgets and spends 5 percent of its operating budget on grants to a local homeless shelter. One of the nonprofit's donors makes a large gift to the nonprofit with a restriction stipulating that the gift must be used to support homelessness. Would it be ethical for the nonprofit to use these restricted funds to replace the funds that the nonprofit would normally spend from its operating budget on grants to the local homeless shelter—thereby freeing such funds for general use?

EXAMPLE Following is an example of a capital expenditures budget incorporating the use of donor-restricted gifts as an element of the budget:

CAPITAL EXPENDITURES BUDGET

New literacy building	$ 500,000
New computers	$ 12,000
New vehicles	$ 60,000
Total capital expenditures	**$ 572,000**
Sources of funds	
Release of restricted gift—Gertrude Johnson bequest for literacy	$ 500,000
Operating surplus	$ 72,000
Total sources of funds	**$ 572,000**

Using donor-restricted funds to replace regularly budgeted expenses is viewed by some as an unethical practice. Such a practice can be perceived as "sleight-of-hand" in the arena of financial administration. Additionally, such a practice has the potential to offend donors or, in the case of donors who are deceased, their families. If a donor makes a gift to a nonprofit that is restricted for a particular purpose, the donor should have a reasonable basis for believing that the restricted gift will be used to fund programs, activities, or initiatives that would not otherwise be funded by the nonprofit's regular operating budget. It is a best practice to avoid using donor-restricted gifts to replace regularly budgeted operating expenses. Failure to follow such an approach may cause reputational damage. Nonprofits that adhere to such a philosophy may wish to adopt policy language to that effect.

Budgeting for use of donor-restricted funds as a control mechanism

A nonprofit can avoid tragic occurrences like the one described in the example on page 12 by having a clear policy governing the expenditure of donor-restricted funds. As a best practice, the policy needs to have clearly delineated lines of authority for approving the release of donor-restricted funds and for making individual expenditures of such funds. The policy should also require planned expenditures of donor-restricted funds to be incorporated into specific budgets (e.g., the operating budget, capital expenditures budget, or debt principal reduction budget) as appropriate. To incorporate the expenditure of donor-restricted funds into the operating budget, a line item adjacent to the estimated revenues can be included that represents "release of donor-imposed restrictions" or "resources provided from donor-restricted gifts." Including such a line item would reflect the authorization to use donor-restricted gifts. The expenditures related to use of the funds would be included in the appropriate section of the budget for expenditures. Requiring that the release of donor-restricted funds and related expenditures be incorporated into the budgeting process adds an element of healthy control to the use of such funds.

BUDGETING AS AN EXPENSE CONTROL MECHANISM

Nonprofit leaders have widely varying views on the purpose and function of the nonprofit's operating budget. For some, the operating budget is merely an estimate or a rough guideline of expectations for financial activities during the applicable period. For nonprofit leaders who have this view of the operating budget, the budget is not an authoritative document, nor is it an expense control mechanism. For others, an operating budget—once approved—is an official expression of limitation on the amount of expenses that may be incurred by the nonprofit. For nonprofits that have this view, any expenditure in excess of what is authorized in the operating budget may not be incurred without specific approval.

A nonprofit's view on whether the budget acts as an expense control mechanism or is simply a helpful guide depends in large part on the nonprofit's governance model and nonprofit polity. Traditionally, it has been common for nonprofits to view the annual operating budget as an official limitation on the nonprofit's spending that cannot be exceeded without specific authorization.

Regardless of a nonprofit's view of the role and authority of the budget with respect to expense control, every nonprofit should still actively engage in a meaningful and thorough budgeting process as a best practice for financial planning purposes, good stewardship, and as an element of sound internal control.

> Every nonprofit should still actively engage in a meaningful and thorough budgeting process as a best practice for financial planning purposes, good stewardship, and as an element of sound internal control.

So we're going over budget...now what?

For nonprofits that view the operating budget as an expense control mechanism, the matter of how to deal with expenditures in excess of budgeted amounts is an important element of policy that is often poorly developed. For example, a nonprofit operating budget will typically include line items for each of the nonprofit's main areas of program operations.

Suppose a nonprofit develops and approves an operating budget for the year 20X1 reflecting total expenses of $1.5 million, of which $200,000 relates to educational activities. Also suppose that, due to unexpected developments, it appears the nonprofit's expenses for its educational activities will exceed the amount budgeted by $50,000 for the year.

Is it acceptable for the nonprofit's executive leadership (staff) to make the additional expenditures for the educational activities, so long as total expenses do not exceed the total amount of expenses budgeted for the nonprofit of $1.5 million? Even if nonprofit staff leaders are permitted to reallocate budget line items so long as the total amount spent remains within the amount of total expenses authorized by the budget, who on the nonprofit leadership staff has the authority to make such a reallocation decision? The CFO? The CEO? Or should nonprofit leaders be required to obtain specific authorization to incur expenses that exceed the amount budgeted for the educational activities? If authorization is required in order to exceed expenses for an individual line item or for the budget as a whole, who must provide that authorization? If the organization's board of directors has a finance committee, must the finance committee approve such a variance? Or must such approval be granted by the board of directors or by some other group? Would the answer to these questions change, depending on the amount by which actual expenditures are expected to exceed budgeted amounts?

Many nonprofits do not have good answers to these questions. For nonprofits that view the operating budget as an expense control mechanism, it is essential to have an appropriate budget policy that clearly addresses such matters and leaves little room for misunderstanding.

The following sample budget policy statement may help nonprofits wishing to adopt a policy of their own:

> **Sample Nonprofit Budget Policy** *(For nonprofits in which budgeting serves as an expense control mechanism)*
>
> **1. Budget methods and approvals—operating**
> Annually, the CFO shall, in cooperation with department heads, develop a detailed proposed operating budget for each department, reflecting revenue and expenses using the same method of accounting used by the Nonprofit in preparing its regular financial statements for Finance Committee and Board consideration. The detailed proposed operating budget shall be presented to the Finance Committee for approval no later than _____ (date). Upon approval by the Finance Committee, the approved budget (with any modifications) shall be summarized by department and submitted to the Board for approval no later than _____ (date). Upon approval by the Board of the summarized budget (with any modifications), the budget shall be officially adopted for the respective year. Notwithstanding the official adoption of any budget, management of the Nonprofit is not permitted to authorize expenses in excess of revenue for any year-to-date period without specific approval of the Finance Committee. The Finance Committee is not permitted to authorize expenses in excess of revenue of more than $_____ for any year-to-date period without specific approval of the Board.
>
> Subject to the limitations described in the preceding paragraph, the CFO is permitted to reallocate budgeted amounts from one department to another, so long as the total budget remains unchanged. Subject to the limitations described in the preceding paragraph, department heads are permitted to incur expenses for their respective departments which vary from the amounts budgeted for individual line items, so long as the total expenses for each such department remain within the total amount budgeted for the department.
>
> Variances (expenses in excess of budgeted amounts) by individual departments must be approved by the CFO. Variances in the total operating budget of up to $_____ annu-

ally must be approved by the Finance Committee. Variances in the total operating budget in excess of $_____ annually must be approved by the Board.

All approvals of budgets and variances should be duly recorded in the minutes of the body exercising such authority.

2. Budget methods and approvals—capital expenditures and debt principal reduction

Annually, the CFO shall develop a detailed proposed capital expenditures budget and a proposed debt principal reduction budget reflecting expected sources of funds and proposed expenditures for capital items and principal reduction. The detailed budgets shall be presented to the Finance Committee for approval no later than _____ (date). Upon approval by the Finance Committee, the approved capital expenditures and debt principal reduction budgets (with any modifications) shall be summarized and submitted to the Board no later than _____ (date) for approval. Upon approval by the Board of the summarized capital expenditures and debt principal reduction budgets (with any modifications), the budgets shall be officially adopted for the respective year. Capital expenditures and debt principal reduction may only be made from fund sources identified in and approved as part of the respective budgets. Notwithstanding the official adoption of any budget, management of Nonprofit is not permitted to authorize expenditures in excess of actual authorized fund sources received or available for any year-to-date period without specific approval of the Finance Committee. The Finance Committee is not permitted to authorize expenditures in excess of authorized fund sources received or available of more than $_____ for any year-to-date period without specific approval of the Board. Funds from new borrowings of debt are considered authorized fund sources only if the proceeds of the specific debt are included in the authorized capital expenditures or debt principal reduction budget and the specific debt is approved in advance by the Board pursuant to applicable provisions of the Articles of Incorporation and/or Bylaws.

All approvals of budgets and variances should be duly recorded in the minutes of the body exercising such authority.

3. Budget methods and approvals—auxiliary activities

Annually, the CFO shall, in cooperation with department heads, develop a detailed proposed auxiliary activities budget for ABC Nonprofit, reflecting revenue and expenses using the same method of accounting used by ABC Nonprofit in preparing its regular financial statements for Finance Committee and Board consideration. The detailed proposed auxiliary activities budget shall be presented to the Finance Committee for approval no later than _____ (date). Upon approval by the Finance Committee, the approved auxiliary activities budget (with any modifications) shall be summarized and submitted to the Board no later than _____ (date) for approval. Upon approval by the Board of the summarized auxiliary activities budget (with any modifications), the budgets shall be officially adopted for the respective year. Notwithstanding the official adoption of any budget, management of ABC Nonprofit is not permitted to authorize expenses in excess of income for any year-to-date period without specific approval of the Finance Committee. The Finance Committee is not permitted to authorize expenses in excess of income of more than $ _____ for any year-to-date period without specific approval of the Board.

As an alternative to providing a separate budget for auxiliary activities as described in the preceding paragraph, budgeted revenues and expenses for auxiliary activities may be incorporated into the nonprofit's annual operating budget.

All approvals of budgets and variances should be duly recorded in the minutes of the body exercising such authority.

4. Disbursement and use of restricted funds
All disbursements of donor-restricted funds, to the extent not covered in specifically approved budgets (for example, capital expenditures budgeted from building fund contributions included in the capital expenditures budget) must be approved in advance by the Finance Committee.

Management of ABC Nonprofit must establish proper accounting and tracking of donor-restricted contributions so as to ensure that donor-restricted funds are held until spent for authorized purposes, and that expenditures of such funds are in accordance with applicable donor restrictions. The nonprofit shall not utilize donor-restricted funds to replace funds for regular, recurring operating activities that are ordinarily and customarily budgeted and funded by the nonprofit's general revenues.

ALTERNATIVES TO THE ANNUAL BUDGETS

Nonprofits tend to operate with the mindset that budgeting is a formal, annual process that must be performed in a manner and timeframe that aligns with the nonprofit's fiscal year.

In reality, there is no legal requirement for such a formal or annual process.[1] With improved technologies and availability of more timely financial information on a regular basis, nonprofits are able to monitor and forecast activities and costs on a more dynamic basis than has been the case in the past. As a result, some nonprofits have adopted alternatives to (either as a supplement or in lieu of) the formal, annual budgeting process. These alternatives are more fluid and dynamic. Such an approach allows nonprofit leaders to adapt on an ongoing basis to changing expectations regarding revenues and other dynamic developments. A more dynamic budgeting or forecasting process is likely essential for a nonprofit undergoing rapid change—particularly a nonprofit experiencing rapid growth or a nonprofit that has experienced a sudden and unexpected challenge or crisis. Whether a nonprofit chooses to abandon formal, annual budgeting or not is a decision to be made by its governing body and possibly (depending on the nonprofit's governance model) its membership.

A commonly used alternative to the formal, annual budgeting process is some form of rolling forecast or rolling budget. For example, a nonprofit may adopt a rolling forecast looking forward for the next 12 months and update the forecast each quarter. For obvious reasons, utilizing a rolling forecast or rolling budget in which forecasted or budgeted amounts change frequently presents challenges for a nonprofit that wishes to use its budget as an expense control mechanism. Accordingly, it may be wise for a nonprofit that utilizes a rolling forecast or rolling budget model to officially adopt policies or constraints on spending. For example, a nonprofit may adopt a resolution providing that the financial management of the nonprofit shall result in a minimum cash flow surplus for each calendar quarter or for a calendar year. Such a resolution may also adopt targeted benchmarks for the nonprofit to reach each quarter, or year, as progress toward its longer-term targets for improved liquidity and financial position.

If a rolling forecast or rolling budget model is used, it is still important for the nonprofit to utilize its forecast or budget as a tool for effective fiscal management and internal control. Comparing actual results with budgeted or forecasted amounts for the applicable periods of time is a particularly effective financial oversight exercise and an important element of sound internal control. The fact that the nonprofit may not utilize a formal, annual budgeting process is not a basis for abandoning the process of comparing actual results with forecasted or budgeted amounts.

---

1 Consideration must be made, however, of an individual nonprofit's governing documents (articles of incorporation and bylaws) or, if applicable, requirements of accrediting organizations or other oversight bodies that may impose specific, formal, annual budgeting requirements.

IDENTIFYING EXPENSE REDUCTIONS

No discussion of budgeting would be complete without addressing the topic of reducing expenses. As a normal part of the budgeting process, nonprofits find themselves wishing to conduct more programs, activities, and initiatives than available funds will allow. Additionally, nonprofits that wish to improve their liquidity and financial position may need to reduce expenses in an effort to generate reasonable and appropriate cash flow surpluses to reach their targets.

The obvious places to look

Nonprofits looking to reduce their expenses will typically look first at the rather obvious areas of potential opportunity for cost savings, such as:

- Eliminating staff positions;
- Reducing staff work hours and compensation;
- Reducing employer-paid staff benefits;
- Renegotiating costs with vendors;
- Renegotiating debt terms; and
- Deferring maintenance on property and equipment.

Five not-so-obvious places to look

Following are some not-so-obvious ways that nonprofits may be able to reduce expenses:

1. Mission and purpose exercise

This chapter begins with the observation that "It all starts with mission and purpose." The exercise of clearly identifying a nonprofit's specific mission and purpose, followed by critically evaluating its programs, activities, and initiatives, can be an extraordinarily effective process for ferreting out waste or marginally beneficial programs and activities. The evaluation should help nonprofit leaders determine whether each program, activity, or initiative significantly and effectively contributes to the accomplishment of the nonprofit's mission and purpose. Coupled with a zero-based budgeting approach (described earlier in this chapter), such an exercise can efficiently help nonprofit leaders identify those aspects of the nonprofit's operations that are prime candidates for expense reductions. It can also assist nonprofit leaders in reallocating expense priorities toward those activities that are more effective in accomplishing the nonprofit's mission and purpose.

2. Streamlining processes and systems

Addressing the following questions and many others like them can help a nonprofit streamline its processes and systems and, as a result, operate more efficiently and at a lower cost.

- How much does it cost for your nonprofit to pay a bill with a check? (Not the bill itself—the **process** of paying the bill.) As mentioned in Chapter 6, a *Wall Street Journal* article stated that a business check costs between $4 and $20 to fully prepare and process, and that the cost of writing a check can be as much as five times the cost of an e-payment.
- Does your staff use computerized bank account reconciliation applications? How much time does the account reconciliation process take?
- Are your expense reports submitted on paper with paper receipts attached? How much collective staff time (all staff) is spent preparing and addressing paper expense reports for reimbursement?
- How much collective staff time does your nonprofit spend completing, approving, and otherwise addressing purchase orders and similar authorizations?
- Is giving to your nonprofit as easy as buying a book on Amazon.com? How much time does your staff spend processing check-based contributions?
- When people make a purchase in your nonprofit gift shop or store with a credit card, must they sign a receipt, and must you then store that receipt? Have you considered that many vendors now do not require signatures for payment card transactions?
- How much time does your staff spend filing documents and retrieving (or searching for) documents in paper files? If your nonprofit operates with a paperless filing system, how many steps are involved when your staff members scan documents for electronic storage? Does the scanning process involve them leaving their desks to scan the documents at a central scanner? Do they then return to their desks to find the document they just scanned on the network server?
- Do all of your desk-based employees have multiple computer monitors, allowing them to easily navigate multiple documents at a time?
- Do you still have a person answering your telephones? If yes, is that based on the belief that callers prefer that? Have you reconsidered that belief?

__Illustration of Cost of Lost Efficiency for One Factor - Scanners Not on Desks__
Assume ABC Nonprofit has 10 administrative employees that regularly scan documents an average of 10 times a day each. Assume the average total com-

pensation cost for these employees is $20 per hour. Each time an employee scans a document, she walks to a centralized scanner, scans the document, and returns to her desk. The process takes 3 minutes longer than it would if the employees had individual scanners on their desks. The time differential is 30 minutes per day per employee (based on 3 minutes each time and 10 trips a day). Multiply the 30 minutes per day (a half hour) by the average pay rate of $20 per hour. For five days a week, 48 weeks out of the year, for 10 employees, that's a total cost of 0.5 x $20 x 5 x 48 x 10, or **$24,000 per year for simply not having scanners on employees' desks.**

Nonprofits typically have many processes and systems that have not been seriously evaluated for efficiency. A nonprofit that wishes to reduce its expenses should consider whether there is a significant opportunity to do so by streamlining its processes and systems.

Nonprofit leaders may decide to undertake an effort to streamline the nonprofit's processes and systems themselves. Larger nonprofits may seek out a consultant to assist. A professional discipline exists around the practice of streamlining processes and systems. Much of the professional work conducted in this area utilizes principles of "Lean Six Sigma"—a term attributed to authors Michael George and Robert Lawrence, Jr. Various levels and types of certification exist in this arena. A nonprofit considering engaging a consultant to assist with streamlining its activities should perform appropriate due diligence and check references for comparable clients of the consultant.

3. Energy studies and adaptations

Many nonprofits throughout the United States have found it helpful to engage experts to perform energy usage analyses. Such an expert will typically recommend adaptations to equipment, fixtures, insulation, lighting, software, and usage management systems in order to help the nonprofit operate with greater energy efficiency. The changes necessary to generate significant energy savings may require a substantial initial investment. Of course, a nonprofit must evaluate its expected return on that investment to determine whether making it is a wise decision. Analyses performed for larger nonprofits by reputable energy consulting companies (and, in some cases, utility companies themselves) have generally brought cost savings and satisfaction to the nonprofits that performed them. A nonprofit interested in pursuing the possibility of an energy study should reach out to other nonprofits for referrals to a reputable service provider. The nonprofit may also wish to consult its own electrical utility company to identify energy analysis options that may be available.

4. Outsourcing

Many nonprofits outsource certain aspects of their operations. In many cases, the nonprofit believes the function or activity can be performed more effectively, more efficiently, and less costly by persons or companies that concentrate their work and expertise in the particular field. For example, nonprofits commonly outsource the administration of their employee retirement plans, cafeteria (Section 125) plans, and other employee benefit plans. Many nonprofits with investment portfolios outsource the asset management function for those portfolios. Nonprofits commonly outsource the processing and disbursement of their payrolls. Other services commonly outsourced include grounds maintenance, information technology (IT) services, vehicle maintenance, and security. Nonprofits may also outsource:

- Regular accounting and financial reporting activities
- Bill-paying activities
- Human resources (or some aspects of it, such as employee screening)
- Document printing, preparation, and graphic design
- Document editing and proofing
- Website and social media management
- Public relations
- Food service operations

5. Collaboration

To more effectively and efficiently carry out their mission and purpose, nonprofits sometimes collaborate with each other. While such collaboration is very common in connection with international missions and humanitarian relief activities, collaboration in the arena of domestic program activities is an area of growing interest among nonprofits. Collaboration can take forms that are similar to outsourcing (described previously) and can offer many of the same advantages. The primary differences between collaboration and outsourcing are that:

1. In collaboration arrangements, the nonprofit often participates directly in conducting the respective activities along with the other organizations with which it is collaborating.

2. Outsourcing is most commonly a purely contractual arrangement with a vendor or service provider, whereas some aspects of collaboration may not involve formal contractual agreements.

Here are some examples in which a nonprofit may collaborate with other nonprofits to carry out particular programs, activities, or initiatives:

- XYZ Charity has a desire to meet the needs of some of the homeless people in its area. Rather than starting its own direct service program for the homeless, XYZ Charity collaborates with a local nonprofit homeless shelter in the same community. One of XYZ Charity's staff members works directly with the staff of the local homeless shelter as part of his duties for XYZ Charity. XYZ Charity also provides volunteers from its supporter base to serve at the homeless shelter, and XYZ Charity makes grants to the homeless shelter to help fund its operations.
- XYZ Community Services, a nonprofit organization, has a desire to provide mental health counseling for members of a particular community. Rather than starting its own direct counseling program, XYZ Community Services collaborates with Lighted Way Counseling, a reputable local nonprofit organization dedicated to providing mental health counseling. XYZ Community Services encourages its clients and their families to utilize the services of Lighted Way Counseling. XYZ Community Services enters into a cooperation agreement with Lighted Way Counseling that stipulates certain principles and practices that will be followed whenever Lighted Way counselors work with clients referred by XYZ Community Services. XYZ Community Services provides financial support to Lighted Way Counseling on a regular basis.

A nonprofit that considers collaborating with other nonprofits should take care to ensure that the expectations of all parties involved are clearly spelled out. Depending on the nature and extent of the collaboration, a legal agreement may be appropriate and necessary. Collaboration agreements can take various forms. However, it is wise for a nonprofit considering such an arrangement to consult with its legal counsel in order to ensure that a proposed collaboration arrangement and its related agreements are appropriate for the nonprofit and do not subject the nonprofit to unintended risks or other unanticipated consequences.

CHAPTER 1 | Mission, Purpose, and Budgeting

12 Steps for Sound Nonprofit Budgeting

1	Identify and/or evaluate the nonprofit's mission and purpose.	7	Determine capital expenditures and principal reduction requirements for the relevant period.
2	Identify, evaluate, and critically screen the programs, activities, and initiatives that significantly assist the nonprofit in carrying out its mission and purpose.	8	Identify and determine the costs for carrying out the programs, activities, and initiatives in an excellent manner as identified in Step 3, applying the nonprofit's spending philosophy and compensation philosophy. Aggregate costs with capital expenditures and principal reduction requirements identified in Step 7.
3	For each program, activity, and initiative the nonprofit plans or wishes to conduct, determine and define the markers of excellence.	9	Estimate the resources/funds (revenues) expected to be available for the applicable period.
4	Identify or define the nonprofit's spending philosophy.	10	Assess the estimated revenues as compared with the total costs determined in Step 8 and the desired progress toward liquidity and financial position targets identified in Step 6.
5	Identify or define the nonprofit's compensation philosophy. • Well above average • Above average • Average • Modest • Vow of poverty	11	Make prioritization decisions as necessary to reduce specifically identified costs so that resulting estimated excess of revenues over costs is satisfactory.
6	Identify the nonprofit's targets for sound liquidity and financial position and the timeframe for reaching them, with annual milestones/interim targets.	12	Pursue approval of operating, capital expenditures, and debt reduction budgets in accordance with the organization's policy. Identify specific sources of funds for capital expenditures and debt reduction budgets.

CHAPTER 2

Accounting and Financial Reporting

Nonprofit officials responsible for the nonprofit's accounting and financial reporting should view the nonprofit's decision-making leaders like drivers of an automobile. Driving a car requires continuously using information from numerous sources. A driver keeps within the lines of the highway, follows road signs, watches other vehicles, checks dashboard gauges, and listens to GPS directions. A good and healthy system of accounting and financial reporting is much like the sources of information for a driver on the highway. The accounting and financial reporting system provides nonprofit leaders with critical information necessary for good decision-making and safe navigation toward the goal of carrying out the nonprofit's mission and purpose. As such, the accounting and financial reporting system must provide accurate, timely, and relevant information.

GENERAL DEFINITIONS

Accounting is the process by which the nonprofit's financial operations and transactions are observed, measured, processed, recorded, organized, stored, and formatted. The primary purpose and result is to facilitate **financial reporting**, which may be either **internal** or **external**.

Internal financial reporting provides nonprofit leaders with financial information to assess the financial condition of the nonprofit and to make informed decisions about the operations and activities of the nonprofit.

External financial reporting provides financial statements, which cover a specific period of time, to users who are external to the leadership of the nonprofit. These financial statements facilitate an understanding of the nonprofit's financial position and financial activities. External users of the financial statements may include, but are not limited to, nonprofit constituents, lending institutions, denominational organizations, and accrediting organizations, such as educational accreditation bodies for schools, the Better Business Bureau's Wise Giving Alliance, or (for Christian churches and ministries) ECFA.

INTERNAL FINANCIAL REPORTING

Given the previous analogy about the information a driver uses on the highway, a few key points about the role of internal financial reporting in a nonprofit setting are worthy of consideration.

The internal financial reporting function is a *means*, not an end. Just as a driver uses a variety of sources of information to make decisions while driving toward a destination, nonprofit leaders use financial reporting for wise decision-making regarding the nonprofit's operations and activities. The accounting and financial reporting function serves a supporting and informational role with respect to the leadership of the nonprofit. The accounting function and its people are not, and never should be, viewed as the "driver" or the "destination" with respect to a nonprofit's activities or operations.

Information provided by the financial reporting process must be *timely, accurate,* and *relevant*. Drivers need to know that their automobile is low on fuel before it is empty. Similarly, nonprofit leaders need *timely, accurate*, and *relevant* financial information; this information keeps them apprised of current conditions so that they can make the best possible decisions.

Financial reports must be clear and understandable. Financial reports presented in a highly detailed or technical format typically have limited value for nonprofit leaders. Those who prepare financial reports must take into consideration the fact that the internal users of the reports are not generally accountants. Financial reports must be provided to decision makers in a format and language that they understand.

> **Nonprofit leaders need *timely, accurate,* and *relevant* financial information; this information keeps them apprised of current conditions so that they can make the best possible decisions.**

Who says internal financial reports must look like financial statements?

The most helpful financial reporting information for nonprofit leaders is likely to include a combination of financial and nonfinancial information. Financial information alone presents an incomplete picture. For example, if a nonprofit leader learned that contribution revenues increased for the first half of the year by 20 percent, that statement alone may sound excellent. However, if the 20 percent increase in contributions were annotated with information that a single donor made a large gift accounting for more than the 20 percent increase, and that the number of "giving units" actually declined during the first half of the year, then the nonprofit's leadership would receive a more complete picture—and likely reach different conclusions.

CHAPTER 2 | Accounting and Financial Reporting

With respect to internal financial reporting, there are no rules or laws that dictate the nature, scope, or format of the reports.[1] Accordingly, financial reports should be presented in the manner most helpful to those who use them. Graphs, charts, dashboard-like "gauges," and plain-language narratives are likely to provide the most helpful information in most circumstances.

Examples of financial reports

1. Sample narrative report on liquidity and financial position

The Organization's overall financial position improved during the month of October as compared with September. Weekly contributions from donors averaged approximately $28,000 for the month of October, compared to approximately $24,000 for September. The Organization's operating cash balance increased from approximately $230,000 at the end of September to approximately $270,000 at the end of October. The average number of giving units for October also increased to approximately 750 people compared to about 680 for September. The age of accounts payable invoices remains consistent at approximately 17 days. The Organization continues to pay its bills in a timely manner. Debt payments as a percentage of overall revenue year-to-date is at approximately 20.2 percent, which is within the range the Organization has deemed acceptable. Given the upward trend in the number of giving units and total giving, the overall outlook is good at this time.

We have not yet made meaningful progress toward achieving our goal of maintaining a debt service reserve equal to six months of debt service costs. We plan to begin to address that goal as part of the upcoming year's budgeting process.

2. Gauges

On page 30 is a more visually driven approach to providing the same information described in the sample narrative above.

Who are the users?

The users of internal financial reports typically include members of the nonprofit's leadership team, financial oversight committee, and governing body. In designing a system of internal financial reporting, those who are responsible for preparing financial reports must consider the specific people who will read and use them. They must also consider the nature and scope of information that each user or group of users needs in order to effectively carry out

---

[1] Of course, there are laws prohibiting fraud, misappropriation, and other similar activities.

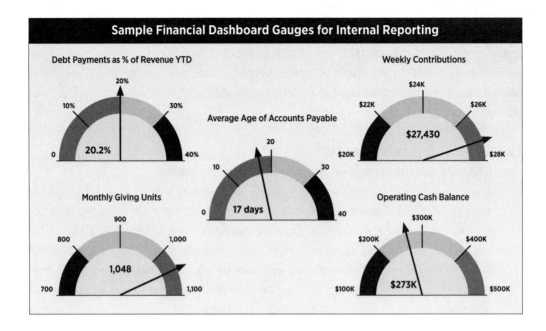

their roles. For example, the CFO of a nonprofit will likely need financial information that is more detailed in nature and scope than the information needed by the nonprofit's governing board. Additionally, the CFO will likely need specific information regarding the financial activities of all areas of the nonprofit's operations, whereas department heads may only need information regarding the financial activities of their respective departments.

What information should be covered by the internal financial reporting process?

Nonprofit leaders should determine the nature and scope of information they need in order to carry out their respective responsibilities. An effective way to make such a determination is to identify the "key questions" they need answered. Once the key questions are identified, nonprofit leaders can evaluate and modify the financial reporting content and format to ensure that the financial reports adequately address the key questions. Questions that nonprofit leaders might incorporate into their list include:

1. Is the organization's current liquidity sound or strong? How do we know?
2. Is the trending in the organization's liquidity improving or declining? Elaborate.
3. What is the organization's current balance for cash and other liquid assets? What is the balance net of donor-restricted and designated amounts? Provide details.

CHAPTER 2 | Accounting and Financial Reporting

4. If current accounts payable and other similar liabilities were paid, how many months of cash operating expenses would the current cash and liquid assets balance (net of donor-restricted and designated amounts) cover?
    a. How does the answer to this question compare to the organization's objectives for this matter?
    b. Is there a plan in place to improve the operating cash reserves balance? What is the plan? How are we doing with respect to implementing the plan?
5. Is the organization paying all of its bills on time?
6. Has the organization had any trouble in recent weeks or months meeting its cash flow demands? If yes, elaborate.
7. Does the organization expect to have any trouble in the foreseeable future with respect to meeting its cash flow demands? If yes, elaborate.
8. Has the organization borrowed any money to fund regular operations or noncapital outlays? If yes, elaborate.
9. Has the organization dipped into donor-restricted or designated cash or investment balances to fund operations at any point during the last year? If yes, elaborate.
10. What is the current balance of the organization's mortgage debt?
11. Are debt payments being made in a timely manner, without any difficulty?
12. Are there any specific financial covenants contained in the organization's loan agreements that stipulate specific financial requirements the organization must meet as a condition of complying with the terms of the loan? If yes, provide details with respect to the nature of each covenant as well as the organization's compliance with the terms of the covenant.
13. What percentage of the organization's total revenues is being spent on servicing the organization's mortgage debt? How does the answer to this question compare to the organization's targets?
14. What is the ratio of the organization's total liabilities to the organization's net assets without donor restrictions?
    a. How does the answer to this question compare to the organization's targets with respect to this matter?
15. What is the balance of the organization's debt service reserves?
    a. How many months of debt service for the organization's existing mortgage debt will this balance cover?
    b. How does the answer to this question compare with the organization's targets with respect to this matter?

c. Is there a plan in place to improve the debt service reserves balance? What is the plan? How are we doing with respect to implementing the plan?
16. Is there any other information not addressed in the previous questions regarding the organization's overall liquidity or financial position that the organization's leadership should know? If yes, provide details.
17. Is the trending with respect to overall contribution revenue favorable or declining?
    a. If declining, what are the causes and what is the organization's leadership doing to address the matter?
    b. Does the trending in the organization's overall contribution revenue align with the trending in the organization's per capita giving? Elaborate and provide details. Is per capita giving from donors trending favorably or unfavorably? Provide details.
18. What other information about the organization's revenues (especially revenues not related to contributions) is relevant to organization leadership?
19. With respect to expenditures, is organization leadership adhering to budget parameters? How do we know?
20. Are expenditures increasing or decreasing? Elaborate as necessary.
21. Are appropriate approval processes in place for all expenditures? Elaborate and describe the approval process for all areas of expenditure.
22. Is there any additional information about the organization's expenditures not covered that would be relevant to the organization's leaders?
23. Is the organization generating a cash flow surplus from its operating activities? Why or why not?
24. How do the organization's financial operating results compare with expectations as set forth in the approved budget?
25. Are there any current vulnerabilities, specific risks, threats, or other similar matters that could adversely affect the organization's financial condition? If yes, elaborate.
26. On a scale of 1 to 10, with 1 very weak and 10 extraordinarily strong, how would the organization's staff leadership rate the organization's current financial condition? Explain the basis for the rating.

NOTE: *Responses to key questions should be provided in plain language. A perfectly acceptable format for a portion of the organization's internal financial reporting may be a Q&A format, with questions like these along with appropriate responses by members of the accounting and financial management team. Such a format can cover a particular period of time. Once responses are formulated to the questions, the responses can be updated each time new reports are required. If changes to the responses are highlighted, users of the reports can* *quickly and easily identify new information. Of course, the organization's accounting and finance team should have appropriate schedules and details available to support the responses.*

Nonprofit leaders shouldn't be intimidated

If a nonprofit leader does not completely understand the internal financial reports, or feels that additional information is needed, that leader should work with the organization's accounting team to revise and improve the financial reporting process. A nonprofit leader should never be intimidated if he or she does not understand information in the financial reports. If the leader has significant overall management responsibilities for the nonprofit and does not adequately comprehend the financial reporting information, the leader cannot carry out his or her duties responsibly. While a nonprofit leader responsible for overseeing the business activities of a nonprofit should have business experience, if the financial reports do not provide information in a manner that facilitates understanding, the problem is not likely with the leader. More likely, the problem is with the internal financial reporting process.

Effective internal financial reporting is always based on the idea that meaningful, usable, relevant, and timely information is provided to decision-makers in a format they can easily understand. When that is not happening, the solution is not to attempt to convert a decision-making nonprofit leader into an accountant. Rather, the nonprofit's accounting team must adapt to the needs, language, and experience of the nonprofit's decision-makers. If the nonprofit's accounting team is unable to do so, the nonprofit leadership may need to evaluate the makeup of the accounting team.

Reporting to people charged with financial oversight

Nonprofit leaders do not need to be accountants in order to carry out and manage the day-to-day business activities of a nonprofit. But those charged with overseeing the nonprofit's financial activities—be it the members of the governing body, such as a board, or a committee—should have financial expertise. Often, the board assigns a finance committee or its equivalent to oversee the nonprofit's financial operations. The members of this committee must diligently and consistently perform their tasks and responsibilities. Otherwise, the board can't effectively govern in the manner required. And even worse, it will fall short of fulfilling its legal duties.

> **While a nonprofit leader responsible for overseeing the business activities of a nonprofit should have business experience, if the financial reports do not provide information in a manner that facilitates understanding, the problem is not likely with the leader. More likely, the problem is with the internal financial reporting process.**

Because so much is at stake, at least some of the people responsible for performing governance-level financial oversight should be financial professionals—accountants, corporate finance executives, bankers, and so on.

Since at least a portion of those serving on the body responsible for the nonprofit's financial oversight will—or should—be composed of financial professionals, the nature and format of reporting to the financial oversight body may vary from the reporting provided to other nonprofit leaders. For example, financial professionals may be accustomed to reading and evaluating formal financial statements. An effective nonprofit financial reporting system will include the ability to produce accurate and timely financial statements in a proper format for the financial oversight body. The nonprofit's accounting team should also produce whatever other reports the oversight body requires and should do so in the format prescribed by the oversight body.

As further described in Chapter 8, appropriate financial oversight may involve the use of audits or other accountability measures designed to evaluate the veracity and propriety of financial reports and other information on which nonprofit leaders rely.

NONPROFIT ACCOUNTING DEFINITIONS

Certain key terms are central to nonprofit accounting. Here are the ones most commonly used:

Assets

Assets represent items of value that the nonprofit owns or to which the nonprofit has certain rights that relate to future benefits. The most common assets recognized in the financial reports of nonprofits include cash, investment securities, and property and equipment (frequently referred to as "PP&E"—the second "p" is for "plant"). Property and equipment is also sometimes referred to as "fixed assets." Other types of assets include accounts receivable (such as amounts due from families for school tuition for nonprofits that operate schools), inventories (such as bookstore or food service inventory items), loans receivable, and prepaid expenses (payments made in advance of receiving goods or services).

Liabilities

Liabilities represent obligations of the nonprofit to pay money or to provide goods or services to another party. The most common liabilities recognized in nonprofit financial reports include accounts payable (amounts due to vendors), accrued expenses (expenses that have been incurred but not invoiced by a vendor, such as payroll earned by employees but not yet paid, interest that has accumulated with respect to outstanding debt but is not yet due, and so on), and debt payable (frequently referred to as "notes payable," "mortgages payable," or "loans payable"). Another type of liability sometimes seen in nonprofit financial statements is unearned revenue (for example, tuition money that has been received from parents for education services to be provided by the nonprofit's school in future months).

Net assets

In the purest and simplest sense, net assets comprise the difference between a nonprofit's assets and its liabilities. However, in accounting for nonprofit organizations, net assets are classified into one or two categories, depending on whether the nonprofit has received contributions subject to donor-imposed restrictions.

The two major categories of net assets that a nonprofit may have are as follows:

> **1. Net assets *with* donor restrictions.** Net assets with donor restrictions arise when a donor makes a gift to the nonprofit and stipulates that the gift is to be used for a specific purpose, at a specific future time, or is to be invested permanently and not expended.
>
> Donor restrictions on net assets can either be **permanent** or **temporary.**
>
>> **Permanent** restrictions on net assets arise when a donor makes a gift to the nonprofit and stipulates that the gift amount (or some portion of it) is to be invested permanently and not expended by the nonprofit. Donors who make permanently restricted gifts frequently stipulate how the distributions or earnings from the invested gift are to be utilized. An example of a contribution that results in permanently restricted net assets is a permanent endowment gift—the donor stipulates that the gift amount is to be invested permanently and that distributions from the endowment fund are to be used for certain purposes, such as funding scholarships.
>
>> **Temporary** restrictions on net assets arise when a donor makes a gift to the nonprofit and stipulates that the gift is to be used for a specific purpose or at a specific future time. A common example of a gift that results in a temporary restriction is a gift by a donor to the nonprofit's building fund, where donors have been advised that such contributions will be used to fund a particular building project.

NOTE: Net assets with donor restrictions represent the nonprofit's "equity" in the related assets. A nonprofit's net assets balance is distinct from the nonprofit's "actual" assets (cash, investments, and so on). For example, if a donor makes a cash gift of $1 million to a nonprofit to fund a permanent scholarship endowment, the accounting entry is to recognize an asset (cash) of $1 million and contribution revenue with donor restrictions of $1 million. The contribution revenue with donor restrictions results in an increase in net assets with donor restrictions of $1 million. The ultimate effect on the nonprofit's financial position is that the nonprofit has additional assets of $1 million (cash) and net assets with donor restrictions of $1 million.

While net assets and actual assets are distinct, a nonprofit should always ensure that it has actual assets (typically in liquid form) sufficient to cover its net assets with donor restrictions (whether such restrictions are permanent or temporary). Failure to do so typically constitutes a violation of one or more donor-imposed restrictions, which can be a significant legal matter.

2. Net assets *without* donor restrictions. Net assets without donor restrictions comprise the balance of net assets that are not subject to donor restrictions. A nonprofit's governing body may "designate" a portion of the nonprofit's net assets for a particular purpose. Designations made by the nonprofit itself (as contrasted with a donor-imposed restriction) do not constitute net assets *with* donor restrictions, but rather, are a component of net assets *without* donor restrictions. The fundamental reason for such treatment is that internal designations made by nonprofit leaders may be undone or reversed, whereas restrictions imposed by donors are subject to legal limitations on the nonprofit's ability to use the funds in ways that vary from the donors' restrictions.

Income, revenue, and gains

Income, revenue, and gains generally result from the nonprofit receiving one or more assets, experiencing an increase in the recognizable value of one or more assets, or experiencing a decrease in the recognizable value of one or more liabilities. In plain words, income, revenue, and gains generally result when positive (good) things happen to the nonprofit's assets or liabilities. Common examples of income and revenue are contributions, interest and dividend income from investments, and fees received for program activities conducted by the nonprofit. Gains commonly occur from appreciation of a nonprofit's investment assets.

Expenses or losses

Expenses or losses generally result when the nonprofit transfers assets (e.g., cash) to other parties to cover operating costs, experiences a decrease in the recognizable value of one or more assets, or experiences an increase in the recognizable value of one or more liabilities. The most common expenses incurred by a nonprofit are the cash operating costs associated with regular activities (e.g., salaries, utilities, repairs, maintenance, transportation, and so on). The most common example of a non-cash expense incurred by nonprofits is depreciation. A common way a nonprofit may experience losses is a decline in the value of a nonprofit's investment assets.

> **Depreciation** – is a non-cash expense that represents the "using up" or deterioration of a long-lived asset. Property and equipment other than land generally deteriorate over time and ultimately must be either repaired, refurbished, replaced, or simply discarded. Accountants estimate the useful life of a particular asset and then recognize its deterioration over the estimated useful life. For example, assume that a nonprofit acquires an item of electronic equipment for $50,000. The estimated useful life of the equipment is 5 years. The nonprofit may recognize depreciation expense of $10,000 per year over the 5-year estimated useful life of the asset. As another example, assume that the nonprofit constructs a new building for a cost of $4 million and estimates that the building has a useful life of 40 years. The nonprofit may recognize depreciation expense of $100,000 per year over the 40-year estimated life of the building. (While nonprofits commonly recognize depreciation expense evenly over the life of an asset, other methods of recognizing depreciation [typically, accelerated] may be permissible. In reality, nonprofits rarely use depreciation methods other than recognizing the expense evenly over the estimated life of an asset—a method that is referred to as "straight-line" depreciation.)
>
> The accounting entry necessary to recognize depreciation expense involves increasing an expense account (depreciation expense) and increasing an account commonly referred to as "accumulated depreciation." Accumulated depreciation is a "contra-asset" account, which simply means that it is a negative account in the nonprofit's assets. For example, using the information described in the preceding paragraph for the electronic equipment, the equipment is originally recognized as an asset on the books of the nonprofit for $50,000. After the first year the depreciation expense is recognized, accumulated depreciation in the amount of $10,000 will be recognized as a contra-asset, thereby reducing the net amount of the equipment asset on the nonprofit's books from $50,000 to $40,000.

Even though depreciation expense is a non-cash expense in the year in which it is recognized, it is a very real economic expense in the sense that it represents the genuine deterioration of an asset that is being used up over time. As further described in Chapter 1, nonprofits often overlook or ignore the reality of depreciation expense, which can adversely affect a nonprofit's ability to reach its targeted financial objectives.

NONPROFIT ACCOUNTING METHODS

Nonprofits apply a variety of accounting methods in their financial statements and reports. Current professional accounting literature refers to a comprehensive method of accounting as a *"financial reporting framework."* The three financial reporting frameworks most commonly used by nonprofits in the United States are:

1. Generally Accepted Accounting Principles (GAAP);
2. The cash basis; and
3. The modified cash basis.

Generally Accepted Accounting Principles (GAAP)

Accounting principles that are formally and officially recognized by the accounting profession in the United States are commonly referred to as "generally accepted accounting principles," a term that is frequently abbreviated using the acronym "GAAP." The official accounting literature comprising GAAP is promulgated by the Financial Accounting Standards Board—an independent nonprofit organization. GAAP is used by many regulated businesses (e.g., banks) and companies whose stock is publicly traded on US stock exchanges. GAAP is also used by many privately held businesses, as well as many nonprofit organizations. The GAAP framework is used most frequently for external financial reporting. Outside the context of regulated and publicly traded companies, its use for *internal* financial reporting is much less common.

The primary distinction between GAAP and the other frameworks described is that GAAP generally attempts to recognize revenues and expenses as they are *incurred*, rather than when an organization receives or pays the cash (or other assets) related to the revenues and expenses.

For example, when a nonprofit has a company repair the nonprofit's air-conditioning equipment, the repair expense is *incurred* at the time the repair is performed. Under GAAP, the nonprofit would recognize the repair expense at the time the repair is performed and would recognize a payable to the vendor for the amount due.

As another example, assume that a nonprofit operates a school and families are required to pay tuition for the school year in advance. When the nonprofit receives the tuition money from the families, it has not yet provided the services for the tuition paid. Under GAAP, the nonprofit would recognize the cash it receives as an asset and it would also recognize a liability associated with the nonprofit's obligation to provide services in the future. Such a liability is frequently referred to as "unearned revenue." The nonprofit would then recognize the revenue over the period during which the services are provided.

As a final example, assume that a nonprofit's fiscal year ends on June 30, which happens to fall in the middle of the nonprofit's payroll period. As of that date, the nonprofit's employees have worked several days for which they have not yet been paid, since the payroll date has not yet arrived. Under GAAP, the nonprofit will recognize "accrued payroll expense"—a liability for the services that have been provided to the nonprofit but for which the nonprofit has not yet paid.

Due to the fact that the GAAP framework typically involves recognizing "accruals" such as those described in the preceding paragraph, GAAP is sometimes referred to as the "full accrual" method of accounting.

Even though the GAAP framework is formally and officially recognized by the accounting profession, use of the GAAP framework for external financial reporting by nonprofit organizations varies. For organizations subject to state charitable solicitation registration laws, some states impose external financial reporting requirements that include the requirement to use the GAAP framework for required financial statements. Additionally, the use of GAAP for external financial reporting purposes may be required as a contractual or legal condition for nonprofits in certain circumstances. For example, a bank or other lender may require a nonprofit to apply the GAAP framework to financial statements submitted to the lender on an annual basis. Similarly, a government agency or other grant-funding nonprofit may require a nonprofit to submit GAAP-basis financial statements as a condition of receiving a grant. Regardless of whether a legal or contractual requirement applies, a nonprofit may still voluntarily choose to use the GAAP framework for its external financial reporting. Regardless of whether a legal or contractual requirement applies to the use of GAAP in external financial reporting, and regardless of whether a nonprofit voluntarily uses GAAP in its external financial reporting, the nonprofit is free to use whatever financial reporting framework it considers most helpful for its internal accounting and financial reporting purposes.

The primary advantage of the GAAP framework is that it is almost universally accepted by all parties for external financial reporting. Lending institutions, regulatory bodies, taxing authorities, grant-making organizations, prospective donors, accrediting organizations, and virtually all other external users of the nonprofit's financial statements will accept financial statements prepared using GAAP. GAAP is the "highest common denominator" of the financial reporting frameworks. There is no higher method of financial reporting.

Accordingly, a nonprofit that applies the GAAP reporting framework to its external financial statements will be in a position to provide acceptable financial statements to virtually any party who may require them in virtually any scenario. That is not the case with respect to the other reporting frameworks described below. For example, if a nonprofit were to apply for a new mortgage loan, it is possible that the lender would require the use of the GAAP reporting framework in the nonprofit's financial statements. If the nonprofit's external financial statements are not ordinarily prepared using the GAAP framework, the nonprofit may be required to rework its accounting and financial reporting in order to satisfy the lender.

> GAAP is the "highest common denominator" of the financial reporting frameworks. There is no higher method of financial reporting.

The cash basis

The cash basis financial reporting framework is really quite simple. Sometimes colloquially referred to as the "pure cash basis" of accounting (to distinguish it from the "modified cash basis"), the premise of the cash basis framework is to recognize only cash transactions in the nonprofit's financial statements. For this purpose, organizations frequently define the term "cash" to include balances in bank deposit accounts as well as highly liquid investment securities. Accordingly, under the cash basis framework, the only assets recognized in the nonprofit's financial statements are cash and highly liquid investment securities. No other assets are recognized, and no liabilities are recognized.

Income and revenues are recognized when cash is received, and expenditures are recognized when cash is paid. With GAAP, cash spent to purchase a long-lived asset would result in the recognition of the long-lived asset in the nonprofit's financial statements (and not an immediate expense), but the cash basis framework dictates that any such expenditure is simply a cash disbursement that reduces the nonprofit's cash balance. Similarly, while GAAP would dictate that a principal payment made by a nonprofit to reduce its outstanding debt would reduce the liability on the financial statements of the nonprofit, the cash basis framework

CHAPTER 2 | Accounting and Financial Reporting

does not recognize liabilities, meaning a payment to reduce the outstanding principal of debt is simply another type of cash expenditure that reduces the nonprofit's cash balance.

Accordingly, a financial statement prepared using the cash basis framework for a particular period of time will generally report only the following items:

- Beginning cash and investment balances;
- Receipts;
- Disbursements; and
- Ending cash and investment balances.

(The financial statement may provide descriptions or categories of cash receipts and cash disbursements.)

Given the fact that the cash basis financial reporting framework is so simple and limited, it is typically used only by very small organizations with very simple financial operations. For a very small nonprofit, the cash basis framework may be adequate to meet the needs of nonprofit leaders for both *internal* and *external* financial reporting. This is especially true for nonprofits that do not have significant property and equipment or significant outstanding debt. The primary virtue of the cash basis framework is its simplicity. Very little, if any, accounting experience is required to maintain an accounting system using the cash basis financial reporting framework.

While the simplicity of the cash basis financial reporting framework may be a virtue for very small nonprofits, its limitations make it an inadequate framework for most larger nonprofits—especially nonprofits with significant property and equipment or significant outstanding debt. Due to the fact that the cash basis framework does not recognize assets other than cash or any liabilities, applying the cash basis framework to a nonprofit with significant property and equipment or debt will produce financial statements that do not reflect the nonprofit's significant assets or obligations. The absence of such information would make it difficult—if not impossible—for nonprofit leaders or others to accurately and adequately assess the nonprofit's financial condition.

While the simplicity of the cash basis financial reporting framework may be a virtue for very small nonprofits, its limitations make it an inadequate framework for most larger nonprofits—especially nonprofits with significant property and equipment or significant outstanding debt.

The modified cash basis

The modified cash basis reporting framework takes the cash basis framework and adds to it the recognition of limited types of assets in addition to cash and limited types of liabilities. As is the case with the cash basis framework, the term "cash" in the modified cash basis framework is typically defined to include highly liquid investment securities. Generally, in the modified cash basis framework, property and equipment is recognized as an asset (along with its contra-asset, accumulated depreciation) in addition to cash. Additionally, outstanding debt and other "hard" liabilities (not regular accounts payable or accruals) are recognized as liabilities.

Other types of assets and liabilities are generally not recognized under the modified cash basis reporting framework. For example, accounts receivable, inventories, and prepaid expenses are not generally recognized as assets under the modified cash basis. Similarly, regular accounts payable, accrued expenses, and unearned revenue are not generally recognized as liabilities. Some professional judgment may be required in determining whether it is appropriate to recognize a particular asset or liability under the modified cash basis framework. The basic concept of the modified cash basis framework is to recognize "hard" assets and liabilities, and not to recognize accrual-type assets and liabilities.

Many nonprofits use the modified cash basis framework for financial reporting. The primary advantage that the modified cash basis offers over the GAAP basis is its relative simplicity. Since accrual-type assets and liabilities are not recognized, the accounting is simpler. For many nonprofits, including some larger nonprofits, the modified cash basis reporting framework may be used for both *internal* and *external* financial reporting (if acceptable to external users). Nonprofits that use the modified cash basis often favor it because, while it is relatively simple (as compared to the GAAP basis), it does provide information about the nonprofit's most significant assets and liabilities—its cash and investments, its property and equipment, and its outstanding debt. For many nonprofit leaders, the omission of accrual-type assets and liabilities is not a significant factor in their evaluation of the nonprofit's financial condition. Further, if nonprofit leaders want to assess information about the nonprofit's accrual-type assets and liabilities, such as accounts receivable, inventories, and accounts payable, that information can be measured and reported to nonprofit leaders as of any given date separately from the nonprofit's financial statements.

> **NOTE:** *While some variations of the modified cash basis framework exist that differ slightly from that described above, the methodology and principles described represent the most commonly used version of the modified cash basis framework.*

EXTERNAL FINANCIAL REPORTING

External financial reporting typically involves the nonprofit issuing formal financial statements to users who are external to the nonprofit's governing body and staff leadership. The nature, content, and format of the external-use financial statements will vary based on the reporting framework used by the nonprofit. Following is a summary description of the financial statements typically included for nonprofits with respect to each of the three financial reporting frameworks.

Generally Accepted Accounting Principles (GAAP)

Statement of financial position. Sometimes informally referred to as the "balance sheet," the statement of financial position reports the assets, liabilities, and net assets of the nonprofit. The balance of each of the two components of net assets is also reported—without donor restrictions and with donor restrictions (if applicable).

Statement of activities. Sometimes informally referred to as the "income statement" or the "P&L" (which stands for "profit and loss"—a term commonly used in the business sector), the statement of activities reports the income, revenues, gains, expenses, and losses of the nonprofit. The net amount of these items is reported as the "change in net assets." The statement of activities reports the change in each of the two components of net assets—without donor restrictions and with donor restrictions (if applicable).

Statement of cash flows. The statement of cash flows reports the nonprofit's sources and uses of cash. Inflows and outflows of cash are grouped into three categories—operating cash flows, investing cash flows, and financing cash flows.

Statement of functional expenses. Nonprofit organizations issuing GAAP-basis financial statements must include certain information about the categorizations of the organization's expenses. An organization can choose to provide the required information in a statement of functional expenses. A statement of functional expenses is not a required statement in the GAAP reporting framework, but it can be used as a means of providing the required information about expense categorization. Alternatively, an organization can provide the required information either in the statement of activities or in the notes to the financial statements. Expenses are required to be categorized according to both their *functional classification* and their *natural classification.* Functional classification includes the categories of *program* expenses (those that relate specifically to carrying out the organization's purposes) and *supporting* expenses (those that do not specifically relate to carrying out the organization's purposes). Supporting expenses may include both *management and general* expenses and *fundraising* expenses. For expenses that relate to more than one function, allocations are necessary. Natural classification includes traditional operating categories of expenses such as salaries and employee benefits, occupancy costs, interest expense, etc. The methods used to allocate costs to each function are also required to be disclosed in the notes to the financial statements.

Notes to the financial statements. Specific disclosures regarding various aspects of the organization's financial position and activities are required by GAAP.

See the sample GAAP-basis nonprofit financial statements on page 59.

The cash basis

Statement of cash receipts and disbursements. The statement of cash receipts and disbursements is a very simple statement that includes the following components:

- Beginning cash and investment balances;
- Receipts;
- Disbursements; and
- Ending cash and investment balances.

Appropriate detail should be provided for each of the components.

Notes to the financial statement. A statement of cash receipts and disbursements prepared under the cash basis reporting framework may or may not be accompanied by notes to the financial statement providing additional disclosures about the nonprofit and the information in the statement. *It is a best practice to provide notes to the financial statement under the cash basis framework. Appropriate notes are required if the financial statement is to be audited and the nonprofit wishes to receive an unqualified ("clean") audit opinion.*

The modified cash basis

Statement of financial position–modified cash basis. The statement of financial position–modified cash basis reports the cash (including highly liquid investment securities), property and equipment (net of accumulated depreciation), and outstanding debt of the nonprofit, along with the resulting net assets balance. It is a generally accepted practice for the statement of financial position–modified cash basis to include the balance of each of the two components of net assets—without donor restrictions and with donor restrictions (if applicable).

Statement of activities-modified cash basis. The statement of activities–modified cash basis reports the income, revenues, gains, expenses, and losses of the nonprofit in a manner consistent with the modified cash basis financial reporting framework. The net amount of these items is reported as the "change in net assets-modified cash basis." It is a generally accepted practice for the statement of activities–modified cash basis to report the change in each of the two components of net assets—without donor restrictions and with donor restrictions (if applicable).

Notes to the financial statements. Financial statements prepared under the modified cash basis reporting framework may or may not be accompanied by notes to the financial statements providing additional disclosures about the nonprofit and information in the statements. *It is a best practice to provide notes to the financial statements under the modified cash basis framework. Appropriate notes are required if the financial statements are to be audited and the nonprofit wishes to receive an unqualified ("clean") audit opinion.*

NONPROFIT ACCOUNTING SOFTWARE

Virtually all nonprofits use some type of accounting software to create and maintain appropriate accounting records and financial reporting. Some smaller nonprofits use software with functionality that is limited to the accounting and financial activities arena (e.g., QuickBooks). Larger nonprofits generally use "nonprofit management" applications with both accounting and other capabilities—including tools that assist with various operational areas of the nonprofit (e.g., donor records, facilities usage, inventory management, school administration, and so on). Some accounting and nonprofit management applications are run on the nonprofit's own computer network, while others are offered as "cloud-based" applications accessible by users through the Internet.

> In determining whether a specific nonprofit accounting and financial management application is appropriate for a particular nonprofit, nonprofit leaders should take into consideration not only the operating functionality of the application, but also the strength and reputation of the application with respect to internal control.

In determining whether a specific nonprofit accounting and financial management application is appropriate for a particular nonprofit, nonprofit leaders should take into consideration not only the operating functionality of the application, but also the strength and reputation of the application with respect to internal control. (See Chapter 7 for more information about maintaining sound internal control.) Additionally, nonprofit leaders should evaluate the financial strength and viability of the company providing the application to address the possible risk of the provider going out of business. Cessation of business by a nonprofit's accounting and operations application provider could have adverse implications with respect to the nonprofit's accounting and other important records—especially if the application is cloud-based and becomes inaccessible. Lastly, the nonprofit will want to fully understand the security controls put into place by the provider to keep sensitive private data protected.

Commonly used accounting, financial management, and donor management applications

In my book, *Church Finance* (Second Edition), I provided information related to identifying accounting and financial management software applications specifically directed at churches. For nonprofits other than churches, I would observe that in my experience in serving nonprofit organizations across the United States for more than 30 years, the most commonly used accounting application for smaller nonprofit organizations is *QuickBooks*. For larger organizations, we commonly see either Blackbaud's application (named *Financial Edge*) or Sage's application (named *Intacct*). For donor database management, we commonly see Blackbaud's *Raiser's Edge* in use by larger organizations. We also see *Studio Enterprise* by DonorDirect with some frequency. Another widely used application is *DonorPerfect*. Of course, numerous applications exist to serve the nonprofit sector in the arena of donor database management in addition to the ones I have mentioned here.

Cloud-based paperless accounts payable applications

Certain cloud-based applications for accounts payable management exist which are independent of accounting and general ledger software applications. Independent cloud-based accounts payable applications typically integrate or interface with a variety of general ledger and accounting software packages. A nonprofit considering such an application should evaluate whether it will integrate or interface with the nonprofit's accounting software package. Even if the cloud-based accounts payable application does not directly interface or integrate with the nonprofit's accounting software package, other advantages of the cloud-based application may still outweigh that disadvantage.

Cloud-based accounts payable applications may offer significant advantages over applications that are built into a nonprofit's in-house accounting software. For example, with a cloud-based application, nonprofit leaders may use their computer, smart phone, iPad, or similar device to review, approve, and pay bills from literally anywhere in the world at any time, so long as they have an Internet connection. Additionally, the better cloud-based applications incorporate user rights and user profiles with built-in internal controls as a standard feature. Accordingly, nonprofit leaders can receive reminder emails at selected intervals (daily, weekly, and so on) of bills requiring review, approval, and payment. When the leader who is vested with the authority to approve actual payments (bills that have been properly approved by others) selects specific bills for payment and executes the "pay" command, the bills are paid.

Disbursements are either made electronically or the cloud-based application service provider prints checks at its location and mails them to the respective vendors. The cost of such applications is typically insignificant in light of the dramatic streamlining and improvement in efficiency that typically result from their use.

Two popular examples of cloud-based accounts payable management applications are *Bill.com* and *Concur Invoice*.

In addition to providing significant efficiencies, electronic accounts payable management systems generally facilitate improved internal control by requiring multiple individuals to provide approvals in connection with disbursements (assuming the application has been properly set up with segregated user rights). For example, such an application offers "roles," such as the accountant role, with duties that align with the principle of segregation of duties. An accountant, for example, would not be permitted to execute a "pay" command. Another feature that enhances internal control is that such systems do not produce physical checks to be signed by nonprofit employees and mailed or delivered from the nonprofit's office. Instead, disbursements are either made electronically through the ACH system or checks are prepared and mailed by the service provider directly to the vendors. Cloud-based paperless accounts payable management systems offer significant advantages over traditional paper-check-based systems.

An overall observation about data access and cloud-based applications

As cloud-based software applications become more prevalent and increasingly become the norm rather than the exception for most computerized functions, nonprofits must consider some unique implications. When cloud-based applications first began to emerge, the idea of an organization having its data stored "somewhere in the cloud" on the application provider's servers was both novel and, for many, uncomfortable. For better or worse, many nonprofits liked the idea of having "their data" on "their servers" and were uneasy with alternatives. Over time, cloud-based application providers have responded to such concerns with a variety of safeguards, including enhanced security measures, use of fortified data centers, redundant backups, and the like. Over time, nonprofits and other organizations have not only warmed to the idea of cloud-based applications and data storage, there has been a steady movement toward "cloudifying" everything, including the very servers used by the organizations.

Use of cloud-based applications, data storage, and servers has brought with it many, many advantages. Many in the IT profession would argue that data stored and backed up in the cloud is safer now than having it onsite, even when backed up offsite. Data backup is often effortless and exposure to hacker risk is greatly reduced with security enhancements such as user filters and multi-factor authentication.

But loss of data due to a disaster or hacking is only one aspect of data protection. Another very important factor is accessibility of the data in the event the application provider were to cease operations. Addressing this factor requires a multi-faceted assessment. Perhaps first and foremost, an assessment should be made of the viability of the provider. I have observed numerous instances of "cool new apps" popping up, offering to make some aspect of management or operations easier, only to later go defunct—along with the users' data. Ideally, such providers give their users some advance notice of their impending demise, but that does not always happen. Nonprofit leaders should make a risk-based assessment of a cloud-based provider's viability. The more severe the impact would be in the event of data loss, the more thorough the assessment of viability should be. It's one thing to have an application provider go defunct that simply provides the users with reminders to complete certain tasks at certain times. That would be a very low-risk scenario. On the other hand, having your accounting, payroll, and donor management application provider go defunct with your nonprofit's data would be quite another thing. That would be a very high-risk scenario and warrants a full assessment of the provider's viability, including reference checks, credit checks, financial assessment, etc.

In addition to assessing the strength of a cloud-based application provider's viability, nonprofits should also ensure that they download their data periodically in case it becomes irretrievable from the application provider. Applications that house important data should offer an "export" function that allows its users to export their data to a generic file format and download it. The idea is that if the need were to arise, the user could import the data into a new application (at least to the extent possible). In addition to periodically exporting and downloading their data, nonprofits should consider "printing" their data in reports that would be helpful in the event of a data loss. Reports can be "printed" to PDF files and saved by the nonprofit periodically as an additional measure of protection.

AUTHOR'S NOTE: Early in my accounting career, I audited banks and a software company that provided operations software for banks' main operations (the software that handled data for customers' bank accounts, loan accounts, and the banks' own accounting). Talk about a high-risk scenario! When banks would consider using the software company's applications, they would review the audited financial statements of the software company. They also required the software company to engage an independent CPA firm to attest to the fact that the software company kept a working copy of its software applications on media in an offsite vault for use in the event of a disaster. While the specific nature of a risk assessment today would be different, the same concept of risk assessment applies to nonprofits entrusting their core operations and data to a cloud-based application provider.

Data security in general

Data security is a front-and-center issue today, as it should be. The topic of data security is beyond the scope of this book, but it is a critically important aspect of nonprofit administration.

Any attempt to provide a limited summary of key elements of healthy data security practices here would be inadequate. What is important is that the organization's governing body and staff leadership have a healthy regard for the need to proactively and holistically address data security risk in the organization. The organization's IT service providers, whether internal, external, or both, must be specifically charged with the responsibility for proactively managing data security. If your organization's IT support team is internal, the responsibility to effectively and proactively manage data security should be a prominent aspect of each employee's job description and duties. If your organization has an external IT support team, that responsibility should be a prominent provision in the contractual agreement with the service provider. These responsibilities of your internal and/or external IT support team should include an obligation to regularly report to your organization's management about the state of the organization's data security.

Establishing and maintaining healthy data security practices is not a once-and-done exercise. It is a continuous exercise in which the ever-changing risks continue to evolve, and in which the organization continuously and proactively responds to the evolving risks as appropriate.

In addition to the role of the IT support team, nonprofit leaders must recognize that every employee—every user of the organization's applications—is responsible for being vigilant and watchful for data security risks. Healthy data security practices will involve regular education of your organization's employees about data security risks and how they are expected to help.

Establishing and maintaining healthy data security practices is not a once-and-done exercise. It is a continuous exercise in which the ever-changing risks continue to evolve, and in which the organization continuously and proactively responds to the evolving risks as appropriate.

OUTSOURCING ACCOUNTING AND FINANCIAL REPORTING

As the complexity of the accounting, tax, and regulatory compliance environment for nonprofits continues to increase, more nonprofits are outsourcing their accounting and financial reporting functions to others. As was the case with payroll processing beginning in the 1980s and 1990s, nonprofits are beginning to find that outsourcing their accounting and financial reporting can, in some cases, result in better information with less risk and at a cost that is lower than performing the functions internally. Nonprofit accounting, financial reporting, and tax compliance are very different from the accounting, financial reporting, and tax compliance conducted in the business sector. Accordingly, when a nonprofit hires an accountant or bookkeeper from the general business sector, there is typically a steep learning curve with respect to the unique attributes of the nonprofit sector. The availability of accountants and bookkeepers with significant and high-quality nonprofit experience is limited.

True outsourcing of a nonprofit's accounting and financial reporting function is very different from traditional bookkeeping services. Traditional bookkeeping services are typically "after the fact" and involve preparing financial statements and reports for the nonprofit after the end of each month (or quarter). Under the traditional bookkeeping service model, nonprofit employees typically prepare checks and pay the nonprofit's bills on a day-to-day basis. The bookkeeper takes the information from the nonprofit after the end of each month (or quarter) and uses it to prepare financial reports.

True outsourcing of a nonprofit's accounting and financial reporting function, however, involves having the outsourcing firm actually coordinate the day-to-day bill paying process, payroll, and similar functions as they occur. In some outsourced accounting and financial reporting arrangements, the outsourcing firm maintains real-time financial reports and dashboards that are accessible to nonprofit leaders on a continuous basis. Additionally, in some outsourced accounting arrangements, nonprofit bills are paid through an electronic bill-paying process, thereby eliminating the need for anyone to print, sign, and mail checks. When outsourcing of a nonprofit's accounting and financial reporting function is performed by a firm with significant experience in the nonprofit arena, the quality of the accounting and information available to nonprofit leaders may exceed anything available to the nonprofit if the nonprofit were to hire an accountant or bookkeeper internally from the general business sector. Also, since outsourcing by definition involves having people external to the nonprofit performing the accounting and financial reporting function, outsourcing typically facilitates an improvement in internal controls by enhancing the segregation of incompatible duties.

Outsourcing the accounting and financial reporting function is most commonly done by moderate to large-sized nonprofits (e.g., those with annual revenues between $500,000 and $4,000,000). Very large nonprofits do not commonly (currently) outsource their accounting and financial reporting functions—although an increasing number of larger organizations are doing so. Outsourcing can be an affordable option, often costing less than performing services of comparable quality internally. The cost of outsourcing will vary based on a variety of factors, including the nature of the specific services provided and the experience of the people performing the outsourced services. A nonprofit with an internal accounting team understandably may be reluctant to consider switching to outsourcing if doing so would mean that one or more of the nonprofit's employees would be terminated. If the nonprofit's internal accounting person or people are performing well, the nonprofit may wish to wait until a change in their employment occurs naturally (e.g., when the key accounting person resigns or retires).

RETENTION OF NONPROFIT RECORDS

The federal Sarbanes-Oxley law includes provisions prohibiting the destruction or falsification of documents subject to certain federal proceedings. Additionally, federal tax law and other laws allow regulatory authorities to examine the records of nonprofit organizations for various reasons (compliance with tax law, employment law, employee benefits law, etc.). Such laws also require organizations to maintain appropriate records related to compliance with the laws. It is important for organizations to maintain records that may be required to be produced in the event of an IRS or other regulatory examination. Attorneys generally advise nonprofit organizations to adopt a record retention policy prescribing the types of records to be maintained and the duration of time that they will be maintained. In some cases, attorneys specifically advise that such policies require destruction of documents after the applicable retention period.

A record retention policy is necessarily unique to the type of organization adopting it. Additionally, different attorneys have very different views about the approach to record retention policies. (For example, some attorneys advocate strongly for purging records at the end of the required retention period and others do not.) I recommend that each organization's board adopt a record retention policy drafted uniquely for that organization under the specific advice of appropriately experienced legal counsel.

An organization's record retention and destruction policy should ensure that necessary records and documents are adequately protected and maintained and ensure that records that are no longer needed or are of no value are discarded at the proper time. In addition, it can aid employees in understanding their obligations in retaining electronic documents—including email, web files, text files, sound and movie files, PDF documents, and other electronic documents and files.

Following is a sample record retention and destruction policy—provided solely for educational purposes. This sample policy can serve as a basis for discussion by a nonprofit's leaders with its legal counsel about a policy that is appropriate for that nonprofit, and **it should not simply be used or adopted as is.**

Sample Record Retention and Destruction Policy

1. Policy
This Policy represents the [Name of Organization]'s policy regarding the retention and disposal of records and the retention and disposal of electronic documents.

2. Administration
Following is a Record Retention Schedule that is approved as the initial maintenance, retention and disposal schedule for physical records of [Name of Organization] and the retention, and disposal of electronic documents. The [insert title of policy administrator] (the "Administrator") is the officer in charge of the administration of this Policy and the implementation of processes and procedures to ensure that the Record Retention Schedule is followed. The Administrator is also authorized to make modifications to the Record Retention Schedule from time to time to ensure that it is in compliance with local, state, and federal laws and includes the appropriate document and record categories for [Name of Organization]; monitor local, state and federal laws affecting record retention; annually review the record retention and disposal program; and monitor compliance with this Policy.

3. Suspension of record disposal in event of litigation or claims
In the event [Name of Organization] is served with any subpoena or request for documents or any employee becomes aware of a governmental investigation or audit concerning [Name

of Organization] or the commencement of any litigation against or concerning [Name of Organization], such employee shall inform the Administrator, and any further disposal of documents shall be suspended until such time as the Administrator, with the advice of counsel, determines otherwise. The Administrator shall take such steps as is necessary to promptly inform all staff of any suspension in the further disposal of documents.

4. Applicability

This Policy applies to all physical records generated in the course of [Name of Organization]'s operation, including both original documents and reproductions. It also applies to the electronic documents described above.

This Policy was approved by the Board of Directors of [Name of Organization] on [Date].

RECORD RETENTION SCHEDULE

This Record Retention Schedule is organized as follows:

Section Topic

- A. Accounting and Finance
- B. Contracts
- C. Corporate Records
- D. Electronic Documents
- E. Payroll Documents
- F. Personnel Records
- G. Property Records
- H. Tax Records
- I. Contribution Records

> **NOTE:** *This list of possible records suggests the potential breadth of items for which policies should be established. Every organization may not need all of these categories, but every organization should for itself determine which ones are relevant.*

The following are some common retention periods. These apply to both physical and electronic documents. If no physical copy of an electronic document is retained, the means to "read" the electronic document must also be retained.

A. Accounting and Finance

Record Type	Retention Period
Accounts payable & accounts receivable ledgers and schedules	7 years
Annual audit reports and financial statements	Permanent
Annual audit records, including work papers and other documents that relate to the audit	7 years after completion of audit
Bank statements and canceled checks	7 years
Donor or customer credit card numbers	Full credit card numbers should not be retained any longer than immediate business needs and merchant account agreements dictate.
Employee expense reports	7 years
General ledgers	Permanent
Notes receivable ledgers and schedules	7 years
Investment records	7 years after sale of investment

B. Contracts

Record Type	Retention Period
Contracts and related correspondence (including any proposal that resulted in the contract and all other supportive documentation)	7 years after expiration or termination

NOTE: *Some states may require a longer retention period generally, or for specific types of contracts. A local attorney should be consulted.*

C. Corporate Records

Record Type	Retention Period
Corporate records (minute books, signed minutes of the Board and all committees, corporate seals, articles of incorporation, bylaws, annual corporate reports)	Permanent
Licenses and permits	Permanent

D. Electronic Documents

1. **Email:** Not all email needs to be retained, depending on the subject matter.
    - All email—from internal or external sources—is to be deleted after 12 months.
    - [Name of Organization] will archive email for six months after the staff has deleted it, after which time the email will be permanently deleted.
    - All [Name of Organization] business-related email should be downloaded to a service center or user directory on the server.
    - Staff will not store or transfer email related to [Name of Organization] on non-work-related computers except as necessary or appropriate for [Name of Organization] purposes.
    - Staff will take care not to send confidential/proprietary [Name of Organization] information to outside sources.

2. **Electronic documents:** This includes Microsoft Office Suite and PDF files. Retention depends on the subject matter.

3. **Web page files/Internet cookies:**
    - Web browsers on all workstations should be scheduled to delete Internet cookies once per month.

In certain cases a document will be maintained in both paper and electronic form. In such cases the official document will be the electronic document.

> **NOTE:** *This section may be the appropriate place to include other policies regarding email retention, usage, or subject matter. Whether the paper or electronic document is the "official document" would be determined by each organization.*

E. Payroll Documents

Record Type	Retention Period
Employee deduction authorizations	Termination + 4 years
Payroll deductions	Termination + 7 years
W-2 and W-4 forms	Permanent
Garnishments, assignments, attachments	Termination + 7 years
Payroll registers (gross and net)	7 years
Time cards/sheets	2 years
Unclaimed wage records	6 years

F. Personnel Records

Record Type	Retention Period
Commissions/bonuses/incentives/awards	7 years
EEO-I/EEO-2—employer information reports	2 years after superseded or filing (whichever is longer)
Employee earnings records	Separation + 7 years
Employee handbooks	1 copy kept permanently
Employee personnel records (including individual attendance records, application forms, job or status change records, performance evaluations, termination papers, withholding information, garnishments, test results, training and qualification records)	Separation + 6 years
Employment contracts—individual	Separation + 7 years

CHAPTER 2 | Accounting and Financial Reporting

Record Type	Retention Period
Employment records—correspondence with employment agencies and advertisements for job openings	3 years from date of hiring decision
Employment records—all non-hired applicants (including all applications and resumes—whether solicited or unsolicited, results of post offer, pre employment physicals, results of background investigations, if any, related correspondence)	2-4 years (4 years if file contains any correspondence which might be construed as an offer)
Job descriptions	3 years after superseded
Personnel count records	3 years
Forms I-9	3 years after hiring, or 1 year after separation if later

NOTE: Many employment and employment tax related laws have both state and Federal law requirements. A local attorney should be consulted.

G. Property Records

Record Type	Retention Period
Correspondence, property deeds, assessments, licenses, rights of way	Permanent
Property insurance policies	Permanent

H. Tax Records

Record Type	Retention Period
Tax-exemption documents and related correspondence	Permanent
IRS rulings	Permanent
Excise tax records	7 years

Record Type	Retention Period
Payroll tax records	7 years
Tax bills, receipts, statements	7 years
Tax returns—income, franchise, property, payroll	Permanent
Tax work paper packages originals	7 years
Sales/use tax records	7 years
Annual information returns—federal and state	Permanent
IRS or other government audit records	Permanent

NOTE: *Retention period for sales taxes and property taxes are determined by state law. A local accountant or attorney should be consulted.*

I. Contribution Records

Record Type	Retention Period
Records of contributions	7 years
Documents evidencing terms, conditions, or restrictions on gifts	7 years after funds are expended

This sample policy was adapted by Michael E. Batts, CPA, from a model policy developed by ECFA and is used by permission. Information about ECFA is available at ecfa.org.

Sample GAAP-Basis Financial Statements for external reporting with sample report of independent auditor

Report of Independent Auditor

The Governing Body
ABC Nonprofit
City, State

We have audited the accompanying financial statements of **ABC Nonprofit** ("the Nonprofit"), which consist of the statement of financial position as of June 30, 20XX, and the related statements of activities, functional expenses, and cash flows for the year then ended, and the related notes to the financial statements.

Management's Responsibility for the Financial Statements
Management is responsible for the preparation and fair presentation of these financial statements in accordance with accounting principles generally accepted in the United States of America; this includes the design, implementation, and maintenance of internal control relevant to the preparation and fair presentation of financial statements that are free from material misstatement, whether due to fraud or error.

Auditor's Responsibility
Our responsibility is to express an opinion on these financial statements based on our audit. We conducted our audit in accordance with auditing standards generally accepted in the United States of America. Those standards require that we plan and perform the audit to obtain reasonable assurance about whether the financial statements are free from material misstatement.

An audit involves performing procedures to obtain audit evidence about the amounts and disclosures in the financial statements. The procedures selected depend on the auditor's judgment, including the assessment of the risks of material misstatement of the financial statements, whether due to fraud or error. In making those risk assessments, the auditor considers internal control relevant to the Nonprofit's preparation and fair presentation of the financial statements in order to design audit procedures that are appropriate in the circumstances, but not for the purpose of expressing an opinion on the effectiveness of the Nonprofit's internal control. Accordingly, we express no such opinion. An audit also includes evaluating the appropriateness of accounting policies used and the reasonableness of significant accounting estimates made by management, as well as evaluating the overall presentation of the financial statements.

We believe that the audit evidence we have obtained is sufficient and appropriate to provide a basis for our audit opinion.

Opinion
In our opinion, the financial statements referred to above present fairly, in all material respects, the financial position of ABC Nonprofit as of June 30, 20XX, the changes in its net assets, and its cash flows for the year then ended in accordance with accounting principles generally accepted in the United States of America.

[Audit Firm Signature]

City, State
(Date of Report)

ABC NONPROFIT
Statement of Financial Position
June 30, 20XX

Assets		
Cash and cash equivalents	$	3,210,000
Certificate of deposit		450,000
Investments restricted for long-term purposes		1,480,000
Property and equipment, net		26,400,000
Other assets		50,000
Total assets	$	**31,590,000**
Liabilities		
Accounts payable and accrued expenses	$	760,000
Note payable		4,420,000
Total liabilities		**5,180,000**
Net assets		
Without donor restrictions		
Undesignated		24,010,000
Board designated		700,000
Total without donor restrictions		24,710,000
With donor restrictions		1,700,000
Total net assets		**26,410,000**
Total liabilities and net assets	$	**31,590,000**

ABC NONPROFIT
Statement of Activities
For the Year Ended June 30, 20XX

	Without Donor Restrictions	With Donor Restrictions	Total
Public support and revenue and net assets released from restrictions			
Contributions	$ 10,000,000	$ 2,090,000	$ 12,090,000
Other revenue	1,300,000	—	1,300,000
Gains on investments	—	110,000	110,000
Net assets released from restrictions	1,500,000	(1,500,000)	—
Total public support and revenue and net assets released from restrictions	12,800,000	700,000	13,500,000
Expenses			
Program services			
Educational program activities	6,650,000	—	6,650,000
Community outreach activities	3,700,000	—	3,700,000
Total program services	10,350,000	—	10,350,000
Supporting services			
Management and general	1,650,000	—	1,650,000
Fundraising	150,000	—	150,000
Total supporting services	1,800,000	—	1,800,000
Total expenses	12,150,000	—	12,150,000
Change in net assets	650,000	700,000	1,350,000
Net assets - Beginning of year	24,060,000	1,000,000	25,060,000
Net assets - End of year	$ 24,710,000	$ 1,700,000	$ 26,410,000

ABC NONPROFIT
Statement of Functional Expenses
For the Year Ended June 30, 20XX

	Program Services			Supporting Services			
	Educational Program Activities	Community Outreach Activities	Total Program Services	Management and General	Fundraising	Total Supporting Services	Total Expenses
Personnel costs	$ 3,200,000	$ 2,700,000	$ 5,900,000	$ 1,000,000	$ 100,000	$ 1,100,000	$ 7,000,000
Utilities	700,000	455,000	1,155,000	110,000	10,000	120,000	1,275,000
Grants	1,050,000	—	1,050,000	—	—	—	1,050,000
Food and supplies	750,000	50,000	800,000	10,000	—	10,000	810,000
Depreciation	390,000	330,000	720,000	80,000	—	80,000	800,000
Travel and conferences	306,000	60,000	366,000	110,000	—	110,000	476,000
Office expenses	60,000	50,000	110,000	160,000	5,000	165,000	275,000
Other	25,000	15,000	40,000	78,000	10,000	88,000	128,000
Interest expense	109,000	—	109,000	12,000	—	12,000	121,000
Media and promotion	50,000	30,000	80,000	10,000	25,000	35,000	115,000
Professional fees	10,000	10,000	20,000	80,000	—	80,000	100,000
Total	$ 6,650,000	$ 3,700,000	$ 10,350,000	$ 1,650,000	$ 150,000	$ 1,800,000	$ 12,150,000

ABC NONPROFIT
Statement of Cash Flows
For the Year Ended June 30, 20XX

Operating cash flows	
Cash received from contributors	$ 11,510,000
Other revenue received	1,300,000
Cash paid for operating activities and costs	(11,189,000)
Interest paid	(121,000)
Net operating cash flows	1,500,000
Investing cash flows	
Redemption of certificate of deposit	170,000
Investment purchases	(290,000)
Purchases of and improvements to property and equipment	(1,470,000)
Net investing cash flows	(1,590,000)
Financing cash flows	
Proceeds from contributions restricted for investment in property and equipment and endowments	620,000
Principal payments on debt	(230,000)
Net financing cash flows	390,000
Net change in cash and cash equivalents	300,000
Cash and cash equivalents - Beginning of year	2,910,000
Cash and cash equivalents - End of year	$ 3,210,000
Reconciliation of change in net assets to net operating cash flows	
Change in net assets	$ 1,350,000
Adjustments to reconcile change in net assets to net operating cash flows	
Depreciation	800,000
Contributions restricted for investment in property and equipment and endowments	(620,000)
Gains on investments	(110,000)
Change in other assets	10,000
Change in accounts payable and accrued expenses	70,000
Net operating cash flows	$ 1,500,000

ABC NONPROFIT
NOTES TO FINANCIAL STATEMENTS
June 30, 20XX

NOTE 1
NATURE OF ACTIVITIES

ABC Nonprofit ("the Nonprofit") is a not-for-profit corporation, incorporated in the state of XXXXX. The purpose of the Nonprofit is to provide free educational services to the local community and to engage in local community outreach through a variety of means, including conducting educational classes and seminars, operating a community outreach center, operating a food pantry, and other similar activities. The Nonprofit is located in City, State.

NOTE 2
SUMMARY OF SIGNIFICANT ACCOUNTING POLICIES

REVENUE AND SUPPORT
The Nonprofit recognizes cash contributions as revenue when the contributions are received by the Nonprofit. Contributions received are recorded as without or with donor restrictions, depending on the existence and/or nature of any donor restrictions. When a restriction expires (that is, when a stipulated time restriction ends or purpose restriction is accomplished), net assets with donor restrictions are reclassified to net assets without donor restrictions and reported in the statement of activities as "net assets released from restrictions."

CASH AND CASH EQUIVALENTS
Investment instruments which are purchased or donated with original maturities of three months or less are considered to be cash equivalents.

INVESTMENTS RESTRICTED FOR LONG-TERM PURPOSES
The Nonprofit's investments have been restricted pursuant to agreements with donors which stipulate that the funds be held in perpetuity or are donor-restricted for the acquisition of long-lived assets such as property and equipment.

PROPERTY AND EQUIPMENT
Property and equipment are stated at cost, if purchased, or estimated fair value on the date of donation, if donated. Depreciation is provided using the straight-line method over the estimated useful lives of the assets.

NET ASSETS
Net assets without donor restrictions are available for use at the discretion of the Board and/or management for general operating purposes. From time to time, the Board may designate a portion of these net assets for specific purposes which makes them unavailable for use at management's discretion. The Board has designated a portion of net assets without donor restrictions for a contingency fund for building repairs and maintenance. Net assets with donor restrictions consist of amounts limited by donor-imposed time and/or purpose restrictions.

FUNCTIONAL ALLOCATION OF EXPENSES
The statement of functional expenses presents expenses by function and natural classification. Expenses directly attributable to a specific functional area are reported as expenses of those functional areas. Indirect costs that benefit multiple functional areas are allocated among the various functional areas based primarily on employee time.

INCOME TAXES
The Nonprofit is exempt from federal income tax as a nonprofit described in Section 501(c)(3) of the Internal Revenue Code and from state income tax pursuant to applicable state law. The Nonprofit is further classified as a public charity and not a private foundation for federal income tax purposes. The Nonprofit has not incurred unrelated business income taxes. As a result, no income tax provision or liability has been provided for in the accompanying financial statements.

USE OF ESTIMATES
Management uses estimates and assumptions in preparing the financial statements. Those estimates and assumptions affect the reported amounts of assets and liabilities, the disclosure of contingent assets and liabilities, and reported revenues and expenses. Significant estimates used in preparing these financial statements include those related to the estimated fair value of investments and the useful lives of property and equipment. Actual results could differ from the estimates.

SUBSEQUENT EVENTS
The Nonprofit has evaluated for possible financial reporting and disclosure subsequent events through (Date of Audit Report), the date as of which the financial statements were available to be issued.

ABC NONPROFIT
NOTES TO FINANCIAL STATEMENTS
June 30, 20XX

NOTE 3
LIQUIDITY AND AVAILABILITY OF RESOURCES

Financial assets available for general expenditure within one year of the date of the statement of financial position are as follows:

Cash and cash equivalents	$ 3,210,000
Certificate of deposit	450,000
Investments restricted for long-term purposes	1,480,000
Total financial assets	5,140,000
Less:	
Amounts unavailable for general expenditure within one year, due to donor-imposed restrictions	(1,700,000)
Amounts unavailable for general expenditure by management without Board approval	(700,000)
Net financial assets available within one year	$ 2,740,000

The Nonprofit is primarily supported by contributions from the general public in the local community. As part of the Nonprofit's liquidity management, it structures its financial assets to be available as its general expenditures, liabilities, and other obligations come due. Because a donor's restriction requires resources to be used in a particular manner or in a future period, the Nonprofit must maintain sufficient resources to meet those responsibilities to its donors. Thus, certain financial assets may not be available for general expenditure within one year. Additionally, the Board has designated a portion of net assets without donor restrictions for a contingency fund for building repairs and maintenance. Because of the Board's designation, those amounts are not available for general expenditure within the next year; however, the Board could make them available, if necessary. Management believes the Nonprofit has sufficient cash available for general operations that may be drawn upon in the event of unanticipated financial distress or immediate liquidity need.

NOTE 4
CONCENTRATIONS

The Nonprofit maintains its cash, cash equivalents, and certificate of deposit in deposit accounts which may not be federally insured, may exceed federally insured limits, or may be insured by an entity other than an agency of the federal government. The Nonprofit has not experienced any losses in such accounts, and believes it is not exposed to any significant credit risk related to cash, cash equivalents, and the certificate of deposit.

The Nonprofit's debt is held by a single financial institution.

NOTE 5
INVESTMENTS RESTRICTED FOR LONG-TERM PURPOSES

Investments restricted for long-term purposes consisted of the following as of June 30, 20XX:

Marketable equity securities	$ 1,480,000
Total investments restricted for long-term purposes	$ 1,480,000

Investments restricted for long-term purposes were restricted for the following purposes as of June 30, 20XX:

Corpus of endowments	$ 800,000
Building fund	600,000
Appreciation on endowments	80,000
Total investments restricted for long-term purposes	$ 1,480,000

ABC NONPROFIT
NOTES TO FINANCIAL STATEMENTS
June 30, 20XX

NOTE 6
FAIR VALUE MEASUREMENTS

Accounting principles generally accepted in the United States of America ("GAAP") define fair value for an investment generally as the price an organization would receive upon selling the investment in an orderly transaction to an independent buyer in the principal or most advantageous market for the investment. The information available to measure fair value varies depending on the nature of each investment and its market or markets. Accordingly, GAAP recognizes a hierarchy of "inputs" an organization may use in determining or estimating fair value. The inputs are categorized into "levels" that relate to the extent to which an input is objectively observable and the extent to which markets exist for identical or comparable investments. In determining or estimating fair value, an organization is required to maximize the use of observable market data (to the extent available) and minimize the use of unobservable inputs. The hierarchy assigns the highest priority to unadjusted quoted prices in active markets for identical items (Level 1 inputs) and the lowest priority to unobservable inputs (Level 3 inputs).

A financial instrument's level within the fair value hierarchy is based on the lowest level of any input that is significant to the fair value measurement.

Following is a description of each of the three levels of input within the fair value hierarchy:

> Level 1 – unadjusted quoted market prices in active markets for identical items
>
> Level 2 – other significant observable inputs (such as quoted prices for similar items)
>
> Level 3 – significant unobservable inputs

Estimated fair values of assets measured on a recurring basis as of June 30, 20XX, are as follows:

	Total	Level 1	Level 2	Level 3
Marketable equity securities				
Common and preferred stocks	$ 1,000,000	$ 1,000,000	$ —	$ —
Mutual funds	480,000	480,000	—	—
Total marketable equity securities	$ 1,480,000	$ 1,480,000	$ —	$ —

NOTE 7
PROPERTY AND EQUIPMENT

Property and equipment consisted of the following as of June 30, 20XX:

Land and land improvements	$ 5,400,000
Buildings and building improvements	24,000,000
Furniture and equipment	3,800,000
Vehicles	200,000
Total	33,400,000
Less: Accumulated depreciation	(7,000,000)
Net property and equipment	$ 26,400,000

Depreciation expense for the year ended June 30, 20XX amounted to $800,000.

ABC NONPROFIT
NOTES TO FINANCIAL STATEMENTS
June 30, 20XX

NOTE 8
NOTE PAYABLE

Note payable as of June 30, 20XX consisted of a note payable to a bank which is payable in monthly installments including interest at the one-month LIBOR plus 2.50% per annum and which is collateralized by a mortgage on certain real property. The note matures during May 20XX.

Approximate future maturities of the note payable are as follows:

For The Year Ended June 30,	
20X1	$ 275,000
20X2	300,000
20X3	315,000
20X4	340,000
20X5	360,000
Thereafter	2,830,000
Total	$ 4,420,000

Interest expense for the year ended June 30, 20XX amounted to $121,000.

NOTE 9
NET ASSETS WITH DONOR RESTRICTIONS

Net assets with donor restrictions were restricted for the following purposes:

	Beginning Balance July 1	Contributions and Income	Releases	Ending Balance June 30
Building fund	$ 400,000	$ 420,000	$ (220,000)	$ 600,000
Endowments with distributions restricted for educational opportunities	300,000	200,000	—	500,000
Endowments with distributions restricted for general program purposes	300,000	—	—	300,000
Food pantry	—	1,470,000	(1,250,000)	220,000
Net appreciation on endowments	—	110,000	(30,000)	80,000
Total	$ 1,000,000	$ 2,200,000	$ (1,500,000)	$ 1,700,000

The Nonprofit preserves the estimated fair value of all endowment gifts as of the gift date, which management deems is in compliance with state law. Accordingly, the Nonprofit classifies as "endowment corpus" (a) the original value of gifts donated to the permanent endowments, and (b) the original value of subsequent gifts to the permanent endowments. The Nonprofit has adopted an investment policy for endowment assets that attempts to provide a predictable stream of funding to supported programs while seeking to maintain the purchasing power of the endowment assets and to preserve the invested capital. The Nonprofit seeks the advice of investment counsel, as well as management and the Board, when determining amounts to be spent on supported programs. The Nonprofit has adopted a current annual spending rate of 5% of the estimated fair value of the endowment funds.

NOTE 10
RETIREMENT PLAN

Certain employees of the Nonprofit are enrolled in a retirement plan administered by XYZ ("the Plan"). The Nonprofit contributes 8% of each eligible employee's gross wages to the Plan each pay period. Participating employees may make elective deferral contributions by entering into a salary reduction arrangement. Employer contributions to the Plan amounted to approximately $300,000 during the year ended June 30, 20XX.

CHAPTER 3

Income—Contributions

The primary source of income for many nonprofit organizations is contribution revenue. Some nonprofits generate a substantial amount of their income from sources other than contributions. Other sources of revenue are addressed in Chapter 4. This chapter explores a variety of forms that contributions take.

CONTRIBUTIONS REVENUE

What is a contribution?

Whether labeled contributions, donations, gifts, or any other term, contributions represent a one-way transfer of value from a donor to the nonprofit. In other words, a contribution is a gift—a one-way transaction in which the donor does not receive anything of value in exchange. If a donor does receive something of value in exchange, the transaction (or at least part of it) is not a contribution. A detailed description of tax law and tax compliance considerations related to contributions is beyond the scope of this book. But the reader should be aware that special tax reporting considerations apply when a nonprofit provides donors something of value in exchange for a "contribution." For a very simple example, when nonprofit constituents pay the fee of $7 per person to attend a high school football game at a nonprofit school, that transaction is not a contribution because the member receives something of value (attendance at the game) in exchange for the money paid. Similarly, if a nonprofit sells educational books in a nonprofit bookstore, the purchase of a book is not a charitable contribution.

Contributions come in a variety of flavors and colors

Donors commonly make regular contributions to nonprofits by sending them checks in the mail or by donating electronically, either through online donations (mobile and otherwise) or by use of text messaging applications (where the donation is facilitated by third-party providers). And while such "regular" donations may represent the overwhelming majority of contribution revenue, contributions to nonprofits come in a variety of "flavors and colors." That is, contributions can vary in a number of ways from a simple unrestricted gift made by a nonprofit constituent. Following are some examples with a brief description for each.

AUTHOR'S NOTE: Electronic donations offers advantages over check-based, mailed-in contributions. *For one, many nonprofits report that when their donors give electronically, consistency in their giving improves. Additionally, electronic giving is typically more secure than giving by checks sent through the mail. Funds given electronically go directly into the nonprofit's bank account, eliminating the multiple points in the process in which checks are subject to loss.*

Pledges or expressions of intent to give

Some nonprofits ask their donors to provide an estimate or commitment of their expected donations for the coming year—as a means for the nonprofit to better estimate its revenues, as a means for establishing commitment and accountability on the part of the donors, or both.

Sometimes referred to as "pledges," "giving commitments," "faith promises," or other similar terms, such expressions of intent are not only made for regular giving. Nonprofits sometimes request that donors make such expressions in connection with special donation campaigns, such as campaigns to raise funds for a new building or special project. The expressions of intended donations made by donors help nonprofits estimate what they will receive in response to a campaign, a factor that can be very important for planning purposes.

When are pledges revenue?

When donors make such expressions with respect to their intended future donations, the accounting implications are important. Do such expressions represent revenue to the nonprofit when the expressions are made? Or is revenue recognized only when money is actually received? The correct answer depends on a few variables.

First, let's distinguish between *internal* financial reporting and *external* financial reporting. As we established in Chapter 2, no laws or regulations govern the details of internal financial reporting. Internal financial reporting should be designed to provide the most helpful information in a timely and relevant manner for decision-makers. So, for internal financial reporting purposes, the nonprofit should determine the most helpful way to present donor expressions with respect to their intent to give. It is likely that the most helpful and reasonable approach to internal reporting in this area is to track the estimated future donation amounts outside the actual financial statements of the nonprofit (i.e., do not recognize the pledges as revenue) and to recognize revenue when it is actually received. In my experience, that is the most common method used by nonprofits for internal financial reporting.

With respect to *external* financial reporting, it is first important to address the accounting framework the nonprofit uses in producing external financial statements. The three main accounting frameworks used by nonprofits and described in Chapter 2 are generally accepted accounting principles (GAAP), the cash basis, and the modified cash basis. Neither the cash basis nor the modified cash basis framework for external financial reporting would ordinarily recognize receivables—and so, regardless of the nature of the expression made by donors about their future donations, such amounts would not ordinarily represent revenue in external financial statements following either of those frameworks. Rather, revenue would be recognized when the contributions are actually received.

Under the GAAP framework, we must look a bit deeper into the nature of the expressions of intent made by the donors in order to determine the proper accounting treatment. GAAP accounting rules provide that an "unconditional promise to give" represents revenue at the time the unconditional promise is made. In defining an unconditional promise to give, the GAAP rules stop short of requiring that a commitment to give be legally enforceable. The rules focus on the intent of the donor in making the expression—and it is clear that the GAAP rules contemplate that the giver is expressing an unconditional commitment—that is, not just an estimate of what they *hope* to give but a full-pledged commitment ("promise") of what they *will* give. When a donor makes an unconditional promise to give to a nonprofit, the organization should be expected to rely on that commitment. So, if donors make unconditional promises to give—either for annual operations or for a special campaign—the correct accounting treatment under the GAAP framework is to recognize the amounts of such promises as revenue when they are made. If the period of time over which the promised gifts are to be made exceeds one year, the nonprofit is required to discount the amounts to their estimated present value. Additionally, the nonprofit is required to estimate amounts that will not be paid (amounts that are uncollectible—equivalent to bad debts) and recognize an offsetting allowance for the estimate of uncollectible amounts.

In my experience, the expressions of expected future donations made by nonprofit donors rarely meet the definition of an unconditional promise to give. Both nonprofits and their donors typically have an understanding that such expressions are estimates of what each donor hopes or expects to give, and neither party views the expression as unconditional. Both parties typically understand that a donor's circumstances can change and that what they will actually give may differ significantly from what they have expressed. In cases where donors make an expression of what they expect to give, and not an unconditional promise to give, the correct accounting treatment under the GAAP framework is not to recognize revenue until the contributions are actually received by the nonprofit. Depending on the circumstances, the nonprofit may wish to include a disclosure in the notes to its financial statements describing the expressions of intent to give made by donors.

From a practical perspective, nonprofits should realize that if they do consider donors' expressions of intent to give to represent unconditional promises to give, if the nonprofit's financial statements are audited by an external auditor, the auditor must test the asset amounts that the nonprofit has recognized as receivables due from its donors. Depending on the amounts involved, such testing typically includes a requirement for the auditor to confirm with donors in writing that the amount recognized by the nonprofit correctly represents the amount the donors have unconditionally promised to give. In my experience, nonprofits are often uncomfortable with an auditor having to obtain such confirmations from donors.

It is not always easy to determine whether an expression of intent to give by a donor represents an unconditional promise to give. Given that nonprofits and their donors are understandably not focused on GAAP accounting rules, they often use ambiguous or minimal documentation surrounding such expressions. For example, donors may be asked to fill out a card simply labeled "Giving Pledge for the Year 20XX," on which they are to put their name and a dollar amount. Does that represent an unconditional promise to give? Such a card in and of itself is inadequate for making that determination. Rather, one must look to the true intent of the parties, which is often undocumented. Nonprofits can prevent such confusion by including clear language on forms used for making such expressions. Regardless of what a form may be titled, a nonprofit can clarify the intent of the parties—that an expression of intent is not an unconditional promise to give—by adding language such as the following to the form:

> *This document represents an expression of the donor's current expectation regarding future donations and does not constitute an unconditional promise to give.*

Donor-restricted gifts

In addition to making regular, unrestricted gifts, donors can make restricted gifts to a nonprofit. A donor-restricted gift is one made by a donor and accepted by the nonprofit subject to a restriction as to time, purpose, or both. For example, a gift from a donor may be restricted such that the donated amount is to be invested permanently and only the earnings or distributions from the investment are to be used by the nonprofit. Such a gift, if accepted by the nonprofit, is considered "permanently restricted" given the intent of the donor that the original gift is not to be expended. Permanently restricted gifts are also commonly referred to as "endowments." As another example, a donor may restrict a gift to a nonprofit to be used to support scholarships. Such a gift, if accepted by the nonprofit, is considered "temporarily restricted" given the intent of the donor that the gift may be expended, but only for the stated purpose. Other examples of temporarily restricted gifts are gifts to a building fund or gifts for a special project.

The mere fact that a donor proposes to make a restricted gift to a nonprofit does not mean that the nonprofit must accept the gift or its proposed restriction. Suppose, for example, that a donor proposes to make a gift of $20,000 for the purchase of new signage for the nonprofit's headquarters building when the nonprofit has no need for or interest in new signage. It would be inappropriate for a nonprofit to accept a gift subject to such a restriction because it would be unusable. As another example, suppose a donor proposes to give $3 million to build a new program services building on the condition that the building be named after the donor. In deciding whether to accept such a gift, the nonprofit would need to consider several factors. Does it need a new program services building? Is $3 million enough to build it? If not, does the nonprofit intend to raise the difference in cost? Does the nonprofit wish to name the building after the donor? What happens in the event the donor later engages in some kind of disgraceful conduct? Can the nonprofit remove the donor's name from the building at that time?

Gifts restricted for projects and programs are tax deductible—gifts restricted for specific people are not

This book is not a book on tax compliance for nonprofits, and a detailed description of tax compliance considerations related to charitable contributions is outside the scope of this book. Nonprofit leaders should be aware, however, of an important principle in tax law with respect to restricted gifts made by donors. Contributions to a nonprofit are generally deductible by donors for income tax purposes under US federal income tax law. A restricted gift is deductible just like an unrestricted gift, so long as the restriction is a time restriction or a restriction for use of the gift for a particular project or program. But a gift restricted or earmarked by a donor for the benefit of one or more specific people is not a tax-deductible gift. For example, if a donor were to propose a gift to the nonprofit subject to a restriction that the gift be used to help the Donaldson family, who just lost their house in a fire, such a gift, if accepted by the nonprofit, would not be a tax-deductible contribution and should not be acknowledged by the nonprofit as one. Some nonprofit legal and accounting advisors would suggest that a nonprofit should not participate in such an arrangement regardless of whether it treats the gift as tax-deductible or not. Assuming such arrangements are occasional and not frequent, I do not share that concern, provided that such gifts are not acknowledged (receipted) by the nonprofit as charitable contributions and provided that there is a bona fide reason for a donor to make such a request (e.g., to keep the source of the gift anonymous).

> A restricted gift is deductible just like an unrestricted gift, so long as the restriction is a time restriction or a restriction for use of the gift for a particular project or program. But a gift restricted or earmarked by a donor for the benefit of one or more specific people is not a tax-deductible gift.

Noncash gifts

Donors sometimes offer, and nonprofits sometimes encourage, gifts of property in addition to gifts of money. Donors sometimes have significant tax advantages for donating appreciated property to a nonprofit charity. Noncash contributions to nonprofits commonly come in the form of publicly traded stocks. Donors sometimes make gifts of real estate. Rarer are gifts of tangible personal property, such as jewelry and furniture (unless the nonprofit operates a thrift shop or museum) or gifts of ownership interests in a privately held business.

Of the types of gifts described above, gifts of publicly traded stock are arguably the easiest to administer. The nonprofit needs to open a stock brokerage account with a brokerage firm to allow donors to transfer their stocks to the nonprofit's account. The nonprofit then sells the stocks and transfers the cash to their bank account. (Many nonprofits have a policy or practice of selling donated stocks immediately after they are received to avoid the risk of loss of value after the donation—a good practice. Investment management is a separate discipline that should be carried out pursuant to a well-defined strategy, as described in Chapter 6).

About that adage "Don't look a gift-horse in the mouth"

Other types of noncash property gifts require special consideration. For example, with respect to a proposed gift of real estate, the nonprofit will want to evaluate the potential risks associated with accepting the gift. Are there any liens on the property? Is there any environmental contamination on the property for which the nonprofit could be liable? Have all taxes been paid on the property? Is the property a liability risk? Is the property marketable? Is the nonprofit willing to incur the costs associated with holding the property while it is for sale? These are questions best addressed with the help of legal counsel.

For property gifts other than real estate, reasonable questions include whether the property is marketable and whether there are tax, legal, or other risks associated with the nonprofit's ownership of the property.

A gift acceptance policy
Many questions can arise related to whether to accept a nontraditional, noncash, or restricted gift. Accordingly, it is a good idea for nonprofits to have a gift acceptance policy—a policy that provides guidance in addressing nontraditional or restricted gifts. This chapter includes a sample gift acceptance policy for consideration.

Help with accepting and/or administering nontraditional gifts
One of your nonprofit's donors approaches you, the financial leader of your nonprofit, and offers to make a gift to the nonprofit of a 30 percent interest in a business owned by the donor. The business sells and installs windows in homes. The donor expects that the company or its assets will be sold in the near future at a very substantial gain and he wants your nonprofit to share in the reward. What do you do? On one hand, you appreciate the very generous spirit of the donor and his desire to benefit the nonprofit substantially. On the other hand, you are unsure of the implications or risks associated with the nonprofit owning such an asset, and you are uncomfortable having the nonprofit accept it. The good news is that there is an alternative to what may appear to be a dilemma. A number of nonprofit, tax-exempt organizations exist that have as one of their main purposes helping nonprofit organizations navigate such scenarios. Such organizations will, many times, accept such a gift into a fund that is dedicated to supporting a particular nonprofit 501(c)(3) tax-exempt organization. In the faith-based Christian sector, one such organization is the National Christian Foundation (NCF), headquartered in Atlanta, Georgia, with affiliates in a number of cities across the country. NCF has accepted numerous nontraditional gifts, including ownership interests in private companies, and used the proceeds from such gifts to support the donors' intended nonprofit charity. NCF charges administrative fees for its services. Another organization that offers such services is Barnabas Foundation, headquartered in Crete, Illinois. Barnabas Foundation requires an organization to be a member in order to participate in its programs. Organizations like NCF and Barnabas Foundation can uniquely facilitate some nontraditional gifts that a nonprofit may not be equipped to accept directly. Other religious groups have similar foundations. Similarly, in the non-

faith-based sector, many larger communities have community foundations equipped to facilitate nontraditional gifts for the benefit of a particular charitable nonprofit organization.

Acknowledging contributions for tax purposes

A detailed description of tax compliance considerations related to charitable contribution acknowledgments (receipts) is outside the scope of this book. One excellent resource for guidance on tax compliance considerations for charitable giving is the book, *The Guide to Charitable Giving for Churches and Ministries*, published by ECFA and available through its website at ecfa.org. Nonprofit financial leaders should be aware, however, of some key tax law principles that apply with respect to acknowledging charitable contributions.

1. Donors are required to obtain a proper acknowledgment for their cash and *non-cash* contributions prior to filing their tax returns. (This rule applies to all contributions except relatively small ones, and for practical reasons, most nonprofits issue proper acknowledgments for all contributions, regardless of size, so as to make sure the bases are covered.) Failure by a donor to obtain a proper written contribution acknowledgment from the nonprofit will result in the contribution being disallowed by the IRS in the event of an examination. The IRS has very strictly enforced this requirement, and the courts have backed up the IRS in its enforcement.
2. Nonprofits can easily overlook providing a proper acknowledgment to donors for nontraditional or noncash gifts because such gifts are not processed using the nonprofit's regular contribution processing systems. Nonprofits should review their records carefully at the end of each year to make sure that all nontraditional and noncash contributions are "on the radar" so that they can issue proper acknowledgments to donors.
3. Special rules exist for acknowledging contributions in which the donor receives something of value in exchange (e.g., payments to attend a dinner banquet or payments to participate in a fundraising golf tournament sponsored by the nonprofit). The full amount of such payments is not deductible. This type of contribution is referred to in the tax law as a *quid pro quo* contribution.
4. Nonprofit finance leaders should be well aware of the requirements for proper contribution acknowledgments and issue them to donors either at the time of each gift or early in the year following the year in which the contributions were made. Financial penalties apply to the nonprofit for failure to issue proper acknowledgments for *quid pro quo* contributions. While there are not financial penalties for failure to issue proper acknowledgments for other types of

contributions, the adverse impact on donors for such failure could be disastrous. Due to the requirement that donors have proper acknowledgments in hand prior to filing their tax returns, it is considered a best practice to issue all charitable contribution acknowledgments for the prior year by January 31 each year.
5. Gifts of donated services and gifts of the use of property are not tax deductible and should not be acknowledged as tax-deductible contributions. (Note, however, that out-of-pocket expenses incurred by volunteers while performing their volunteer services are generally deductible—subject to proper substantiation.)
6. As described previously in this chapter, gifts restricted by donors to benefit one or more specific people are not tax deductible and should not be acknowledged as tax-deductible contributions.
7. Gifts of automobiles, boats, and airplanes, if accepted, are subject to special documentation requirements.
8. If the nonprofit accepts a noncash property donation (other than publicly traded stock), the nonprofit may be subject to a requirement to file a form with the IRS when it sells or otherwise disposes of the property.

PLANNED AND DEFERRED GIVING

The terms "planned giving" and "deferred giving" are often used interchangeably to refer to any method of giving by a donor to a nonprofit charitable organization at some point in the future, after the donor's execution of an agreement or other gift instrument gives effect to the gift. This book uses the terms "planned giving" and "planned gift" to refer to such methods of giving.

The most common examples of planned giving by nonprofit donors in the United States are:

- Charitable bequests pursuant to a will or similar document;
- Gifts of life insurance;
- Charitable gift annuities; and
- Charitable remainder trusts.

Other less common forms of planned giving by nonprofit donors exist and are outside the scope of this book. A few examples are charitable lead trusts, pooled income funds, and gifts of remainder interests in property. A nonprofit that is approached by a donor interested in making a planned gift should consider the donor's proposal together with knowledgeable legal and tax counsel. The mere fact that a proposed planned gift may seem complex is not a reason for a nonprofit to reject such a proposal. To do so could represent poor fiscal management. With proper legal and tax advice, a nonprofit may determine that accepting a seemingly complex proposed planned gift is in its best interests.

Some larger nonprofits have one or more staff members dedicated to encouraging and overseeing planned gifts from donors. Commonly, organizations that have been in existence for a long time and that have developed a mature base of donors can benefit by educating their donors about the availability and benefits of various planned giving arrangements.

The mere fact that a proposed planned gift may seem complex is not a reason for a nonprofit to reject such a proposal. To do so could represent poor fiscal management.

Charitable bequests

One of the simplest ways donors may make a planned gift is to leave assets to their nonprofit charity of choice as part of a will or other similar estate document (such as a revocable living trust). Since the provisions of a will or revocable living trust may be changed from time to time, a donor is not entitled to an income tax deduction during his or her lifetime for simply naming a nonprofit charity as a beneficiary in a will or similar document.

Requests by donors for estate planning assistance

At times, donors may seek advice or referrals from leaders of a nonprofit organization they support regarding their estate planning. Sometimes, donors seek such advice from the nonprofit because they wish to include the nonprofit as a beneficiary in their estate plans. Nonprofits should obtain advice from experienced legal counsel in determining whether or to what extent the nonprofit should assist a donor with estate planning. On one hand, a nonprofit wants to encourage and (to the extent appropriate) facilitate a donor's desire to make a planned gift to the nonprofit. On the other hand, a nonprofit is not a law firm and if the nonprofit provides advice to a donor regarding legal matters, the nonprofit would likely be in violation of state law. Additionally, if the nonprofit facilitates a donor's decision to include the nonprofit in his/her will or other estate planning documents as a beneficiary, the nonprofit could be open to allegations of undue influence over the donor's decisions. If family members of the donor or others protest the validity of the designation of the nonprofit as a beneficiary, there is a risk that a court may rule that the designation by the donor of the nonprofit as a beneficiary was invalid. Nonprofits and their legal counsel should consider these issues carefully in determining how to properly address a request by a donor for estate planning assistance.

Gifts of life insurance

As has long been the case, there are perfectly acceptable ways for donors to make gifts of life insurance to a nonprofit charitable organization. Unfortunately, due to negative publicity in recent years surrounding questionable practices involving donors, charities, and life insurance providers, much confusion exists in the area of tax law associated with gifts of life insurance.

Inappropriate life insurance transactions

The negative publicity in recent years in the area of charitable gifts of life insurance relates primarily to practices involving "charitable split-dollar life insurance." Charitable split-dollar life insurance arrangements typically involve a donor or a member of the donor's family being entitled to certain benefits in connection with the contribution of all or part of a life insurance policy to a nonprofit charity, along with payments by the donor to cover the premiums of such a policy.

In *Notice 99-36,* the Internal Revenue Service addressed charitable split-dollar life insurance arrangements by stating:

> In general, a charitable split-dollar insurance transaction involves a transfer of funds by a taxpayer to a charity, with the understanding that the charity will use the transferred funds to pay premiums on a cash value life insurance policy that benefits **both the charity and the taxpayer's family**. Typically, as part of this transaction, the charity or an irrevocable life insurance trust formed by the taxpayer (or a related person) purchases the cash value life insurance policy. The designated beneficiaries of the insurance policy include both the charity and the trust. **Members of the taxpayer's family (and, perhaps, the taxpayer) are beneficiaries of the trust.** [Emphasis added.]
>
> In a related transaction, the charity enters into a split-dollar agreement with the trust. The split-dollar agreement specifies what portion of the insurance policy premiums is to be paid by the trust and what portion is to be paid by the charity. The agreement specifies the extent to which each party can exercise standard policyholder rights, such as the right to borrow against the cash value of the policy, to partially or completely surrender the policy for cash, and to designate beneficiaries for specified portions of the death benefit. The agreement also specifies the manner in which it may be terminated and the consequences of such termination. Although the terms of these split-dollar agreements vary, the common

feature is that, over the life of the split-dollar agreement, the trust has access to a disproportionately high percentage of the cash-surrender value and death benefit under the policy, compared to the percentage of premiums paid by the trust.

Charitable split-dollar insurance transactions
As part of the charitable split-dollar insurance transaction, the taxpayer (or a related person) transfers funds to the charity. Although there may be no legally binding obligation expressly requiring the taxpayer to transfer funds to the charity to assist in making premium payments, or expressly requiring the charity to use the funds transferred by the taxpayer for premium payments in accordance with the split-dollar agreement, both parties understand that this will occur.

The structure of charitable split-dollar insurance transactions varies. In some cases, a member of the taxpayer's family, a family limited partnership, or another type of intermediary related to the taxpayer is used as an intermediary rather than an irrevocable life insurance trust. This notice applies to any charitable split-dollar insurance transaction, regardless of whether a trust or some other type of related intermediary is used in the transaction.

Generally, to be deductible as a charitable contribution, a payment to charity must be a gift. A gift to charity is a payment of money or transfer of property without receipt of adequate consideration and with donative intent. However, regardless of whether a taxpayer receives a benefit in return for a transfer to charity or has the requisite donative intent, sections 170(f)(3) and 2522(c)(2) provide that generally no charitable deduction is allowed for a transfer to charity of less than the taxpayer's entire interest (i.e., a partial interest) in any property. **Thus, no charitable contribution deduction is permitted when a taxpayer assigns a partial interest in an insurance policy to a charity.** [Emphasis added.]

The IRS considers charitable split-dollar life insurance arrangements to be abusive transactions, as is made clear by the following excerpts from *Notice 99-36*:

Depending on the facts and circumstances, **the Service may challenge, on the basis of private inurement or impermissible private benefit, the tax-exempt status of a charity that participates in charitable split-dollar insurance transactions.** [Emphasis added.]

In addition, the Service may impose penalties on participants in charitable split-dollar insurance transactions, including the accuracy-related penalty under section 6662, the return-preparer penalty under section 6694, the promoter penalty under section 6700, and the penalty under section 6701 for aiding and abetting the understatement of tax liability.

Clearly the IRS is not a fan of charitable split-dollar life insurance arrangements. **Nonprofits should avoid participation in such arrangements.**

Permissible life insurance gifts

Donors may make life insurance-related gifts to nonprofits in a variety of acceptable ways:

Simply naming the nonprofit as a beneficiary of a life insurance policy
A donor may simply name a nonprofit charity as a beneficiary of a life insurance policy. In doing so, the donor may make the nonprofit either the sole beneficiary or one of multiple beneficiaries. In such an arrangement, the donor retains ownership of the insurance policy and makes the related premium payments. There is no transfer of ownership of the insurance policy to the nonprofit, nor does the nonprofit have any responsibility with respect to making premium payments. Additionally, the owner of the insurance policy is typically permitted to change the beneficiaries of his or her life insurance policy while the insured person is living.

Since no ownership transfer is made to the nonprofit in connection with naming the nonprofit as a beneficiary, and since a donor may change a beneficiary designation, a donor is not entitled to a charitable contribution deduction for federal income tax purposes in connection with naming the nonprofit as a beneficiary of a life insurance policy. As is the case with many other types of planned gifts, a nonprofit may not be aware of the fact that it has been named by a donor as a beneficiary of a life insurance policy. The nonprofit may simply receive a death benefit payment upon the death of the insured person. Such arrangements are both common and permissible.

Transferring ownership of an insurance policy to the nonprofit
A donor may transfer ownership of an insurance policy to the nonprofit. Of course, in so doing, the beneficiary designation should be changed as well so that the nonprofit is the sole beneficiary. It is important to note here that a transfer of the

entire ownership interest of an insurance policy to the nonprofit is an acceptable charitable practice, unlike the scenario described for charitable split-dollar life insurance arrangements.

Life insurance policies typically exist in one of two broad types: term insurance (which does not accumulate cash value and typically only pays a death benefit) and insurance that can accumulate cash value as well as provide a death benefit (often referred to as "whole," "universal," "variable," or "cash value" life insurance). The provisions of life insurance policies, including premium payment obligations, vary widely and no attempt to provide simple descriptions or categorizations of such policy variations would be adequate here.

When a donor transfers his or her entire interest in a life insurance policy to the nonprofit, the donor may be entitled to a charitable contribution deduction for federal income tax purposes. A contribution of a life insurance policy to a nonprofit is considered a noncash contribution and is subject to the ordinary rules that apply to noncash charitable contributions. A term life insurance policy may have little or no economic value, especially if premiums must continue to be paid in order to keep the policy in force. On the other hand, a term life insurance policy may have significant value if the person whose life is insured has a short life expectancy. A cash-value type life insurance policy may have economic value if the owner may surrender the policy in exchange for cash. A donor making a gift of a life insurance policy must determine the value of the policy contributed to the nonprofit. If the donor wishes to claim the value of the policy as a charitable contribution deduction, the donor should follow guidance for noncash contributions such as that found in *IRS Publication 561* and *IRS Publication 526*, as well as IRS Form 8283 and its related instructions. If the donor claims a value for a contributed life insurance policy in excess of $5,000, the donor likely will request the nonprofit to sign Form 8283 acknowledging receipt of the life insurance policy.

Determining whether to accept a gift of a life insurance policy
When a donor offers to contribute ownership of a life insurance policy to a nonprofit, the nonprofit should evaluate the form and economics of the proposed gift. For policies that do not require future premium payments, the decision likely will be quite simple. For policies that require future premium payments, the nonprofit should evaluate whether the donor intends to make future contributions to the nonprofit that are sufficient to cover the premiums. (Such plans are permissible

under federal tax law, provided that the nonprofit is the sole owner and beneficiary of the policy. In such arrangements, assuming that the nonprofit is the sole owner of the life insurance policy as well as the sole beneficiary, the donor is not receiving anything in exchange for contributions that are intended to help the nonprofit make future premium payments. Accordingly, such contributions would ordinarily be deductible just like other charitable contributions.)

With most insurance policies, the only adverse consequence of failing to pay premiums is that the policy lapses. If the nonprofit accepts a gift of a policy that requires future premium payments and the donor fails to make contributions to fund the payments, the nonprofit must decide whether to make the premium payments without a subsidy from the donor, or to stop making the payments and allow the policy to lapse. Cash-value type life insurance policies may have accumulated value that will permit deferral of premium payments for a period of time. The nonprofit may also wish to consider the life expectancy of the donor in making a decision about whether to accept a proposed gift of a life insurance policy or to continue making premium payments for a policy it owns. The nonprofit should consider all relevant economic factors in making the decision. It would be wise for the nonprofit to consult with a knowledgeable life insurance broker or agent and legal counsel in evaluating proposed gifts of life insurance.

Charitable gift annuities

Charitable gift annuities represent a method of accommodating an **irrevocable** planned gift. A charitable gift annuity is an agreement between a donor and a nonprofit charity pursuant to which the donor transfers something of value to the nonprofit (typically money) in exchange for the nonprofit's promise to make regular payments to the donor for a stated period of time. The stated period of time may be a fixed number of years or the remainder of the donor's life. Payments may begin immediately, or they may be deferred for an agreed-upon period of time.

When payments are to be made only to one beneficiary, such arrangements are commonly referred to as "single-life" gift annuities. A donor may stipulate that payments are to be made as long as one of two beneficiaries is still living. Such arrangements are commonly referred to as "joint and survivor" gift annuities. Other variations of gift annuities exist as well.

Gift annuity payments are typically described in terms of a percentage of the value of property or money that the donor transfers to the nonprofit at the time the annuity is established.

EXAMPLE Ted and Mildred Wilson entered into a gift annuity agreement with Do Good Charity pursuant to which Mr. and Mrs. Wilson transferred $100,000 to the nonprofit. Ted is 70 years old and Mildred is 68. The agreement calls for the nonprofit to make 6-percent annuity payments in monthly installments to the couple so long as either of them is living beginning on the first month after the annuity agreement is executed. Accordingly, the nonprofit will make payments of $6,000 per year (6 percent multiplied by $100,000) to the couple in monthly installments of $500 so long as either of them is living. This is an example of a typical joint and survivor immediate charitable gift annuity arrangement.

If the facts stated previously were the same, except that the annuity payments did not begin until five years after the annuity agreement was executed, such an agreement would represent a joint and survivor *deferred* charitable gift annuity arrangement.

Legal and regulatory considerations for gift annuities

A nonprofit must consider legal and regulatory implications prior to offering gift annuities to its donors. The offering of gift annuities and the related administration of gift annuities is an activity that is regulated by many states in the US. For states that regulate gift annuities, statutory requirements are typically part of the state's insurance laws and the regulatory agency that oversees gift annuities is typically the same agency that oversees insurance regulation in the state. States that regulate gift annuities typically have specific requirements for the content of annuity agreements, the annuity rates that nonprofits may pay, the manner in which charitable gift annuity funds must be invested, and the amount of "reserves and surplus" that an issuing organization must maintain in connection with its outstanding gift annuities.

Nonprofits must have experienced legal counsel advising them with respect to the issuance and administration of charitable gift annuities under applicable state law.

Tax aspects of charitable gift annuities

A donor is typically entitled to a charitable contribution deduction for federal income tax purposes in connection with establishing a charitable gift annuity. A calculation must be made of the present value of estimated future annuity payments to be made under the agreement. The present value of the future annuity payments is subtracted from the value of money or property transferred by the donor to the nonprofit at the inception of the agreement. The net result, which is the present value of the nonprofit's estimated remainder interest in the annuity, is typically the amount deductible by the donor. Additionally, annuity payments made to the beneficiaries (or "annuitants") are typically only partially taxable, as a portion of the annuity payment is considered a return of the donor's original investment in the agreement.

Nonprofits offering gift annuities should do so only under the advice of knowledgeable tax and legal counsel, who can assist in compliance matters as well as in making the present value calculations described previously.

Alternatives to administering charitable gift annuities directly

Some organizations offer to accept and/or administer charitable gift annuities for the benefit of nonprofit charitable organizations that do not wish to engage in such activities themselves. A nonprofit's legal counsel can assist the nonprofit in evaluating the advisability of such arrangements.

The American Council on Gift Annuities

Significant additional information about gift annuities and related topics is available from the American Council on Gift Annuities (ACGA) at acga-web.org. The ACGA publishes recommended charitable gift annuity rates which are updated periodically and are typically utilized by nonprofits that issue gift annuities.

Charitable remainder trusts

A charitable remainder trust has features that are similar to a charitable gift annuity, but unlike a charitable gift annuity (which is an agreement directly between the donor and the issuing nonprofit organization), a charitable remainder trust is actually a separate legal entity created by a donor for the purpose of accommodating a planned gift. A trust is typically created pursuant to a trust document and must generally have one or more trustees and one or more beneficiaries. A charitable remainder trust will have one or more **income beneficiaries**, who receive payments initially, and one or more **remainder beneficiaries**, such as the donor's chosen nonprofit charity.

Nonprofit as trustee?

It is possible that a donor may ask the nonprofit to serve as trustee of a charitable remainder trust. Since the nonprofit will be a remainder beneficiary of the trust, and because there are significant legal considerations, nonprofits should not accept the role of trustee of a charitable remainder trust unless they have evaluated the matter carefully under the advice of legal counsel and determined that serving as trustee would be appropriate in the circumstances. The risks can be greater for a trust in which the nonprofit is not the sole remainder beneficiary (due to the fact that the nonprofit is responsible for managing the trust's assets for the ultimate benefit of another nonprofit organization, in addition to itself). Some nonprofit organizations will not, as a matter of internal policy, accept the role of trustee for charitable remainder trusts.

If the nonprofit does not wish to serve as trustee, other options include banks with trust departments and independent nonprofit foundations.

Types of charitable remainder trusts

There are *many* variations of charitable remainder trusts. The two broadest categories of charitable remainder trusts (of which there are many subtypes) are:

1. Charitable remainder annuity trusts; and
2. Charitable remainder unitrusts.

A common form of **charitable remainder annuity trust** (often referred to as a "CRAT") is a trust wherein a donor transfers money or property to the trust in exchange for **equal annual payments** to be made over an agreed-upon period of time, with the remainder interest going to a designated charity.

A CRAT operates in a manner very similar to a charitable gift annuity. However, since a trust is a separate legal entity and the nonprofit is not the "issuer," such arrangements are not subject to the same regulatory requirements that apply to charitable gift annuities under the laws of many states. State law may, however, govern the manner in which the trustee of such a trust must administer it. Note that as a remainder beneficiary, a nonprofit may be unaware that a donor has formed such a trust until it is notified of its right to receive the remainder proceeds. Such occurrences are rather common.

> **EXAMPLE** Ted and Mildred Smith formed a charitable remainder annuity trust and named their bank as trustee and Do Good Charity as the remainder beneficiary. Mr. and Mrs. Smith contributed $100,000 to the trust. The trust document stipulates that Mr. and Mrs. Smith will receive 6 percent of the original trust principal annually for as long as either one of them is living. Accordingly, Mr. and Mrs. Smith will receive $6,000 per year from the trust as long as either one of them is living. At the second death, Do Good Charity will receive the remaining assets of the trust.

Ted and Mildred Smith are entitled to an income tax deduction at the time they fund the trust. The deduction is determined in a manner similar to that for gift annuities as described previously.

A common form of **charitable remainder unitrust** (often referred to as a "CRUT") is a trust wherein a donor transfers money or property to the trust in exchange for payments equal to **a fixed percentage of the value** of the trust's assets each year for a stated period of time. A remainder interest goes to a designated charity. Since the value of the trust's assets may change from year to year, the amount of the payments to the beneficiaries may vary from year to year, while the percentage remains fixed.

As is the case with CRATs, CRUTs are not regulated in the same manner as charitable gift annuities under the laws of many states. State law may, however, govern the manner in which the trustee of such a trust must administer it. Note that as a remainder beneficiary, a nonprofit may not be aware that a donor has formed such a trust until it is notified of its right to receive the remainder proceeds. Such occurrences are rather common.

> **EXAMPLE** Ted and Mildred Smith formed a charitable remainder unitrust and named their bank as trustee and Do Good Charity as the remainder beneficiary. Mr. and Mrs. Smith contributed $100,000 to the trust. The trust document stipulates that Mr. and Mrs. Smith will receive 6 percent of the value of the trust's assets as of the beginning of each year annually for as long as either one of them is living. Accordingly, Mr. and Mrs. Smith will receive $6,000 from the trust in the first year. Assume that at the beginning of Year 2, the value of the trust's assets is $110,000. In Year 2, Mr. and Mrs. Smith will receive 6 percent of $110,000, or $6,600. This annual process will continue as long as either one of them is living. At the second death, Do Good Charity will receive the remaining assets of the trust.

Ted and Mildred Smith are entitled to an income tax deduction at the time they fund the trust. The deduction is determined by calculating the estimated present value of the nonprofit's remainder interest pursuant to guidelines prescribed by the IRS.

CLAWBACKS OF CHARITABLE CONTRIBUTIONS—A CONTINUING CHALLENGE

One of the more insidious risks nonprofits face with respect to charitable contributions is the risk that contributions received from a particular donor may later be ruled "fraudulent transfers" or "fraudulent conveyances" under federal bankruptcy law or applicable state law. The nonprofit that receives the contributions may have no idea that a donor is facing bankruptcy or that a donor may have obtained the donated funds in an ill-gotten manner (such as a Ponzi scheme). If such conditions are present, a bankruptcy trustee, creditors of a donor, or law enforcement authorities may assert that contributions made to the nonprofit were "fraudulent" and, as a result, must be returned by the nonprofit to a receiver, trustee, or other party to pay the creditors or to be used for other purposes. The laws that require such refunds are often referred to as "clawback" laws.

> One of the more insidious risks nonprofits face with respect to charitable contributions is the risk that contributions received from a particular donor may later be ruled "fraudulent transfers" or "fraudulent conveyances" under federal bankruptcy law or applicable state law.

Clawbacks of charitable contributions can be particularly damaging to a nonprofit, especially in cases where the contributions are large, and the nonprofit has spent the money on operations or assets before learning of the clawback claim. Accordingly, **nonprofit leaders would be well-advised to carefully evaluate large or unusual gifts. If there is any concern about the possibility of a clawback claim, the organization should consult with legal counsel and consider holding the assets for a period until it is deemed safe by the nonprofit's legal counsel to spend them—possibly three years or more.**

Numerous instances of clawbacks of charitable contributions occurred during the Great Recession and they still occur today.

The federal government and many states have laws that provide nonprofits ***very limited protection*** from clawbacks. For example, Florida law (which is comparable to the laws of a number of states) provides that **a natural person's (in other words, an actual person and not a business or other legal entity) charitable contributions are fraudulent transfers if they were received within two years before the commencement of a Florida Uniform Fraudulent Transfer Act, bankruptcy, or insolvency proceeding, unless:**

a. **The transfer was made consistent with the debtor's practices in making charitable contributions; or**

b. **The transfer was received in good faith and did not exceed 15 percent of the debtor's gross annual income for the year in which the transfer was made.**

(These provisions are also comparable to those found in the federal Bankruptcy Code's protection for charitable contributions against a bankruptcy trustee's clawback action.)

SAMPLE GIFT ACCEPTANCE POLICY

[Note that the Nonprofit may choose to substitute an appropriate committee in lieu of the Board for certain decisions and may select an appropriate official in lieu of the top business official where appropriate.]

Donor-restricted cash gifts

Cash gifts over $10,000 that are given with a donor restriction (other than gifts to a special fund already approved by the Board) must be brought before the Board for approval prior to acceptance. Recommendations for special recognition of donors (such as publicizing names, naming buildings, rooms, etc.) will be referred to the Board for approval. For donor-restricted cash gifts approved by the Board and exceeding $100,000, the top nonprofit business official shall ensure that the Nonprofit's legal counsel assists in the drafting or review of the documents constituting the gift transfer.

The top nonprofit business official or his/her designee is responsible for addressing proposed donor-restricted cash gifts of $10,000 or less where the proposed restriction is not to a fund already approved by the Board. Such gifts, if accepted, must be for purposes consistent with the Nonprofit's mission and must involve complete expenditure of the gifts within one year of receipt.

Gifts of noncash property

Receiving gifts of noncash property can result in additional expenses for the Nonprofit. This policy establishes a minimum standard for matters to be reviewed in making the determination of whether to accept or reject a gift of noncash property. Once a gift of property is accepted, a proper acknowledgment that conforms to current federal tax law shall be provided to the donor.

Real property

Prior to accepting a gift of real property, the top nonprofit business official or his/her designee shall perform an initial evaluation of the practicality of accepting the offered donation. If the initial evaluation is positive, the top nonprofit business official or his/

her designee shall oversee the performance of reasonable due diligence, including assessment of environmental matters, title, and other such matters deemed appropriate by the top nonprofit business official or his/her designee under the advice of legal counsel. The top nonprofit business official or his/her designee will make a recommendation to the Board regarding acceptance of the donation. The Board must approve, in advance, acceptance of real property. The top nonprofit business official or his/her designee shall ensure that the Nonprofit's legal counsel assists in the drafting or review of the documents constituting the gift transfer.

Intangible personal property
The top nonprofit business official or his/her designee shall address proposed gifts of intangible personal property as follows, provided, however, that contributions with donor restrictions are subject to the policy on donor-restricted cash gifts as set forth previously. Contributions of publicly traded securities with a ready market may be accepted and should be sold as soon as possible after receipt. Contributions of other types of intangible personal property including, but not limited to, stock in privately held entities, limited liability company membership interests, partnership interests, or private debt instruments, must first be evaluated for potential value and marketability. If the top nonprofit business official or his/her designee believes the potential value and marketability of a proposed gift warrants further consideration, he/she shall consult with legal counsel and tax counsel as necessary to evaluate the implications of accepting the gift. If the top nonprofit business official or his/her designee, after such consultations, considers it desirable to pursue acceptance of the proposed gift, he/she shall present his/her findings and recommendations to the Board for final approval prior to acceptance of the proposed gift. Except in the case of a transfer of publicly traded securities with a ready market, the top nonprofit business official or his/her designee shall ensure that the Nonprofit's legal counsel assists in the drafting or review of the documents constituting the gift transfer.

Tangible personal property
Prior to accepting a gift of tangible personal property, the top nonprofit business official or his/her designee shall perform an initial evaluation of the practicality of accepting the offered donation. If the initial evaluation is positive, the top nonprofit business official or his/her designee shall oversee the performance of reasonable due diligence.

a. Tangible personal property will be accepted only if:
   (i) The property is in good condition and can be used by the Nonprofit in its mission; or
   (ii) The property can be sold for an amount adequate to exceed costs associated with accepting, holding, and disposing of the gift.
b. Tangible personal property having a value of $5,000 or more shall be accepted only after the top nonprofit business official or his/her designee has consulted with legal counsel to address risks of unpaid liens or other liabilities, taking into consideration possible UCC-1 lien searches or similar lien searches.
c. All gifts of tangible personal property valued at more than $1,000 must be approved by the top nonprofit business official or his/her designee before they can be accepted. Any tangible personal property gifts valued over $50,000 also require approval of the Board prior to acceptance. For gifts of tangible personal property valued at more than $100,000, the top nonprofit business official or his/her designee shall ensure that the Nonprofit's legal counsel assists in the drafting or review of the documents constituting the gift transfer.

CHAPTER 4

Other Revenue Sources

While the primary source of revenue for many nonprofits is contributions, nonprofits often generate revenue from other sources. For purposes of this chapter, we will refer to revenue from sources other than contributions as *alternative source revenue.* Alternative source revenue may be generated by nonprofit activities and programs (such as food service programs in which patrons are charged for meals or school programs in which patrons are charged tuition) or by more passive activities (such as investing funds to produce income). In this chapter we will explore the variety of alternative sources of revenue, as well as some of the implications that nonprofits must consider in this area.

ALTERNATIVE SOURCE REVENUE

Here are some of the more common forms of alternative source revenue:

Investment income (from investment of liquid funds)

Investment income (interest, dividends, and capital gains) is one of the most common sources of alternative source revenue for nonprofits, as they invest cash reserves in various income-producing investments, such as interest-bearing bank accounts, certificates of deposit, stocks, bonds, mutual funds, and so on. Important considerations related to investment management practices and related topics are addressed in detail in Chapter 6.

Rental income

Rental income is a form of investment income, typically generated by nonprofits that allow other parties to use all or a portion of their real estate in exchange for rent. (Rental income also may be generated by allowing other parties to use *tangible personal property,* such as furniture and equipment, although such arrangements are rare among nonprofits.) Nonprofits may generate rental income from real estate in a variety of scenarios. For example, nonprofits may rent unused office space to other organizations. In some cases, nonprofits may own real estate as investment property (either residential or commercial) and generate rental income. For example, some nonprofits own commercial office buildings and rent space in them to commercial tenants. Some nonprofits own retail shopping centers and rent space in the property to retail merchants.

Income from parking lots or garages

Some nonprofits are located in areas where parking is scarce and needed by people in the area during times when the nonprofit's use is minimal. For example, a nonprofit located in an urban commercial area, such as the "downtown" area of a city, may have significant parking capacity that is not used by the nonprofit during the evening and on weekends. In many such situations, a nonprofit will allow others to use its parking facilities for a fee. Such arrangements may be made in bulk, where the nonprofit rents its entire parking lot to another party, or the nonprofit may directly operate the parking facility, charging individual patrons for using it. As another example, some nonprofit offices are located near venues that attract large crowds, such as sports stadiums and arenas. Nonprofits in such locations often generate income from their parking areas in connection with events at those venues. As described in the section below related to tax considerations of alternative source revenue, the manner in which a nonprofit generates revenue from its excess parking capacity will dictate whether the income is considered rental income for federal income tax purposes, which will affect the federal income tax treatment of the income generated.

Activity revenues

Many nonprofits conduct a variety of activities that generate revenue—some with more of a connection to the nonprofit's exempt purpose activities than others. Motivations for conducting such activities vary widely. Here are some common examples:

Bookstores or gift shops

A nonprofit may operate a bookstore or gift shop selling educational books and other items that help educate users about matters relevant to the organization's exempt purposes. Some nonprofit stores sell other types of merchandise, including clothing, jewelry, and cosmetics. Some nonprofit stores are operated in locations deep within the nonprofit's facilities, are open only at limited times, and are intended primarily to serve the people in attendance at the nonprofit's activities. Other nonprofit stores are located in high-traffic street-front retail locations (either on or off the nonprofit's regular operating premises) and are open during typical retail hours in an effort to attract the general public.

Thrift shops

Some nonprofits operate thrift shops in which they sell used household goods and clothing that have been donated by supporters of the nonprofit. Nonprofit thrift shops vary in sophistication from small spaces on the nonprofit's operating premises to large, appealing retail thrift stores operated in high-traffic commercial areas.

Schools and other educational programs

Many nonprofits operate educational programs such as schools (kindergarten through 12th grade, or portions thereof), colleges and universities, preschools, day care programs, and so on and generate revenue from tuition and fees from such programs.

Cafés, coffee shops, and restaurants

In recent years, many nonprofits have begun operating cafés, coffee shops, and other similar activities—typically in connection with program activities. The nature and sophistication of such activities range from simple kiosks selling coffee and pastries in the nonprofit's facilities, to food courts comparable to those found in shopping malls, to full-service restaurants at which members of the public can make reservations. For organizations like museums and zoos, cafes are available to patrons visiting the facility in order to allow them to stay longer. For schools, lunch programs are central to the overall program. The nonprofit's primary motivation for conducting such activities is typically to serve the people who attend or participate in the nonprofit's program activities. For some very large nonprofits that have relatively continuous activities at their facilities, foodservice operations are often more extensive and elaborate. Some nonprofits even offer catering to patrons at offsite locations.

Special events

Some nonprofits conduct special events that generate revenue, such as festivals, carnivals, banquets, concerts, and similar activities. Motivations for conducting such events vary and may be primarily related to the nonprofit's mission or, alternatively, primarily related to generating income for the nonprofit. The sophistication of such events also varies widely. A simple nonprofit banquet celebrating Mother's Day, for example, may consist of providing a meal and a simple program in exchange for an admission fee. As a contrast, a nonprofit might conduct a multi-day festival featuring carnival rides, games, concessions, and entertainment that may be funded by sales of admissions, concessions revenues, sales of tickets for individual entertainment activities, and corporate sponsorships. Nonprofits may also host music concerts featuring popular recording artists or entertainers, or other similar activities, typically in exchange for admission fees.

Event hosting

Nonprofits may also host events for nonprofit constituents and, in some cases, for outside groups. For example, some nonprofits will host weddings, banquets, reunions, business meetings, private parties, and other gatherings, for which the group uses the nonprofit's facilities and for which the nonprofit provides banquet-type services.

For example, at a wedding, the nonprofit may provide the entertainment, decorations, foodservice, and more. While seemingly similar to the rental activity described above, event hosting is distinct because it involves the provision of significant services in addition to the use of the nonprofit's property.

Broadcasting activities

Some nonprofits operate radio and television stations licensed by the Federal Communications Commission (FCC). The FCC license may be an "educational" or "noncommercial" license (restricting the content to noncommercial content) or it may be a regular "commercial" license (which permits advertising and other commercial content). Operators of noncommercial television and radio stations may sell noncommercial programming time on the station and/or accept corporate sponsorships as a way to generate revenue. Commercial license operators may sell programming time on the station, corporate sponsorships, and/or spots for regular commercials.

ISSUES TO CONSIDER: MISSION AND PURPOSE

Surprisingly, many nonprofits embark on the conduct of alternative revenue source activities without much thought for whether the activities are "on mission" for the nonprofit or not. In fact, as addressed in Chapter 1, many nonprofits do not have a clearly defined and specific expression of mission and purpose—which can make it impossible to determine whether a given activity is "on mission." Such considerations should be the starting place for any nonprofit contemplating an alternative source revenue activity. If the nonprofit does not have a clear and specific sense of mission and purpose, developing and expressing that is the first step. (See Chapter 1 for more details on the topic of Mission and Purpose.)

"Watershed" criteria

There really are only two possible valid motivations for a nonprofit to engage in a particular revenue-generating activity, and at least one of them should be present to justify further consideration of an activity by the nonprofit. The activity should:

> **Surprisingly, many nonprofits embark on the conduct of alternative revenue source activities without much thought for whether the activities are "on mission" for the nonprofit or not.**

a. significantly help the nonprofit advance its mission and purpose,
b. generate significant net income or positive cash flow for the nonprofit, or
c. do both of the above.

Some nonprofits will not consider an activity that does not meet the first criterion, regardless of whether it meets the second criterion—an understandable position.

In addition to the "watershed" criteria described previously, nonprofits should evaluate other aspects of a proposed activity before conducting it. Any nonprofit considering generating income from an alternative revenue source should do so utilizing a rubric that takes into consideration questions such as the following:

10 Questions to ask before starting an alternative revenue source activity

1. Does conducting the activity help the nonprofit carry out its stated mission and purpose? If so, how, and to what extent? Is the activity's positive impact in carrying out the nonprofit's mission and purpose truly expected to be significant and worth the effort? What are the metrics for success in this context, and how will they be measured?
2. Does the nonprofit believe that the financial impact of conducting the activity will be significantly positive for the nonprofit? If the analysis in #1 is such that the activity is not expected to contribute significantly to the nonprofit's overall mission and purpose, is the nonprofit's motivation for conducting the activity to generate net income or positive cash flow for the nonprofit?
3. What are the expected financial outcomes of the activity and how well can we predict them? Does conducting the activity present significant financial risk to the nonprofit?
4. Have we adequately evaluated the legal implications of conducting the activity? (See "Issues to Consider: Legal" in the section following.)
5. Have we adequately evaluated the tax implications of conducting the activity? (See "Tax Considerations" in the section following.)
6. Can we adequately insure for the risks related to the activity?
7. Are there public relations risks associated with the activity?
8. Are there other risks associated with the activity?
9. Do we have the leadership, management, and staff capacity to adequately conduct, account for, and oversee the activity?
10. Are the potential risks and disadvantages of conducting the activity outweighed by the expected benefits to the nonprofit—either financially or in terms of accomplishing the nonprofit's mission and purpose?

ISSUES TO CONSIDER: LEGAL

Legal considerations associated with alternative revenue source activities should be addressed with legal counsel experienced in the applicable area(s) of law. For example, when religious organizations address compliance matters associated with public accommodations laws, it is likely necessary to consult with legal counsel specifically experienced in addressing such matters.

A detailed description of legal considerations in this area is beyond the scope of this book. However, nonprofit leaders should be aware that engaging in alternative revenue source activities can have significant legal implications. Legal considerations to be addressed with experienced legal counsel include, but are not limited to the following:

- Zoning and land use laws (whether the nonprofit is permitted to conduct the activity on the property)
- Risk of legal liability (injuries or other incidents occurring in connection with the activity)
- Insurance coverage (related to the risk of legal liability, but an important specific consideration—addressing whether the nonprofit is adequately insured and/or whether other parties engaging in certain activities should have their own insurance naming the nonprofit as an additional insured party)
- Public accommodation laws (consideration of whether conduct of the activity could result in the nonprofit violating such laws if the nonprofit prohibits certain activities based on its religious beliefs—example: weddings where a couple wishing to be married does not meet the nonprofit's religious criteria)
- Risk of reputational damage with respect to the nature of the activity or its participants

TAX CONSIDERATIONS: UNRELATED BUSINESS INCOME

The scope of this book does not include a detailed description of tax compliance considerations for most topics covered. The book is focused primarily on financial operations and not tax compliance and there are other resources available that address tax compliance matters in significant detail with respect to most relevant topics. However, very few resources exist that describe in detail the applicability of federal income tax to alternative revenue source activities conducted by nonprofits. For that reason, I have included in this chapter specific guidance with respect to tax compliance in this area.

CHAPTER 4 | Other Revenue Sources

A primary tax consideration for an alternative source revenue activity is whether the activity constitutes an "unrelated business activity" subject to special rules under federal income tax law.

US federal law imposes an income tax on a nonprofit if the nonprofit generates net income from one or more unrelated business activities. Congress adopted the tax on unrelated business income ("UBI") primarily for the purpose of eliminating unfair competition between nonprofit, tax-exempt organizations and for-profit, taxable businesses.

An unrelated business activity is a revenue-generating activity that:

- **Constitutes a trade or business;**
- **Is regularly carried on; and**
- **Is not substantially related to the nonprofit's exempt purposes.**

The law also considers the activity of generating income from "debt-financed property" to constitute an unrelated business activity (see **Specific Exclusions from Unrelated Business Income** on page 103 for additional information on this topic).

What constitutes a trade or business?

For purposes of the tax on UBI, a trade or business generally includes any activity carried on for the production of income from the sale of goods or performance of services. Ordinarily, a nonprofit must have a motive (but not necessarily its primary motive) of generating profit from an activity in order for the activity to be considered a trade or business. Most fundraising activities would meet the definition of a trade or business, since fundraising activities are generally conducted for the purpose of generating additional funds for the nonprofit.

> **EXAMPLE** A charity sells T-shirts in connection with its theme of promoting breast cancer awareness for the year. Each shirt costs the charity $8.00 and the charity sells them to the general public for $8.00 each. The T-shirt selling activity is not carried on for the production of income and is not, therefore, a trade or business.

> **EXAMPLE** A charity sells Christmas trees to the public in a high-traffic area during the period leading up to the Christmas holiday. The charity conducts this activity each year for the purpose of raising money for its charitable activities. Christmas trees are generally sold for approximately twice the charity's cost. The activity of selling Christmas

trees is a trade or business, because one of the charity's motives is to generate income from the activity.

When is an activity regularly carried on?

In determining whether an activity conducted by a nonprofit is regularly carried on, the frequency and continuity of the activity must be addressed. If the activity is of a type normally conducted by taxable, for-profit businesses, the frequency and continuity of the nonprofit's activity is compared to the industry norm. An activity will generally be considered to be regularly carried on if the nonprofit conducts the activity with a frequency and continuity that is similar to that of the industry.

> **EXAMPLE** A charity operates an ice cream stand in connection with a county fair that is held each year. At the ice cream stand, which is open to the public, a variety of ice creams and other frozen confections are promoted and sold. The sale and fair last two weeks each year. In addressing the frequency and continuity of the activity, the charity compares its annual ice cream stand to the activities of the retail ice cream industry and with retail stores that sell ice cream. The charity's activity is conducted for two weeks each year, while the industry norm for taxable businesses is to conduct their activities year-round. Even though the charity's ice cream stand is operated every year, it is not conducted with a frequency or continuity that is similar to the business industry norm. Therefore, the charity's annual ice cream stand operation is not regularly carried on.

> **EXAMPLE** A charity sells Christmas trees to the public in a high-traffic area during the period leading up to the Christmas holiday. The charity conducts this activity each year for the purpose of raising money for its charitable activities. In addressing the frequency and continuity of the activity, the charity compares its annual Christmas tree sale to the activities of for-profit businesses that sell Christmas trees. The for-profit businesses generally sell Christmas trees at the same time of year and for approximately the same duration of time as does the charity. The charity's Christmas tree-selling activity is regularly carried on.

How does the nonprofit determine whether an activity is substantially related to its exempt purposes?

A revenue-generating activity is not considered to be substantially related to a nonprofit's exempt purposes merely because the income generated from the activity is used to fund the nonprofit's exempt purpose activities. In order to support the position that an activity is substantially related to a nonprofit's exempt purposes, the nonprofit must show that the conduct of the activity itself (and not the money from it) contributes importantly to the accomplishment of the nonprofit's exempt purposes.

In making this determination, the nonprofit must first identify its exempt purposes. This often-overlooked area of the law is extremely important. Many nonprofits (and their tax advisors) assume that their exempt purposes are obvious and that the general concept of having a religious, educational, or charitable purpose is adequate. However, according to IRS Regulations, in determining whether an activity contributes importantly to a nonprofit's exempt purposes, the IRS looks to "the purposes for which exemption is granted." Accordingly, a nonprofit should be very deliberate when it comes to defining the exempt purposes for which it exists. Some of a nonprofit's purposes may be religious, some may be educational, and others may be charitable. The nonprofit itself establishes the purposes for which it exists, and such purposes are often stated in the nonprofit's governing documents (articles of incorporation and bylaws). A nonprofit's stated exempt purposes should be drafted broadly so as to include all of its intended purposes and not merely the most common activities of nonprofits. (While a purpose statement should be broadly worded to include all of the nonprofit's intended objectives, the statement should be specific and unique to the nonprofit's calling. In other words, a purpose statement shouldn't be a laundry list of everything the nonprofit may ever want to do. The list should represent a current statement of the nonprofit's true purposes). A nonprofit with a more broadly worded purpose statement will be better able to defend a broader array of revenue-generating activities as contributing importantly to its exempt purposes.

> **A revenue-generating activity is not considered to be substantially related to a nonprofit's exempt purposes merely because the income generated from the activity is used to fund the nonprofit's exempt purpose activities.**

> **According to IRS Regulations, in determining whether an activity contributes importantly to a nonprofit's exempt purposes, the IRS looks to "the purposes for which exemption is granted."**

EXAMPLE An example of a **narrowly worded** nonprofit purpose statement is:

> This corporation shall have as its purpose the operation of a homeless shelter in Orlando, Florida.

EXAMPLE An example of a more **broadly worded** nonprofit purpose statement is:

> This corporation is dedicated exclusively to charitable, religious, educational, scientific, and literary purposes. This corporation's primary purpose is to alleviate poverty and the causes of poverty by and through as many methods and means as possible (including by the operation of homeless shelters; conduct of emergency aid activities; educational activities; creation, sale, and distribution of educational media; provision of affordable housing and basic necessities; and other related activities).

In addition to establishing a sufficiently broad purpose statement, the nonprofit should ensure that the relationship between each of its revenue-producing activities and its purposes is clear. In some cases, such as tuition revenue generated by a school, the relationship may be obvious. In cases where the relationship is not obvious, the nonprofit should maintain documentation to support the relationship.

> **EXAMPLE** A charity whose purpose is to provide life skills training to troubled teenagers operates a soda shop, in which all of the labor is provided by teenagers enrolled in the life skills training program. Motivational presentations and other supervised activities are also conducted at the soda shop, and the soda shop serves as a safe place for troubled teenagers to "hang out." The charity should maintain a document approved by the Board of the charity outlining how the operation of the soda shop provides teenagers with hands-on training opportunities and a safe social environment in order to help them develop positive life skills. The document supports the charity's position that the operation of the soda shop contributes importantly to the charity's exempt purposes. The document should make specific reference to the stated exempt purpose(s) supported by the activity.

Activities that include some related and some unrelated elements

A nonprofit may engage in some revenue-generating activities that include elements that are substantially related to its exempt purposes and others that are not. For example, a local art museum may operate a gift shop that sells gift items bearing likenesses of the art found in the museum, along with cosmetics. The fact that an activity (such as operating a bookstore) includes both unrelated and related elements does not cause the entire activity to be considered unrelated to the nonprofit's exempt purposes. Federal tax law applies a "fragmentation" rule that requires such activities to be separated into their related and unrelated elements. In this example, the sale of cosmetics would be considered *not* substantially related to the nonprofit's exempt purposes, while the sale of gift items bearing the likenesses of the museum's art would be substantially related.

Examples of unrelated business activities

Unrelated business activities in a nonprofit may include:

- Operating a public restaurant;
- Operating a revenue-generating parking lot;
- Selling items in a bookstore that are unrelated to the charity's exempt purpose;
- Owning an interest in a business (including a limited liability company [LLC]) that is taxed as a partnership or S-Corporation;
- Providing administrative services to other unrelated organizations for a fee;
- Conducting travel tours that do not significantly further the nonprofit's exempt purpose; or
- Selling advertising in the nonprofit's newsletter or other periodicals.

SPECIFIC EXCLUSIONS FROM UNRELATED BUSINESS INCOME

Federal law provides a number of specific exclusions from the tax on unrelated business income. While there are some exceptions with respect to how certain exclusions apply, income from the following sources is generally excluded from UBI:

1. Dividends, interest, annuities, capital gains, and other investment income;
2. Gains from the sale of property other than inventory;
3. Royalties; and
4. Rent from real property;

   NOTE: For income of the types listed in 1 – 4, the exclusion does not apply if the income is "debt-financed income" as described later. Also, special rules apply if interest, annuities, royalties, or rents are received from an entity that is controlled by the organization receiving the income. Nonprofits should consult highly experienced tax counsel to assist in addressing the tax implications of such arrangements.

5. A trade or business in which substantially all of the work is performed by persons who are not compensated for their work (the "volunteer exception");
6. A trade or business conducted primarily for the convenience of the nonprofit's members, students, officers, or employees (the "convenience of members exception");
7. A trade or business that consists of selling merchandise, substantially all of which was received by the nonprofit as gifts or contributions (the "donated goods exception");

8. Qualified sponsorship activities; and
9. Bingo games that meet certain criteria (the "bingo games exception").

The volunteer exception

Under the volunteer exception (item 5), a trade or business is not a taxable unrelated business activity if "substantially all" of the work conducting the activity is performed by persons who are not compensated. The law is not specific as to the definition of "substantially all." However, there is support for the position that 85 percent or more of the hours of work constitutes "substantially all" of the work for this purpose.

> **EXAMPLE** A nonprofit operates a coffee shop in a retail location that is open to the public. The coffee shop is a trade or business that is regularly carried on and its operation is not substantially related to the nonprofit's exempt purposes. The coffee shop is operated entirely by unpaid nonprofit volunteers, although a minimal amount of work (less than 10 percent) is performed by the nonprofit's paid accounting staff related to the store's record-keeping. Even though the operation of the coffee shop would ordinarily be an unrelated business activity, the fact that substantially all of the work conducting the activity is performed by volunteers causes the coffee shop not to be a taxable unrelated business activity.

The convenience of members exception

Under the convenience of members exception (item 6), a trade or business is not a taxable unrelated business activity if it is conducted primarily for the convenience of the nonprofit's members, students, officers, or employees. For this purpose, court cases and rulings have interpreted the term "members" to include people who attend or participate in a nonprofit's activities, regardless of whether they are actually members of the nonprofit.

> **EXAMPLE** An art museum operates a snack shop during its normal operating hours and during other events held at the charity's facilities in order to provide refreshments to those attending or participating in the events. Even if operation of the snack shop meets the ordinary criteria to be an unrelated business activity, it will be excluded in this case, since it is conducted primarily for the convenience of the charity's "members."

The donated goods exception

Under the donated goods exception (item 7), a trade or business of selling merchandise is not a taxable unrelated business activity if "substantially all" of the merchandise sold is donated to the nonprofit. There is support for the position that "substantially all" for this purpose means 85 percent or more of the merchandise sold.

> **EXAMPLE** A nonprofit operates a thrift shop in a retail location on Main Street. The store is open six days per week on a schedule comparable to that of other retailers in the area. The store's workers are all paid employees of the nonprofit. Virtually all of the items sold in the thrift shop are items received by the nonprofit as donations. The shop also sells a few items of new clothing because the nonprofit is able to purchase and sell those items at a substantial discount. Sales of purchased inventory comprise approximately five percent of the shop's total sales. The nonprofit's operation of the thrift shop is not a taxable unrelated business activity because substantially all of the shop's sales consist of merchandise donated to the nonprofit.

Qualified sponsorship activities

Revenue received by a nonprofit as payment for a qualified sponsorship activity (item 8) is not unrelated business income. A qualified sponsorship activity is an activity in which an outside party (typically a business) pays a nonprofit to sponsor an event or activity conducted by the nonprofit and in exchange receives certain limited types of recognition or acknowledgment. As long as the acknowledgment or recognition made by the nonprofit of the sponsor meets certain criteria, and the nonprofit does not provide the sponsor with a "substantial return benefit," the transaction constitutes a qualified sponsorship activity.

Permissible recognition

The following information about a business sponsor may be displayed, used, recognized, and acknowledged by the nonprofit as part of a qualified sponsorship arrangement:

- Name;
- Logos or slogans that do not contain qualitative or comparative descriptions of the sponsor's products, services, facilities, or company;
- Product lines;
- The fact that the sponsor is an exclusive sponsor of all or part of an event or activity;
- A list of locations, telephone numbers, or Internet addresses;
- Value-neutral descriptions, including displays or visual depictions, of the sponsor's product-line or services; and
- The sponsor's brand or trade names and product or service listings.

Federal regulations state that logos or slogans that are an established part of a sponsor's identity are not considered to contain qualitative or comparative descriptions. Additionally, the display or distribution of a sponsor's product by the sponsor or the nonprofit to the general public at the sponsored activity is permissible.

Advertising is not permissible recognition

Advertising provided by the nonprofit in exchange for payment is considered a "substantial return benefit" and is not permissible recognition. For this purpose, the term advertising means any message which is broadcast or otherwise transmitted, published, displayed, or distributed and which promotes or markets any trade or business, or any service, facility, or product. Advertising includes messages containing qualitative or comparative language, price information or other indications of savings or value, an endorsement, or an inducement to purchase, sell, or use any company, service, facility, or product. A single message that contains both advertising and an acknowledgment is advertising.

Acknowledgments provided to a business in a nonprofit's newsletter, magazine, or other regularly distributed periodical in exchange for payment are not permissible acknowledgments in a qualified sponsorship arrangement. A program or brochure produced and distributed in connection with a specific event is not a periodical for this purpose, and acknowledgments in such a document may be permissible recognition if they meet the criteria set forth above.

Payments for exclusive provider rights are not qualified sponsorship payments

If a nonprofit agrees to permit a business to be the exclusive provider of certain types of products or services in connection with the nonprofit's activities or events in exchange for a payment, the payment received by the nonprofit for the value of that benefit is not a qualified sponsorship payment.

Payments in excess of the value of substantial return benefits

Payments by a sponsor that exceed the fair value of substantial return benefits constitute qualified sponsorship payments if the applicable criteria are met.

> **EXAMPLE** A business pays a charity $20,000 to sponsor the charity's golf tournament fundraiser. The charity provides the business with advertising valued at $12,000 in exchange for the payment. Except for the advertising, all other benefits

provided to the business in connection with the arrangement are permissible benefits in a qualified sponsorship arrangement. $8,000 of the payment by the business is a qualified sponsorship payment.

Special note about arrangements that do not meet criteria for qualified sponsorships

If a nonprofit receives a payment in a transaction that does not meet the criteria for a qualified sponsorship payment, the income to the nonprofit is not automatically unrelated business income. The transaction would need to be evaluated in light of the definition of unrelated business income in order for that determination to be made. For example, if the nonprofit received payment from a business in an arrangement in which the nonprofit endorsed the business at one event, one time, the payment may not constitute unrelated business income to the nonprofit, since the activity is not regularly carried on.

EXAMPLE Children's Charity has an annual Family Fun Weekend in October of each year. The event consists of a variety of entertainment, games, and other activities. Big Car Dealer enters into a sponsorship agreement with Children's Charity in which Big Car Dealer pays the charity $20,000. In exchange for the payment, Children's Charity agrees to prominently display Big Car Dealer's name and logo throughout the event and distribute flyers expressing gratitude to Big Car Dealer for its sponsorship and listing its location, website address, and the types of automobiles sold by the dealership. Additionally, Children's Charity agrees to permit Big Car Dealer to park four of its new vehicles at the entrance to the event. The charity provides no other benefits to Big Car Dealer. The income of $20,000 received by Children's Charity in this transaction is a qualified sponsorship payment and is not unrelated business income to Children's Charity.

EXAMPLE The same facts apply as in the previous example, except that in addition to the benefits provided by the charity in that example, the charity also agrees to permit Big Car Dealer to be the exclusive sponsor of the event. No other businesses are permitted to sponsor the event. The result is the same. The income received by Children's Charity is not unrelated business income. Exclusive sponsorship is a permissible form of recognition in a qualified sponsorship arrangement.

EXAMPLE Children's Charity has a Family Fun Weekend in October of each year. The event consists of a variety of entertainment, games, and other activities. In connection with the event, Great Cola Company pays Children's Charity $10,000 (the fair market value) for the right to be the exclusive provider of beverages to the charity for the event. The charity agrees not to procure beverages from any other vendor for the event. The payment by Great Cola Company is not a qualified sponsorship payment because the exclusive provider benefit provided by the charity is not a permissible benefit in a qualified sponsorship arrangement. The determination of whether the payment is unrelated business income to the charity would have to be made based on the regular definition of unrelated business income and other possible exceptions.

The need for good tax counsel for significant sponsorship arrangements

If a nonprofit wishes to generate significant revenue from qualified sponsorship arrangements, it should engage legal counsel to draft a standard sponsorship agreement and tax counsel to ensure that the standard agreement complies with the requirements for qualified sponsorships. Failure to comply with the requirements of the law can cause all or part of the income from the activity to be taxable as unrelated business income to the nonprofit.

The bingo games exception

Bingo games are not considered taxable unrelated business activities if they:

- Meet the legal definition of bingo;
- Are legal where they are played; and
- Are played in a jurisdiction where bingo games are not regularly carried on by for-profit organizations.

A bingo game, as defined by Treasury Regulations, is:

> A game of chance played with cards that are generally printed with five rows of five squares each. Participants place markers over randomly called numbers on the cards in an attempt to form a preselected pattern such as a horizontal, vertical, or diagonal line, or all four corners. The first participant to form the preselected pattern wins the game. As used in this section, the term "bingo game" means any game of bingo of the type described above in which wagers are placed, winners are determined, and prizes or other property is distributed in the presence of all persons placing wagers in that game. The term "bingo game" does not refer to any game of chance (including, but not

limited to, keno games, dice games, card games, and lotteries) other than the type of game described in this paragraph.

EXAMPLE Senior Citizen Charity conducts bingo games every Friday night in Busy City, in which people buy bingo cards and try to be the first contestant to fill a row of spaces on the cards when numbers are called. The winner of each game wins a prize that is distributed at the event. Bingo is legal in Busy City, but only for nonprofit organizations. Income from Senior Citizen Charity's bingo activity is not unrelated business income because it qualifies for the bingo games exception.

EXAMPLE Senior Citizen Charity also sells scratch-off tickets during its Friday bingo nights in Busy City. Players buy individual "$100 Bingo" scratch-off tickets in the hope that each one is a winner. Most tickets are losers. Selling scratch-off tickets is legal in Busy City, but only for nonprofit organizations and the state government. Income from the sale of the scratch-off tickets does not qualify for the bingo games exception, since the scratch-off game does not meet the legal definition of bingo. It does not matter that the game is labeled "$100 Bingo." The determination of whether the income is unrelated business income to the charity would have to be made based on the regular definition of unrelated business income and other possible exceptions.

EXAMPLE Slick Charity conducts bingo games every Friday night in Conservative City, in which people buy bingo cards and try to be the first contestant to fill a row of spaces on the cards when numbers are called. The winner of each game wins a prize that is distributed at the event. Bingo is not legal in Conservative City, but local officials do not enforce the law. Income from the bingo activity does not qualify for the bingo games exception, since the bingo activity is not legal in Conservative City. It does not matter that the law is not enforced. The determination of whether the income is unrelated business income to the charity would have to be made based on the regular definition of unrelated business income and other possible exceptions.

DEBT-FINANCED INCOME

The federal tax laws and regulations related to debt-financed income are quite technical and complex. A nonprofit that believes it may have debt-financed income or that wants to proactively prevent or minimize it should consult knowledgeable tax counsel as early in the process as possible. In many cases, good planning may reduce or eliminate a significant tax liability that could otherwise occur.

As stated previously in this chapter, investment income such as interest, dividends, rents, royalties, and capital gains are ordinarily excluded from unrelated business income. The ordinary exclusion does not apply, however, if such income is generated from "debt-financed property."

Debt-financed property

According to federal regulations, debt-financed property is property held to produce income (including a gain on sale) for which there is "acquisition indebtedness" at any time during the tax year or during the 12-month period prior to the date the property is sold.

Acquisition indebtedness

Acquisition indebtedness is debt incurred:

- When acquiring or improving the property;
- Before acquiring or improving the property if the debt would not have been incurred were it not for the acquisition or improvement; or
- After acquiring or improving the property if:
  - The debt would not have been incurred were it not for the acquisition or improvement; and
  - Incurring the debt was reasonably foreseeable when the property was acquired or improved.

In other words, acquisition indebtedness is debt that is incurred because the nonprofit acquired or improved certain property, regardless of whether the debt was incurred before or at the time the nonprofit acquired or improved the property. Debt incurred *after* the acquisition or improvement of certain property could also be acquisition indebtedness if it is incurred because of the acquisition or improvement *and* it was "reasonably foreseeable" that the nonprofit would incur the debt when the property was acquired or improved.

Collateralization is not relevant

In determining whether debt is acquisition indebtedness, it does not matter whether it is collateralized by the property in question. The relevant question is why the debt was incurred—not what serves as collateral for it.

> **EXAMPLE** A charity has a location in Town A and owns 20 acres of vacant land in neighboring Town B. The charity has no outstanding debt. The charity borrows $1,000,000 to buy a new parcel of property near its location in Town A. In doing so, the charity uses

the 20 acres it owns in Town B as collateral for the new loan. The new property it acquires in Town A is not mortgaged and does not serve as collateral for the new loan. The new loan represents acquisition indebtedness with respect to the newly acquired parcel, even though the newly acquired parcel is not collateral for the loan, because the debt was incurred to acquire the new parcel. The debt is not acquisition indebtedness with respect to the 20 acres in Town B, even though that 20-acre property is collateral for the loan, because the debt was incurred to acquire the new parcel, not the 20-acre parcel the charity already owned.

Special rules for identification and tracing of indebtedness

Complex issues may arise in determining whether indebtedness was incurred in connection with the acquisition and improvement of property when debt is refinanced, consolidated with other debt, or when a borrower engages in other similar actions. Federal tax law contains rules governing the manner in which the identity of debt related to a specific property is tracked, or traced, when such transactions occur. The tracing rules and process are extremely complex and should definitely be addressed by knowledgeable tax counsel.

EXAMPLE Do Good Charity buys its first property in Year 1 for $1,000,000 and incurs debt of $800,000 in doing so. In Year 2, Do Good Charity acquires a second parcel of land for $500,000. At the time Do Good Charity acquires the second parcel, the debt related to the first parcel has been paid down to $700,000. Do Good Charity obtains a new loan in the amount of $1,100,000 to pay off the original loan and provide financing for the new property; $400,000 of the new loan (the additional principal borrowed) represents acquisition indebtedness with respect to the second parcel and $700,000 of it relates to the first property acquired. Subsequent principal payments on the combined note must be allocated between the two properties in conformity with federal tax rules for purposes of determining remaining acquisition indebtedness.

Special exception for educational institutions

A special exception (effectively, an exemption) to the ordinary rules for acquisition indebtedness exists in the law for organizations that are specifically classified by the Internal Revenue Service as educational institutions and for certain organizations related to educational institutions. An organization classified by the IRS as an educational institution should have an IRS determination letter indicating that the organization is described in Section 170(b)(1)(A)(ii) of the Internal Revenue Code. The special exception for educational institutions involves several technical criteria which must be met and which should be evaluated by tax counsel.

Exception for property used for exempt purposes

Property used by a nonprofit exclusively for exempt purposes is not debt-financed property, regardless of the existence of acquisition indebtedness. Additionally, if "substantially all" (85 percent or more) of the use of the property is substantially related to the nonprofit's exempt purposes, the property is excluded from debt-financed property. The measurement of exempt use and total use may be made by time, space, or a combination of the two. If a nonprofit uses property with acquisition indebtedness less than 85 percent for exempt purposes, the portion of the property used for exempt purposes is *not* debt-financed property and the remainder is, unless another exception in the law applies.

> **EXAMPLE** Helping Hands Charity owns a building that it acquired with debt financing. The building has 10,000 square feet of space. The charity uses all of the space for charitable activities except a 1,000-square-foot space that it rents to a local restaurant. The building is not debt-financed property because the charity uses 90 percent of the building for exempt purposes.

> **EXAMPLE** Helping Hands Charity owns a building that it acquired with debt financing. The building has 10,000 square feet of space. The charity uses all of the space for charitable activities except a 3,000-square-foot space that it rents to a local restaurant. 7,000 square feet, or 70 percent of the building, is not debt-financed property. The 3,000 square feet (30 percent) of the building rented to the restaurant is debt-financed property, and the rental income received is debt-financed income unless another exception in the law applies.

Sale of debt-financed property not used for exempt purposes

A nonprofit can incur a significant tax liability if it sells debt-financed property that is not used for exempt purposes and generates a gain from the sale. **This is an often-overlooked area of the law.**

> **EXAMPLE** Caring for Animals Charity buys a vacant parcel of land for $1,000,000 in Year 1, incurring debt in the amount of $800,000, with the intent of using the property for exempt purposes at some time in the future. The charity never uses the property for exempt purposes. In Year 10, Caring for Animals Charity sells the property for $10,000,000 at a time when the remaining acquisition indebtedness is $500,000. Caring for Animals Charity will incur a substantial tax liability related to its $9,000,000 gain.

Exception for property used in certain activities

Debt-financed property does not include property that is used to conduct any of the following activities for which the income is exempt from unrelated business income (see the section titled **Specific Exclusions from Unrelated Business Income** on page 103 for descriptions of these activities):

- A trade or business in which substantially all of the work is performed by persons who are not compensated for their work (the "volunteer exception");
- A trade or business conducted primarily for the convenience of the nonprofit's members, students, officers, or employees (the "convenience of members exception"); or
- A trade or business that consists of selling merchandise, substantially all of which was received by the nonprofit as gifts or contributions (the "donated goods exception").

The neighborhood land rule exception

> **AUTHOR'S NOTE:** I have summarized below the neighborhood land rule available under federal tax law as it applies to nonprofits **other than** churches or conventions or associations of churches. As applied to churches and associations or conventions of churches, the neighborhood land rule has unique provisions that are generally more liberal than those applicable to other types of nonprofits. I address the "church version" of the neighborhood land rule in my book Church Finance: The Church Leader's Guide to Financial Operations (Second Edition). A nonprofit organization that is classified by the IRS as a church or an association or convention of churches should apply the "church version" of the rule.

If a charity acquires property with debt financing and intends to use the land for exempt purposes within 10 years of the acquisition date, the property will not be considered debt-financed property. This special rule applies only if: (1) the plan to use the property for exempt purposes requires demolition of any buildings or structures that were on the property at the time of acquisition, (2) the acquired property is in the "neighborhood" of the charity's existing exempt-use property (see below), and (3) the property is not subject to a business lease (generally, a lease for more than five years to the same tenant).

Acquired property is generally considered to be "in the neighborhood" of a charity's existing exempt-use property if the acquired property is contiguous with the exempt purpose property or would be contiguous with such property except for the interposition of a road, street, railroad, stream, or similar property. If the acquired property is not contiguous with existing exempt-use property, it may still be considered in the "neighborhood" of such property if it is within 1 mile of such property and the facts and circumstances of the particular situation make the acquisition of contiguous property unreasonable. Special provisions in the law address a scenario where property is not "in the neighborhood" of a charity's existing property but is converted to exempt use within 10 years of its acquisition. Organizations with such a scenario should address the tax issues with knowledgeable tax counsel.

A charity relying on the neighborhood land rule to exclude rental income from debt-financed income may not abandon its plan to convert the land to exempt use. In the event the charity does abandon its plan, the neighborhood land rule exception fails to apply from that point forward.

Additionally, if the charity has not converted the land to exempt use within five years of the acquisition date, the charity must notify the IRS that it is relying on the neighborhood land rule at the end of the fifth year and provide to the IRS information and documents supporting its claimed intent. The IRS will rule as to whether the charity may continue to rely on the neighborhood land rule for the remainder of the allowable period (up to a total of 10 years). Even if the IRS does not rule favorably on the request, if the charity ultimately does convert the land to exempt use within the allowable period in conformity with the neighborhood land rule, the rule will apply retroactively as if the IRS issued a favorable ruling at the end of the fifth year.

As is the case with other aspects of the debt-financed income rules, the neighborhood land rule involves a number of technical requirements and conditions that should be assessed by knowledgeable tax counsel.

> **EXAMPLE** Save the Planet Charity acquires an office building in the neighborhood of its existing facility with debt financing at the beginning of Year 1 and rents the office space to commercial tenants for periods of up to 4 years each. Save the Planet Charity intends to demolish the office building before the end of Year 10 and construct a new education building on the property to be used exclusively for exempt purposes. At the end of Year 5, Save the Planet Charity notifies the IRS of its intent and provides the IRS with plans and drawings showing its progress toward using the property for exempt purposes within the allowable 10-year period. The IRS issues a ruling stating that Save the Planet Charity may continue to rely on the neighborhood land rule through Year 10. At the beginning of Year 8, the office building is demolished, and Save the Planet Charity builds an education building on the property which is used exclusively for exempt purposes.

The rental income received by Save the Planet Charity for the entire 7-year period prior to demolition is not debt-financed income because of the neighborhood land rule.

EXAMPLE Save the Planet Charity acquires an office building in the neighborhood of its existing facility with debt financing at the beginning of Year 1 and rents the office space to commercial tenants for periods of up to 4 years each. Save the Planet Charity intends to demolish the office building before the end of Year 10 and construct a new education building on the property to be used exclusively for exempt purposes. At the end of Year 5, Save the Planet Charity notifies the IRS of its intent and provides the IRS with plans and drawings showing its progress toward using the property for exempt purposes within the allowable 10-year period. The IRS does not issue a favorable ruling stating that Save the Planet Charity may continue to rely on the neighborhood land rule through Year 10. Save the Planet Charity begins to treat its rental income from the property as debt-financed income starting in Year 6. At the beginning of Year 8, the office building is demolished, and Save the Planet Charity builds an education building on the property which is used exclusively for exempt purposes. The rental income received by Save the Planet Charity for the entire 7-year period prior to demolition is not debt-financed income because of the neighborhood land rule. Since the charity treated the income as debt-financed income for Years 6 and 7, the charity may file amended returns and obtain a refund of all taxes paid on the income during that period.

Calculation of debt-financed income subject to tax

In most cases, not all of the net income generated from debt-financed property is actually taxable. The amount that is taxable is based on the amount of applicable debt and the nonprofit's basis in the property.

Calculation of unrelated debt-financed income from regular activity (such as rental income)

In determining how much income (such as rental income) is actually unrelated debt-financed income with respect to a specific property, the nonprofit needs to know the *average* amount of acquisition indebtedness that was outstanding during the applicable tax year and the *average* tax basis (as defined in the regulations) of the property for the period during the tax year that it held the property. The amount of the rental income that is considered unrelated debt-financed income is determined by multiplying the rental income by the ratio of the average acquisition indebtedness to the average tax basis of the property.

EXAMPLE Missionary Charity owns a building that is debt-financed and rents it to a commercial tenant for $100,000 per year. For the year xxx4, Missionary Charity had average acquisition indebtedness related to the building of $600,000 and its average tax basis for the building was $1,000,000. The ratio of the average acquisition indebtedness to the average tax basis is 60 percent. Therefore, 60 percent of the rental income, or $60,000, is considered unrelated gross debt-financed income. The charity would also apply the 60 percent ratio to allowable expenses associated with the building's rental activity to determine the expenses that are deductible against the gross revenue of $60,000 in arriving at net unrelated taxable income (or loss) from the activity.

Calculation of unrelated debt-financed income from the sale of property

In determining how much gain from the sale of debt-financed property is actually unrelated debt-financed income with respect to the property, the nonprofit needs to know the *highest* amount of acquisition indebtedness that was outstanding during the 12-month period preceding the date of the sale and the *average* tax basis (as defined in the regulations) of the property for the period during the tax year that it held the property. The amount of gain that is considered unrelated debt-financed income is determined by multiplying the gain from the sale by the ratio of the highest acquisition indebtedness to the average tax basis of the property.

EXAMPLE Literary Charity buys a vacant parcel of land for $1,000,000 in Year 1, incurring debt in the amount of $800,000, with the intent of using the property for exempt purposes at some time in the future. The charity never uses the property for exempt purposes. At the end of Year 10, Literary Charity sells the property for $10,000,000. The charity's acquisition indebtedness related to the property was $600,000 at the beginning of Year 10 and had been paid down to $500,000 by the end of Year 10 when the property was sold. The charity's average tax basis for the property was its original purchase price of $1,000,000. The charity has a gain on the sale of the property of $9,000,000 (the difference between the sales price of $10,000,000 and the charity's basis for the property of $1,000,000). The highest acquisition indebtedness related to the property during Year 10 was $600,000. The ratio of the highest acquisition indebtedness to the average tax basis is 60 percent. Therefore, 60 percent of the gain (or $5,400,000) is taxable as unrelated debt-financed income. The gain is taxed at regular federal corporate tax rates. State corporate income tax may also apply, depending on specific state law.)

PLANNING POINTER: *If Literary Charity had paid off the acquisition debt 13 months before it closed on the sale of the property, none of the gain would have been taxable. This is an example of where good tax planning could have resulted in very substantial tax savings!*

FEDERAL AND STATE FILING REQUIREMENTS

When a nonprofit generates more than $1,000 of gross revenue from unrelated business activities, the nonprofit is required to file a federal income tax return (Form 990-T). Form 990-T is due by the 15th day of the 5th month after the nonprofit's year-end (May 15 for a nonprofit operating on the calendar year) and may be extended for up to six months.

On Form 990-T, the nonprofit reports the revenue from its unrelated business activities and the expenses related to generating the revenue are deducted. If the revenue exceeds the deductible expenses, the nonprofit has net income from its unrelated business activities, which is subject to federal tax. If the nonprofit is incorporated (i.e., it is a corporation, as are most nonprofits in the US) the regular US corporate income tax rates apply.

Most states require a nonprofit that files Form 990-T to file a state income tax return as well, and if the nonprofit generates net income as calculated under state law, the nonprofit will likely also owe state income taxes calculated at applicable state income tax rates.

Calculating and minimizing net unrelated business income

Once a nonprofit determines that it has more than $1,000 of gross revenue from one or more unrelated business activities, it must determine its net taxable unrelated business income (or loss). Many organizations that have significant revenue from unrelated business activities actually generate a net loss from the activities after taking into account deductible expenses.

The manner in which unrelated *debt-financed* income is calculated is addressed in the previous section on that topic.

To calculate net taxable income from an unrelated business activity other than debt-financed income, the starting point is gross unrelated business revenue. Allowable expenses attributable to the unrelated business activity are deducted from gross revenue. In addition to expenses incurred by the nonprofit, the law allows one standard deduction of up to $1,000 (but the standard deduction cannot create a net loss or make a net loss larger).

In order to be allowable as deductions, expenses must be "directly connected" with carrying on the nonprofit's unrelated business activities. Some expenses are attributable solely to an unrelated business activity, and the relationship is straightforward. A nonprofit may incur some expenses that are attributable partly to unrelated business activities and partly to exempt activities, in which case a reasonable allocation must be made, and only that portion of the expense attributable to the unrelated business activity is deductible. Expenses incurred that directly relate to more than one unrelated business activity must be allocated between unrelated business activities.

> **In order to be allowable as deductions, expenses must be "directly connected" with carrying on the nonprofit's unrelated business activities.**

A nonprofit that engages in unrelated business activities should carefully evaluate all of its expenses to identify every expense that may be properly and reasonably allocated to and deducted from the unrelated business revenue. When all such expenses are identified and deducted, including a reasonably allocable portion of administrative and overhead expenses, the result is often a net loss.

Net losses from unrelated business activities may be carried forward to offset net income in future years in the same manner that is allowed under federal tax law for taxable corporations. A temporary change in the law was passed in 2020 that allows for limited carrybacks of net operating losses.

> **A nonprofit that engages in unrelated business activities should carefully evaluate all of its expenses to identify every expense that may be properly and reasonably allocated to and deducted from the unrelated business revenue.**

The Tax Cuts and Jobs Act passed by Congress in 2017 and signed by President Trump contains a provision prohibiting tax-exempt organizations from using losses from one unrelated business activity to offset income from other unrelated business activities in years after 2017. This new, complex rule is subject to possible legal challenge. Nonprofits with multiple unrelated business activities should consult with their tax advisor as to whether or how this provision in the law applies to their circumstances.

Can a nonprofit have too much unrelated business activity?

A nonprofit may not devote a substantial amount of its time, resources, or activities to any non-exempt purposes. Accordingly, if a substantial portion of a nonprofit's activities are dedicated to the conduct of one or more unrelated business activities, the nonprofit can lose its federal tax-exempt status under Section 501(c)(3) of the Internal Revenue Code. Unfortunately, the law is not clear with respect to measuring or determining the limits of unrelated business activity. The conclusions reached in various cases and rulings over the years vary dramatically due to the unique facts and circumstances in each of them. Many tax practitioners suggest that when a tax-exempt organization generates more than about 10–15 percent of its revenue from unrelated business activities, it should carefully consider (together with knowledgeable tax counsel) whether it may be exposed to risk of loss of exemption. An insubstantial amount of unrelated business activity is not a threat to a nonprofit's federal tax-exempt status.

> An insubstantial amount of unrelated business activity is not a threat to a nonprofit's federal tax-exempt status.

Generating income from activities without generating unrelated business income

Nonprofits may generate income from a variety of sources other than contributions without generating unrelated business income. Using the information described in the previous sections regarding the definition of unrelated business income and the exceptions and exclusions that apply, a nonprofit can wisely plan its revenue-generating activities to avoid UBI treatment. Here are examples of income-generating activities in which a nonprofit may engage along with descriptions of how to avoid unrelated business income in conducting them.

Bookstores and gift shops

The volunteer exception

Income from a nonprofit bookstore or gift shop may be excluded entirely from unrelated business income if the activity is conducted substantially entirely (more than 85 percent) by volunteers (uncompensated workers). If the activity qualifies for the volunteer exception, it doesn't matter whether the items sold in the store or shop are substantially related to the nonprofit's exempt purposes or not; nor does it matter whether the store or shop is located on the nonprofit's property. When the volunteer exception applies, the activity may be conducted in a regular commercial location without affecting the exemption from unrelated business income.

Selling substantially related items

If all the items sold in the store or shop are of a nature that selling them contributes importantly to one or more of the nonprofit's exempt purposes, the activity will not generate unrelated business income. In some cases, the relationship between an item being sold and the nonprofit's exempt purposes may be obvious (e.g., art history books sold by an art museum). As described previously in this chapter, in cases where the relationship is not obvious, the nonprofit should maintain adequate documentation to support the relationship between each item or category of similar items sold and the specific exempt purposes of the nonprofit.

Selling at off-site locations, through catalogues, and so on
Note that despite popular perception, a nonprofit bookstore does not have to be located on the nonprofit's property, operated with limited hours, or concealed from the public in order to have its activities qualify for exemption. In fact, a nonprofit selling items that are substantially related to its exempt purposes may operate its store or shop in a commercial location, be open during regular commercial hours, promote itself to the public, sell its items in mail-order catalogues or over the Internet, and use other similar methods of promotion without generating unrelated business income. In an authoritative ruling issued in the context of a museum selling substantially related greeting cards, the IRS clearly addressed the issue:

The organization sells the cards in the shop it operates in the museum. It also publishes a catalogue in which it solicits mail orders for the greeting cards. The catalogue is available at a small charge and is advertised in magazines and other publications throughout the year. In addition, the shop sells the cards at quantity discounts to retail stores. As a result, a large volume of cards are sold at a significant profit.

The museum is exempt as an educational organization on the basis of its ownership, maintenance, and exhibition for public viewing of works of art. The sale of greeting cards displaying printed reproductions of art works contributes importantly to the achievement of the museum's exempt educational purposes by stimulating and enhancing public awareness, interest, and appreciation of art. Moreover, a broader segment of the public may be encouraged to visit the museum itself to share in its educational functions and programs as a result of seeing the cards. *The fact that the cards are promoted and sold in a clearly commercial manner at a profit and in competition with commercial greeting card publishers does not alter the fact of the activity's relatedness to the museum's exempt purpose.* (Revenue Ruling 73-104, emphasis added.)

The IRS subsequently reaffirmed the conclusion it reached in the Revenue Ruling cited above when it issued a Technical Advice Memorandum (TAM) in a museum context. The question at hand was whether off-site sales by the museum of substantially related items constituted unrelated business activity. In the TAM, in which the museum is referred to as "M," the IRS stated:

> M carries on extensive off-site sales activities. It uses several vehicles to accomplish these sales: retail stores, gift shops, an outlet located in another city, mail-order catalogues, advertisements in various other publications, corporate/conference program, etc. Clearly, M has developed an off-site outlet network and receives significant revenue from such sales.
>
> It is, therefore, not unreasonable to infer from this that the purpose behind the off-site sales activities is a commercial one. Were this not an exempt organization, such logic would be persuasive. *However, regarding the sale of related items by an exempt organization,* Rev. Rul. 73-104 *holds that neither the proximity of the sale to the museum's location nor the fact that the individual purchaser never sets foot on the property matters.*
>
> In *Rev. Rul. 73-104,* the organization sold large volumes of cards at quantity discounts to retail stores and through its mail order catalogues. The revenue ruling states the following: "The fact that the greeting cards are promoted and sold in a clearly commercial manner at a profit and in competition with commercial greeting card publishers does not alter the fact of the activity's relatedness to the museum's exempt purpose." *Thus, once it is determined that a line of merchandise is related to the purposes of a museum, the broader the market the museum is able to reach, the more it can fulfill its exempt function. ... Therefore, exempt product sales occurring outside the Museum Site do not (for that reason alone) constitute unrelated trade or business under section 513 of the Code. (TAM 9550003—* emphasis added. While a TAM is not authoritative, it is helpful in understanding the IRS's position on a particular issue.)

A nonprofit that wishes to engage in aggressive, commercial-type sales of items that it believes are substantially related to its exempt purposes should obtain advice from tax counsel to ensure that it is in compliance with the law.

Parking lots

The IRS has consistently held that the operation of a revenue-producing parking lot by an exempt organization is not a rental of real estate, but rather, is a trade or business activity.

As an alternative to directly operating a parking lot, the nonprofit could rent the parking lot to an unrelated parking company and the parking company could operate the parking lot. In that scenario, the revenue to the nonprofit is real estate rental income, which is not unrelated business income (unless the property is debt-financed). Even if the property is debt-financed, the nonprofit should consider whether it may qualify for:

- The substantially exempt use exception; or
- The neighborhood land rule exclusion, if the nonprofit plans to convert the property to exempt use within 10 years of the date it was acquired.

Concerts or other special events

The conduct of revenue-generating concerts or other events by a nonprofit will not generate unrelated business income if the event itself contributes importantly to one or more of the nonprofit's exempt purposes, or if such activity is not regularly carried on. The relationship between the event and the nonprofit's exempt purposes (e.g., educational, literary, etc.) should be well-documented to support the nonprofit's position. Again, as with other trade or business activities, conduct of the activity substantially entirely by volunteers will also result in the income being exempt from the tax on unrelated business income.

Thrift shops or other sales of donated merchandise

As described previously, a trade or business of selling merchandise is not an unrelated business activity if "substantially all" of the merchandise sold is donated to the nonprofit. There is support for the position that "substantially all" for this purpose means 85 percent or more of the merchandise sold. Therefore, the operation of a thrift shop selling donated goods is not an unrelated business activity. Similarly, the sale of donated merchandise using other methods (such as online auctions, including eBay) is not an unrelated business activity. (Note: A portion of eBay's website is dedicated specifically to online sales by nonprofit organizations.)

Corporate sponsorship of events

Also as described extensively above, revenue received by a nonprofit as payment for a qualified sponsorship activity is not taxable unrelated business income. A qualified sponsorship activity is an activity in which an outside party (typically a business) pays a nonprofit to sponsor an event or activity conducted by the nonprofit and receives, in exchange, certain limited types of recognition or acknowledgment. As long as the acknowledgment or recognition made by the nonprofit of the sponsor meets certain criteria, and the nonprofit does not provide the sponsor with a "substantial return benefit," the transaction constitutes a qualified sponsorship activity.

Scrip programs

Scrip programs are activities in which an organization purchases gift cards (or their equivalent) at a discount and then sells them to supporters, often for face value. For example, a nonprofit might purchase $100 gift cards from a grocery chain at a price of $90 each and sell them to nonprofit constituents for $100 each. Since the constituents are able to use the cards to buy $100 of groceries, the scrip program is an appealing way for many organizations to raise money. Ordinarily, the regular operation of a scrip program by a nonprofit would constitute an unrelated business activity. The IRS has ruled, however, that when the volunteer exception applies (i.e., when substantially all of the activity is conducted by volunteers) the activity is not a taxable unrelated business activity.

Coffee shops and cafés

The best way for a nonprofit to avoid having a coffee shop or café treated as an unrelated business activity is to limit its activity to providing service in connection with events on the nonprofit's property. Doing so will help the nonprofit take advantage of the "convenience of members" exemption described under **Specific Exclusions from Unrelated Business Income** page 103. If the nonprofit wants to have a full-service coffee shop or café open to the public for regular business hours, it should consider having the activity conducted substantially entirely by volunteers to avoid unrelated business income.

Alternatively, the nonprofit could rent a portion of its real property to an unrelated company to operate the coffee shop or café on the site. If the property is *not* debt-financed, real estate rental income is not unrelated business income. If the nonprofit's real property *is* debt-financed, the nonprofit should determine whether an exception may apply to the debt-financed income rules, such as the rule described previously that exempts debt-financed income if substantially all (85 percent or more) of the property is used for exempt purposes.

IMPLICATIONS FOR STATE AND LOCAL TAXES OTHER THAN INCOME TAXES

When a nonprofit engages in *any* trade or business activity, whether it generates unrelated business income or not, it should consider the possible tax implications in state and local jurisdictions. For example, selling goods or services may subject the nonprofit to state sales tax laws, requiring the nonprofit to collect and remit sales tax on transactions subject to the tax. Renting property to tenants may result in similar obligations.

Laws in some states that provide property tax exemptions for nonprofits require that property be used exclusively for exempt purposes in order to qualify for exemption. Where that is the case, a nonprofit that engages in a trade or business activity or that rents out its property to others should determine whether the conduct of the activity could adversely affect its exemption. The definition of exempt use of property for property tax exemption purposes is state-specific and is often different from the definition of exempt-purpose activity under federal income tax law.

It is possible, therefore, that engaging in *any* trade or business, including an unrelated business activity, could adversely affect a nonprofit's exemptions under various state or local laws and ordinances. Nonprofits should consult with their tax counsel and/or with state and local tax authorities in addressing such matters. Some information may be available on the websites of state departments of revenue or local/county property tax authorities.

CHAPTER 5

Compensation

Compensation expense is often the largest single category of expense incurred by nonprofits with paid staff. Given the pervasive significance of compensation to a nonprofit's overall operations, it is an area that warrants very special attention.

COMPENSATION IS MORE THAN A NUMBER IN THE BUDGET

Clearly, staff compensation is significant to a nonprofit in terms of its financial operations. But staff compensation also involves an essentially personal element. The nonprofit's approach to setting and maintaining compensation can have a deep and long-lasting impact on the lives of its employees. The amount and nature of compensation (including benefits) provided to staff can affect their very livelihood—where they live, what they eat, what they wear, where their kids go to school, what they drive, whether they can afford adequate healthcare, what they have available later in life for retirement, their stress and anxiety levels, and more.

When considering the matter of staff compensation, nonprofit leaders should carefully consider the deeply personal aspects of it. Compensation is not just a budget line item. It is a home, groceries, clothing, healthcare, and retirement preparation for people carrying out the work of the organization. For these reasons, it is appropriate for nonprofit leaders to determine and articulate a philosophy for staff compensation that can serve as a guide. Does the nonprofit want its staff to be compensated at a level commensurate with the average compensation of other similar organizations? Above average? Below average? What about benefits? Do we want those to be average, above average, or below average? What role should the nonprofit have in helping employees with health care costs? What role should the nonprofit have in helping employees prepare for retirement? How does the local cost of living impact these determinations? These types of questions should be addressed before nonprofit leaders begin to put numbers on a page to establish compensation (including benefits) for staff members.

> **Given the pervasive significance of compensation to a nonprofit's overall operations, it is an area that warrants very special attention.**

COMPENSATION PHILOSOPHY

The concept of *compensation philosophy*, described in Chapter 1 in connection with the budgeting process, bears mentioning again here in the context of establishing compensation.

Before making appropriate decisions about staff compensation, the nonprofit must determine its compensation philosophy. Specifically, the nonprofit should decide how the compensation of its staff should compare with the compensation of other comparable organizations. In determining how a nonprofit's compensation compares with that of similar organizations, the organization's leaders should look to nonprofit salary survey information. Among the more widely regarded sources of nonprofit salary survey data are GuideStar and The Nonprofit Times. For foundations, a good source is the Council on Foundations. (For churches, see information on this topic in my book, *Church Finance*.)

Determining how a nonprofit's staff compensation compares to that of its peers is only part of the process. A nonprofit's compensation philosophy dictates how that particular nonprofit *intends* for its staff compensation to compare to its peer group. Some nonprofits express their compensation philosophy in terms of a *percentile* of their peer group. For example, a nonprofit may decide that it generally intends for its staff compensation to be in about the 75th percentile of its peer group. Alternatively, a nonprofit may express its compensation philosophy in terms of a relationship to the *average* (e.g., above average, average, and so on). Whichever way the nonprofit chooses to express its compensation philosophy, it is important and helpful for the nonprofit to do so, and for the nonprofit to express the basis for its particular philosophy. In doing so, the nonprofit should also take into consideration the demographics and expectations of its own constituents.

Consider individuality

While a compensation philosophy will guide the nonprofit broadly in its compensation planning, the nonprofit must take into consideration the individual skills, performance, abilities, and contribution of each employee in setting compensation for specific individuals. As a result, the compensation of individual employees may vary somewhat (within reason) from the norm established by the nonprofit's compensation philosophy. Of course, the nonprofit should document its basis for deciding to compensate an individual at a level that exceeds that supported by comparability data and the nonprofit's general compensation philosophy.

The need to document the nonprofit's basis for an individual compensation decision is particularly important when establishing compensation for the nonprofit's top leaders. As is described in more detail in Chapter 9, federal tax laws provide parameters for determining the reasonableness of the compensation of the top leaders of a nonprofit. Failure to comply with federal tax law in this area can subject the nonprofit's leaders to potential personal financial penalties and can, in extreme cases, jeopardize the nonprofit's federal tax-exempt status.

Don't forget benefits

When establishing compensation for nonprofit staff, nonprofit leaders not only must consider the regular salary or wages paid to each person but also the benefits provided. The benefits package provided to nonprofit employees is just as relevant as salary or wages when it comes to performing any analysis of comparability. Accordingly, when a nonprofit compares the compensation of its staff to that of various peer groups by using salary survey data or other similar information, the nonprofit must be careful to ensure that benefits are not neglected in the analysis.

Additionally, under federal tax law, when determining whether a nonprofit leader's compensation is reasonable, all forms of compensation (including benefits) are taken into consideration—both taxable and nontaxable.

See more information about benefits on the next page.

PLANNING AND SETTING COMPENSATION

Establishing a compensation package for nonprofit staff members includes determining both salary (or wages) and benefits. Some benefits are established using group plans that apply to all or certain groups of employees and some benefits are determined uniquely for certain staff members.

In setting salary or wages, the considerations described previously in the chapter regarding philosophy of compensation and comparability are important first steps. Individualizing salary or wages for each employee also involves taking into consideration the unique skills, experience, education, duties, and responsibilities of each employee.

Once a compensation package is determined initially for an employee, nonprofit leaders should review it at least annually.

BENEFITS

The benefits nonprofits provide or offer to their employees vary widely from nonprofit to nonprofit. There are, however, some common elements found in most nonprofits. Starting below is a list of benefits, along with a brief description of each and comments where applicable. The taxability or nontaxability of employee benefits is beyond the scope of this book, and can vary depending on the facts in each situation.

Benefit	Description	Comments
Nonprofit-provided home for staff	Allowing a staff member to live in a home provided by the nonprofit	Special tax benefits may apply if the employee is required as a condition of employment to live on the nonprofit premises (e.g., for security or maintenance purposes).
Group health insurance	A group insurance plan covering the healthcare needs of employees	The nonprofit will need to determine what portion of the cost the nonprofit will cover for employees, their spouses, and their dependents. The nonprofit should consult a knowledgeable advisor to ensure that its healthcare plan complies with applicable law.
Medical expense reimbursement	Various plans or arrangements in which the nonprofit reimburses employees for out-of-pocket health care costs or premiums	The nonprofit must take great care under the advice of competent counsel in adopting any type of medical reimbursement plan. Current tax and healthcare laws impose extremely severe penalties for plans that violate the law..
Retirement plans	Plans that offer the opportunity for employees to accumulate savings for retirement in a tax-advantaged manner	Nonprofits should consult highly experienced nonprofit retirement plan specialists in order to understand and evaluate the numerous available options. From simply offering a plan in which employees can defer a portion of their salary, to making employer matching contributions, to making employer nonmatching contributions, the options are many. The available tax advantages vary as well.

Benefit	Description	Comments
Group life insurance	An insured group benefit plan that pays an employee's designated beneficiaries a lump sum amount of money in the event of the employee's death	A relatively low-cost benefit that can be very important to employees—especially those with families.
Group short-term disability insurance	An insured group plan that pays an employee a portion of his/her normal wages in the event he/she is unable to work due to a disability lasting more than a certain number of days (typically 7 or 14). Short-term disability insurance benefits have a limited duration, such as 90 or 180 days.	Such plans are typically relatively low-cost and can be very important for employees with short-term disabilities. A very common use for such plans is for maternity leave.
Group long-term disability insurance	An insured group plan that pays an employee a portion of his/her normal wages in the event he/she is unable to work due to a disability lasting more than a certain number of days (typically 90 or 180). Long-term disability insurance benefits typically continue for the duration of the disability up to age 65.	Such plans are typically relatively low-cost and can be very important for employees with long-term disabilities. Employers may wish to provide both short-term and long-term disability plans in tandem with each other. The short-term plan benefits pay after the employee's disability crosses the elimination period (typically 7 to 14 days) and lasts as long as 90 to 180 days depending on the specific plan. The long-term disability plan benefits pay if the disability continues after a longer elimination period (typically 90 to 180 days). If the benefit period for the short-term plan lasts the same number of days as the elimination period for the long-term plan, a disabled employee will not have a gap in benefits coverage. That said, an employer can offer a long-term disability plan without a short-term disability plan or vice versa.

Benefit	Description	Comments
Group long-term care insurance	An insured group plan that provides benefits for an employee (and his/her spouse if covered) if long-term care (assisted living, nursing home) is needed	Such plans may be lower cost than one might expect. Even if the nonprofit pays a minimal portion of the cost, simply making such a plan available to employees on a group basis may allow them to obtain coverage less expensively than they would otherwise be able to obtain on their own. Employee coverage may be "portable" in such plans—that is, the employee may be able to maintain the coverage (and the premium) even if he/she terminates employment with the nonprofit.
Dependent care	A plan in which the nonprofit provides or pays all or a portion of the cost for care of an employee's dependent children	Important tax considerations apply to such plans—they should be considered only under the advice of experienced tax advisors.
Use of a nonprofit-owned vehicle	The nonprofit allows an employee to use a nonprofit-owned vehicle for personal use in addition to use in carrying out nonprofit activities	Special tax considerations apply, including a requirement to keep careful records of the vehicle's use.
Payment of expenses for nonprofit business activities	Payment or reimbursement for nonprofit program-related travel, meals, hospitality, and other business expenses	Special documentation requirements apply under federal tax law. Additionally, the nonprofit may wish to establish a policy for the types of costs the nonprofit will pay or reimburse. (For example, some nonprofits will not pay or reimburse costs for alcoholic beverages, first class travel, movies, or certain other items.)
Payment for spouse or companion travel	Payment for an employee's spouse or a companion to travel with the employee on a nonprofit-related program or business trip	Special rules apply under federal tax law in determining whether such payments are taxable to the employee. The fact that the nonprofit may require a spouse to travel with the employee does not determine the proper tax treatment.

Benefit	Description	Comments
Continuing education	Payment of the cost of continuing education for one or more employees	Special rules apply under federal tax law in determining whether such payments are taxable to the employee. Educational benefits come in a variety of forms. The specifics of each situation should be evaluated under federal tax law.
Tuition discounts in a nonprofit-operated school	Discounts for all or certain employees whose children attend a nonprofit-operated school	Special rules apply under federal tax law in determining whether such payments are taxable to the employee. The nonprofit should address such benefits with experienced tax counsel..
Expense allowances or discretionary funds	The nonprofit makes available to an employee an allowance to cover certain types of expenses (e.g., books and research, travel, an automobile, etc.) or the nonprofit provides a discretionary fund to an employee out of which the employee is permitted to make disbursements	Federal tax law is a critically important consideration in the handling of expense allowances or discretionary funds. A general principle is that allowances and discretionary funds are taxable to the employee unless certain restrictions and documentation requirements are met. The nonprofit should address such benefits with experienced tax counsel.

AUTHOR'S NOTE: Fred's Story

One day, a little over 20 years ago, I was sitting at my desk at my accounting firm office, and our firm's courier, Fred, walked into my office. Fred was a wonderfully positive 50-year-old fellow...a genuine inspiration and pleasure to be around. "What's up, Fred?" I asked, expecting him to ask me a regular question of the day-to-day type. "Mike," he said, "I need to let you know something. I've been diagnosed with Parkinson's disease, and I can't drive or work anymore. I am going to have to leave my job immediately." Fred's statement hit me like a load of bricks. Here is a joyful, hard-working, 50-year-old man with an adolescent child suddenly unable to drive or work. What is he going to do? How will he make it? My mind went immediately to the fact that our firm provided and paid for long-term disability insurance coverage for all of its full-time employees, including Fred. I mentioned that to him, and we were both grateful. Our group policy paid Fred 60 percent of his regular pay from the time he had to quit work at age 50 until age 65, at which point Social Security provided benefits. And we had organized the plan in a way that allowed the benefits to be nontaxable to the employee receiving them. I was very grateful that our firm had that coverage in place. I never expected that anyone would need it, and no one in my firm before had ever used the long-term benefits of such a policy. But in that one situation, having it was life-changing for Fred. At the time of the publication of this book, Fred still lives in a nice assisted living facility in Central Florida. While he has great difficulty moving or engaging in daily activities, Fred is still one of the most wonderfully positive people I have ever met...and still a genuine inspiration and pleasure to be around. Employee benefits really matter. No one will ever convince me otherwise.

SETTING COMPENSATION FOR THE NONPROFIT'S TOP LEADERS

Setting compensation for a nonprofit's top leaders, particularly its president/CEO, requires particular attention. In addition to the considerations addressed previously in this chapter, nonprofit leaders must be aware of the special rules that apply under federal tax law with respect to compensation and benefits paid to top leaders of a nonprofit, tax-exempt organization.

Federal tax law requires that the compensation paid to a tax-exempt organization's top leaders must be "reasonable." For this purpose, the total compensation package is considered, including all forms of compensation, whether taxable or nontaxable. And the term "reasonable compensation" is defined in federal tax law as "the amount that would ordinarily be paid for like services by like enterprises (whether taxable or tax-exempt) under like circumstances." In other words, reasonable compensation is what similar organizations provide to similarly qualified people for doing similar work.

If a nonprofit provides excessive total compensation to one or more of its top leaders, very severe penalty taxes can apply personally to the leaders themselves—both the ones receiving the compensation and, in some circumstances, those who approve the excessive compensation. Accordingly, it is important for nonprofit governing bodies (boards) to ensure compliance in this critically important area of tax law. If there is any question about whether a nonprofit leader's total compensation would be considered reasonable if evaluated by the IRS, the nonprofit's board should consult experienced tax counsel.

ECFA is a national nonprofit, tax-exempt organization that accredits evangelical Christian churches and ministries in the areas of financial integrity and governance. ECFA-accredited member organizations must comply with ECFA's Seven Standards of Responsible Stewardship. One of ECFA's seven standards, Standard 6, addresses the compensation-setting practices for an organization determining the compensation package for its top leader. It is my opinion that following ECFA's Standard and policy in this area is a best practice for nonprofits, regardless of whether they are accredited by ECFA or not.

ECFA Standard 6 states:

> Every organization shall set compensation of its top leader and address related-party transactions in a manner that demonstrates integrity and propriety in conformity with ECFA's Policy for Excellence in Compensation-Setting and Related-Party Transactions.

ECFA's Policy for Excellence in Compensation-Setting and Related Party Transactions, referred to above in ECFA Standard 6, is as follows:

ECFA Policy for Excellence in Compensation-Setting and Related- Party Transactions

Compensation-setting

The board or a committee authorized by the board of every organization shall annually approve the top leader's total compensation package, and shall be notified annually of the total compensation package of any member of the top leader's family who is employed by the organization or any of its subsidiaries or affiliates. Such approval and notification shall be documented in the minutes of the organization's board or committee meetings.

The following compensation-setting process is required for organizations with top leaders at annual compensation levels of $150,000 or more and is recommended for the compensated leaders of all organizations:

1. The board or a committee authorized by the board shall make the decision regarding total compensation, and those participating in the decision-making process may not have any conflict of interest in the decision, whether direct or indirect. That is, no person in the decision-making process may:
    a. be related to the person whose compensation is being addressed,
    b. be subordinate to the person whose compensation is being set,
    c. be a person whose compensation is determined in a manner that involves input or decision-making by the person whose compensation is being set, or
    d. otherwise have a conflict of interest.
2. The board or committee shall obtain reliable comparability data with respect to the position for which compensation is being set. Such comparability data shall be for functionally comparable positions, and shall be for organizations as similar as possible to the organization and shall be updated at least every five years.

3. The board or committee shall determine appropriate total compensation, taking into consideration the comparability data referred to above, as well as the skills, talents, education, experience, performance, and knowledge of the person whose compensation is being set.
4. The board or committee shall document its compliance with the requirements described above.
5. The board or committee shall contemporaneously document its decision regarding total compensation and, if applicable, its rationale for establishing compensation at a level that exceeds that which is supported by the comparability data.
6. If the process described in steps 1–5 above is conducted by a committee, the board shall determine its role in affirming, ratifying, or otherwise approving the total compensation package. Board members who have a conflict of interest in determining total compensation (such as employees of the organization) should be recused from any deliberations regarding the compensation of the top leader.

Related-party transactions

The board or a committee authorized by the board of every organization shall properly address related-party transactions pursuant to a sound conflicts-of-interest policy. An organization may not enter into a business transaction with a person or entity that meets the definition of a "disqualified person" under federal tax law applicable to public charities unless the organization takes affirmative steps in advance to ensure that the following is true with respect to the transaction:

1. All parties with a conflict of interest (direct or indirect) are excluded from the discussion and vote related to approval of the transaction;
2. The organization obtains reliable comparability information regarding the terms of the transaction from appropriate independent sources such as competitive bids, independent appraisals, or independent expert opinions;
3. The board or committee has affirmatively determined that entering into the transaction is in the best interests of the organization; and
4. The organization contemporaneously documents the elements described above, as well as the board's or committee's approval of the transaction.
5. If the process described in steps 1–4 above is conducted by a committee, the board shall determine its role in affirming, ratifying, or otherwise approving the transaction. Board members who have a conflict of interest with respect to the transaction should be recused from any deliberations regarding the transaction.

Tax counsel

Organizations are encouraged to consult with tax counsel in establishing compensation for their top leaders, including any person who meets the definition of a disqualified person, and in entering into related-party transactions to ensure compliance with federal tax law and other applicable law. Tax counsel may assist an organization and its leaders in taking steps to avail themselves of protections that may be available under the law in connection with compensation-setting and related-party transactions.

MANAGING COMPENSATION EXPENSE

Nonprofits sometimes struggle with managing the cost of staff compensation. On one hand, the nonprofit may wish to be generous to its employees with respect to compensation. On the other hand, as the nonprofit grows and expands its programs, adding staff brings significant increases to the cost of the nonprofit's overall operations. Cost increases driven by staff additions can cause stress in the nonprofit's budget—creating a challenge in terms of how to reduce expenses while staying true to the nonprofit's commitment to staff.

Such a challenge can be successfully addressed by keeping two key principles in mind:

1. Resources are *always* limited and the decision to spend money will *always* be limited one way or another—either by prudent planning, budgeting, and self-imposed limits or by running out of money.
2. It all starts with mission and purpose.

Will your nonprofit's spending be limited by prudent management or by running out of money?

Nonprofit leaders are sometimes exasperated that as their nonprofit grows and adds staff, programs, and initiatives, the nonprofit runs out of money. How does that happen? It happens because the decisions to add staff, programs, and initiatives are not governed by an overarching principle of financial responsibility.

As described in Chapter 1, the process of budgeting should include the very important element of having targets for the financial health of the nonprofit. The process of having targets for a healthy financial position is described both in Chapter 1, as it relates to budgeting, and in Chapter 6, as it relates to managing liquidity and financial position.

The constraints on a nonprofit's spending will come one way or another. Either they will be self-imposed, based on a prudent budgeting and planning process designed to keep the nonprofit in a healthy financial position, or they will be imposed when the nonprofit runs out of money. It's that simple. When nonprofit leaders do not employ an overarching principle of healthy financial management on the spending process, the nonprofit will likely stay in a continuous state of financial stress, if not emergency.

I have had conversations with leaders of multiple large nonprofits over the years that have found themselves in such situations. Strapped for cash, sometimes without seeing it coming, these nonprofits have trouble meeting their financial obligations in a timely manner. In some cases, they have trouble making timely payments on bank loans. These are nonprofits with budgets in the millions or tens of millions of dollars—and like many other nonprofits their size, their compensation expense comprises a very large portion of their operating budget.

How did these nonprofits find themselves in such a bind, given that such a large portion of their costs relate to salaries and benefits? The conversations are telling. "We were just growing, and our CEO decided that we needed to add staff and programs to meet the needs of our growing constituency," is a common response. Other responses include statements like: "If we have any extra money in our bank account, our leadership will spend it." It's not difficult to see how nonprofits operated in such a manner end up in financial dire straits.

When engaged in conversations like those described above, I have shared with nonprofit leaders the concept that their spending has limitations—either physical (you run out of money) or self-imposed. There is never enough money to do everything that inspired nonprofit leaders may want to do. There is no limit to the number of good things a nonprofit may want to do. But there is a limit to how much a nonprofit can spend. The question is whether nonprofit leaders will impose that limit by practicing sound fiscal management or whether the bank will impose the limit based on the depletion of the nonprofit's cash.

> **I have shared with nonprofit leaders the concept that their spending has limitations—either physical (you run out of money) or self-imposed. There is never enough money to do everything that inspired nonprofit leaders may want to do. There is no limit to the number of good things a nonprofit may want to do. But there is a limit to how much a nonprofit can spend. The question is whether nonprofit leaders will impose that limit by practicing sound fiscal management or whether the bank will impose the limit based on the depletion of the nonprofit's cash.**

A nonprofit can reduce its expenses much more effectively by carefully evaluating mission and purpose than by trying to reduce expenses at the margins. You can only save so much money by reducing the cost of copy paper and toner.

When seeking ways to manage or reduce costs associated with compensation, nonprofits would be well served to engage in the exercise described in Chapter 1 related to mission and purpose. Chapter 1 begins with the observation that "it all starts with mission and purpose." The exercise of clearly identifying a nonprofit's specific mission and purpose, followed by critically evaluating its programs, activities, and initiatives, can be an extraordinarily effective process for ferreting out waste or marginally beneficial expenses. The evaluation should help nonprofit leaders determine whether each program, activity, or initiative significantly and effectively contributes to the accomplishment of the nonprofit's mission and purpose. Coupled with a zero-based budgeting approach (also described in Chapter 1), such an exercise can efficiently help nonprofit leaders identify those aspects of the nonprofit's operations that are prime candidates for expense reductions.

Let's be clear about what we are saying here. One reason nonprofit budgets expand so significantly as nonprofits grow is that the nonprofit not only scales its existing program activities to the larger size of its constituency, it also adds *new* programs and activities, complete with staff members to carry them out. As the size of the constituency grows and nonprofit revenue grows along with it, nonprofit leaders may decide to start a new educational program, or financial classes, or new special events, or a program for single parents, or a new program for the homeless, or a counseling program, or a crisis pregnancy center, or—you get the idea. Let's agree for the sake of discussion that all of these types of activities are good, or at least *can* be good. That is not the question. The question is whether starting them is the right thing to do for your nonprofit. And the answer to that question should depend in significant part on the extent to which each activity significantly helps your nonprofit carry out its specific mission and purpose. And keep in mind, every nonprofit is unique. It is important for each nonprofit to clearly identify and articulate *its* specific mission and purpose as described in Chapter 1. When carrying out the exercise of evaluating *every single one* of the nonprofit's programs, activities, and initiatives against the nonprofit's core mission and purpose, the objective is to identify those activities that are not central to or highly effective in carrying out your nonprofit's specific mission and purpose. Operating a program to serve the homeless may be a good thing, but it may not be central to your nonprofit's specific mission and purpose. Remember, there is no limit to the number of good things a nonprofit may want to do. But there is a limit to the resources it can employ.

Such an exercise can be a powerful experience. Not only can it help a nonprofit reduce expenses much more effectively than addressing them at the margins, it can also help the nonprofit make sure its resources are being spent on the activities that are *most* important to the nonprofit's core mission and purpose.

A note about eliminating staff positions or terminating employees

Nonprofit leaders who are considering terminating employees for expense reduction purposes should consider whether their employees are covered by their state unemployment compensation tax and benefit system. (Smaller organizations and certain religious organizations are exempt, and employees of such organizations are not ordinarily eligible for unemployment benefits). Nonprofit leaders who terminate staff members who are ineligible for unemployment benefits may wish to consider offering a severance package to terminated employees. Of course, the cost of any severance benefits must be taken into consideration when evaluating the cost savings associated with terminations. A growing nonprofit may be able to accomplish the objective of improving its financial position by limiting the hiring of new employees rather than terminating employees. For nonprofit programs that are eliminated, employees staffing such programs can be redeployed to other areas of nonprofit operations.

CHAPTER 6

Managing Liquidity and Financial Position

PHILOSOPHY OF LIQUIDITY AND FINANCIAL POSITION

As with budgeting (addressed in Chapter 1), a nonprofit's management of liquidity and financial position begins with a philosophical assessment. Some nonprofits, for example, intentionally choose to operate with little or no cash reserves. Nonprofits that adhere to such a philosophy often believe it is appropriate to spend all money soon after it arrives to carry out the work of the nonprofit.

Other nonprofits adhere to the philosophy that maintaining a reasonable level of cash reserves and maintaining strong liquidity is an act of sound fiscal stewardship. Nonprofits in this camp believe that financial stability and viability are essential traits for a nonprofit to do its work consistently and reliably.

During the Great Recession that began to affect the US economy so severely in late 2008, nonprofits with little or no cash reserves felt the most immediate, severe effects. In fact, many nonprofits that had significant debt outstanding and that had little or no cash reserves found themselves in immediate financial peril. A significant number of nonprofits were unable to pay their debt obligations and lost significant assets in foreclosure or its equivalent.

From a practical perspective, any number of unexpected developments can occur that could present cash flow challenges to a nonprofit. For example, if a well-respected leader of the nonprofit left, or committed some discreditable act, then financial support could significantly and immediately suffer. A sudden downturn in the economy like the one that occurred in 2008—brought on by the outbreak of war, a stock market collapse, a pandemic, or any other unpredictable event—could have a similar impact.

Part of effective stewardship involves having a viable and stable program. If nonprofit leaders are frequently focused on addressing urgent or critical cash flow challenges or related concerns, they will focus less on their program objectives.

For nonprofits with significant outstanding debt, healthy cash reserves and financial position are essential in supporting the nonprofit's ability to honor its debt obligations. Failure by a nonprofit to honor its debt obligations can adversely affect the credibility and mission of a nonprofit and its leaders. **A nonprofit with the philosophy of maintaining no significant cash reserves should not incur significant debt obligations.**

References to "cash reserves" herein refer not only to cash maintained in a bank and similar accounts, but also to investments in liquid marketable securities that may be readily converted to cash.

PHILOSOPHY OF DEBT

Whether it is permissible or advisable for a nonprofit to enter into a debt obligation depends upon the nonprofit's philosophy about debt and financial position. Many nonprofits enter into debt obligations, considering it permissible to do so as long as each nonprofit carefully and wisely plans for the ability to honor its debt obligations. Some nonprofits believe they should not incur debt obligations, and the references to debt and its management herein are not intended to disrespect those positions.

PHILOSOPHY OF CASH FLOW SURPLUSES

As addressed much more fully in Chapter 1, I support the idea that positive cash flows from the nonprofit's operations support healthy cash reserves and financial position. A nonprofit that intends to maintain a healthy financial position cannot, by definition, do so without cash flow surpluses. Many nonprofit leaders express their desire to maintain healthy cash reserves and financial position, but then operate in a manner that doesn't support that objective. If a nonprofit spends all of its cash revenue each year, then that nonprofit cannot improve its liquidity or cash reserves no matter how much its leaders may say they want to.

Improving a nonprofit's liquidity and cash reserves requires intentional effort as an essential part of the planning and budgeting process. That effort must include planning to spend less than what the nonprofit receives in cash revenues. For a nonprofit that has been following the habit of spending all of its cash receipts annually, the transition can be challenging. If the nonprofit's revenues are growing, the nonprofit may be able to make progress in this area by slowing or stopping spending increases as revenues rise. For nonprofits whose revenues are not growing significantly, the transition will require pursuing additional revenue (through additional donations or from alternative revenue sources), employing expense reductions, or both.

For information about alternative revenue sources and their implications, see Chapter 4. If expense reductions are necessary, they may be in areas of "overhead" (administrative and supporting activities), in program areas, or in a combination of the two. Nonprofits are often very reluctant to curtail a program—especially one that seems to be doing good work. It is also painful and personal when expense reductions involve employee layoffs or terminations.

An observation about managing expenses described in Chapter 5 is presented here again because of its significance and relevance to the point at hand.

Will your nonprofit's spending be limited by prudent management or by running out of money?

Nonprofit leaders are sometimes exasperated that as their nonprofit grows and adds staff, programs, and initiatives, the nonprofit runs out of money. How does that happen? It happens because the decisions to add staff, programs, and initiatives are not governed by an overarching principle of financial responsibility.

As described in Chapter 1, the process of budgeting should include the very important element of having targets for the financial health of the nonprofit. The process of having targets for a healthy financial position is described both in Chapter 1, as it relates to budgeting, and in this Chapter, as it relates to managing liquidity and financial position.

The constraints on a nonprofit's spending will come one way or another. Either they will be self-imposed, based on a prudent budgeting and planning process designed to keep the nonprofit in a healthy financial position, or they will be imposed when the nonprofit runs out of money. It's that simple. When nonprofit leaders do not employ an overarching principle of healthy financial management on the spending process, the nonprofit will likely stay in a continuous state of financial stress, if not emergency.

I have had conversations with leaders of multiple large nonprofits over the years that have found themselves in such situations. Strapped for cash, sometimes without seeing it coming, these nonprofits have trouble meeting their financial obligations in a timely manner. In some cases, they have trouble making timely payments on bank loans. These are nonprofits with budgets in the millions or tens of millions of dollars and like many other nonprofits their size, their compensation expense comprises a very large portion of their operating budget.

How did these nonprofits find themselves in such a bind, given that such a large portion of their costs relate to salaries and benefits? The conversations are telling. "We were just growing, and our CEO decided that we needed to add staff and programs to meet the needs of our growing constituency," is a common response. Other responses include statements like: "If we have any extra money in our bank account, our leadership will spend it." It's not difficult to see how nonprofits operated in such a manner end up in financial dire straits.

When engaged in conversations like those described previously, I have shared with nonprofit leaders the concept that their spending has limitations—either physical (you run out of money) or self-imposed. There is never enough money to do everything that inspired nonprofit leaders may want to do. There is no limit to the number of good things a nonprofit may want to do. But there is a limit to how much a nonprofit can spend. The question is whether nonprofit leaders will impose that limit by practicing sound fiscal management or whether the bank will impose the limit based on the depletion of the nonprofit's cash.

A nonprofit can reduce its expenses much more effectively by carefully evaluating mission and purpose than by trying to reduce expenses at the margins. You can only save so much money by reducing the cost of copy paper and toner.

When seeking ways to manage or reduce costs associated with compensation, nonprofits would be well-served to engage in the exercise described in Chapter 1 related to mission and purpose. Chapter 1 begins with the observation that "it all starts with mission and purpose." The exercise of clearly identifying a nonprofit's specific mission and purpose, followed by critically evaluating its programs, activities, and initiatives, can be an extraordinarily effective process for ferreting out waste or marginally beneficial expenses. The evaluation should help nonprofit leaders determine whether each program, activity, or initiative significantly and effectively contributes to the accomplishment of the nonprofit's mission and purpose. Coupled with a zero-based budgeting approach (also described in Chapter 1), such an exercise can efficiently help nonprofit leaders identify those aspects of the nonprofit's operations that are prime candidates for expense reductions.

Let's be clear about what we are saying here. One of the reasons that nonprofit budgets expand so significantly as nonprofits grow is that the nonprofit not only scales its existing program activities to the larger size of its constituency, it also adds *new* programs and activities, complete with staff members to carry them out. As the size of the constituency grows and nonprofit revenue grows along with it, nonprofit leaders may decide to start a new educational program, or financial classes, or new special events, or a program for single parents, or a new program for the homeless, or a counseling program, or a crisis pregnancy center, or—you get the idea. Let's agree for the sake of discussion that all of these types of activities are good, or at least *can* be good. That is not the question. The question is whether starting them is the right thing to do for your nonprofit. And the answer to that question should depend in significant part on the extent to which each activity significantly helps your nonprofit carry out its specific mission and purpose. And keep in mind, every nonprofit is unique. It is important for each nonprofit to clearly identify and articulate *its* specific mission and purpose as described in Chapter 1. When carrying out the exercise of evaluating *every single one* of the nonprofit's programs, activities, and initiatives against the nonprofit's core mission and purpose, the objective is to identify those activities that are not central to or highly effective in carrying out your nonprofit's specific mission and purpose. Operating a program to serve the homeless may be a good thing, but it may not be central to your nonprofit's specific mission and purpose. Remember, there is no limit to the number of good things a nonprofit may want to do. But there is a limit to the resources it can employ.

Such an exercise can be a powerful experience. Not only can it help a nonprofit reduce expenses much more effectively than addressing them at the margins, it can also help the nonprofit make sure its resources are being spent on the activities that are *most* important to the nonprofit's core mission and purpose.

TARGETING AND ACHIEVING DESIRED FINANCIAL POSITION

While positive cash flows and surpluses have merit, pursuing them should be part of a broader but specific plan. The nonprofit should have specific, targeted objectives for achieving a desired financial condition as well as a timeframe for doing so. This combination provides a roadmap for the nonprofit's leaders in planning and budgeting. Adopting specific, targeted objectives addresses the reasonable question that some may have about the nonprofit's budget surpluses: *To what end is the nonprofit generating these surpluses?* An appropriate response is: "To achieve the nonprofit's specific objectives for liquidity and financial position."

We hear from expert financial advisors continuously that *individuals* should have a financial plan with specific objectives. "Get out of debt," "build cash reserves," and other phrases are ubiquitous parts of such plans. Interestingly, *nonprofit organizations* do not commonly have specific financial objectives or a roadmap for accomplishing them.

Once the nonprofit is philosophically on board with maintaining reasonable cash reserves and an improved financial position, and has determined that it is willing to take the steps to achieve those objectives, the next step is to define what the nonprofit considers to be appropriate cash reserves and a desired financial condition. The nonprofit should have specific targets. For example, the nonprofit may establish a target for cash reserves of six months of cash operating expenses. The nonprofit may also state its objective of reducing its debt from $5 million to $3 million. These are merely examples. The point is that the targets should be specific. By setting specific targets, the nonprofit knows precisely why and to what extent it is pursuing cash flow surpluses.

Once the financial targets are defined, the nonprofit should establish what it considers to be a reasonable timeframe for achieving the objectives. For a nonprofit that is a long way from achieving its objectives, it is wise not to attempt to get from "Point A" to "Point B" overnight. Depending on the circumstances, the process of reaching the nonprofit's targets may take a number of years. If the nonprofit believes its journey from Point A to Point B will be long-term, it is important for the nonprofit to establish annual benchmarks or milestones (interim targets) to facilitate the monitoring and assessment of progress.

> **Once the nonprofit is philosophically on board with maintaining reasonable cash reserves and an improved financial position, and has determined that it is willing to take the steps to achieve those objectives, the next step is to define what the nonprofit considers to be appropriate cash reserves and a desired financial condition. The nonprofit should have specific targets.**

For example, assume the nonprofit has one month's cash operating expenses as a cash reserve, and it plans to achieve a six-month reserve. Assume the nonprofit decides to achieve its target over a five-year period, by increasing the reserve by one month's operating expenses each year. The nonprofit establishes milestones for the end of each year accordingly. At the end of Year 1, the nonprofit should have two months of operating expenses in its cash reserves. At the end of Year 2, it should have three months, and so on, until the end of Year 5, when it should have six months of operating expenses in reserves, assuming the nonprofit has been able to follow its plan.

RECOMMENDED LIQUIDITY AND FINANCIAL POSITION OBJECTIVES

Nonprofit leaders may desire to improve the nonprofit's financial position and liquidity and to establish appropriate targets, but they may not have a sense for what the targets should be. What constitutes "reasonable" cash reserves and "sound" financial position?

The recommendations provided herein are those of the author, based on more than three decades of professional experience plus input from other highly experienced professionals serving the nonprofit sector. The recommendations herein are general in nature and may not be appropriate for some nonprofits, depending on the individual facts and circumstances. Nonprofits should obtain counsel from advisors with significant professional financial experience in establishing their individual targets and objectives.

Sound *refers to a level that represents the minimum position for establishing healthy liquidity and financial position.* **Strong** *refers to a level where financial position and liquidity should be more than adequate in most circumstances.* The term "cash" as it relates to reserves and balances is intended to include liquid marketable investment securities.

Operating cash reserves

Assume the nonprofit has one month's cash operating expenses as a cash reserve, and it plans to achieve a six-month reserve. Assume the nonprofit decides to achieve its target over a five-year period, by increasing the reserve by one month's operating expenses each year. The nonprofit establishes milestones for the end of each year accordingly. At the end of Year 1, the nonprofit should have two months of operating expenses in its cash reserves. At the end of Year 2, it should have three months, and so on, until the end of Year 5, when it should have six months of operating expenses in reserves, assuming the nonprofit has been able to follow its plan.

> **NOTE:** *The recommended levels are based on the assumption that the nonprofit already maintains cash, including liquid marketable securities, adequate to cover all donor-restricted and designated net assets. Recommended reserves and balances are levels in excess of the amounts required to cover such items.*

> **Sound:** Three months of operating cash expenses plus current liabilities
> **Strong:** At least six months of operating cash expenses plus current liabilities

Debt service reserves (for nonprofits with mortgage or other long-term debt)

> **Sound:** Six months of debt service costs (principal and interest payments)
> **Strong:** At least one year of debt service costs

NOTE: *If a lender requires maintenance of minimum debt service reserves, the actual use of the lender-required reserves will typically create an event of default on the loan if the use of the funds causes the reserve balance to decrease below the required minimum. Accordingly,* *the nonprofit should maintain debt service reserves above and beyond the level required by a lender if the nonprofit wishes to be able to use the funds without defaulting on the loan. See below for more information about debt service reserves.*

Debt level
Sound: Total liabilities should not exceed 2.5 times the nonprofit's net assets without donor restrictions.
Strong: Total liabilities are less than 2 times the nonprofit's net assets without donor restrictions.

Loan-to-value ratio
Sound: Debt should not exceed 70 percent of the current market value of the underlying collateral property.
Strong: Debt is less than 65 percent of the current market value of the collateral property.

Debt service
Sound: Annual debt service payments (principal and interest) do not exceed 15-20 percent of the nonprofit's annual cash operating expenses.*
Strong: Annual debt service payments do not exceed 10 percent of the nonprofit's annual cash operating expenses.*

*To the extent that debt service payments are made from operating expenses. Debt service payments funded by special gifts or separate funds, such as a building fund or debt service fund, would not be counted in this calculation.

Average age of accounts payable invoices
Sound: Accounts payable invoices should not generally be more than 30 days old if the nonprofit is paying its bills in a timely manner. Accordingly, the average age of accounts payable invoices should not exceed about 25 days. If the average age of accounts payable invoices increases much beyond 25 days, the nonprofit's leadership should consider that a warning sign of potential cash flow issues.
Strong: The average age of accounts payable invoices is not more than 15 days.

In any event, in a financially healthy organization, accounts payable should be paid by their due date.

Other benchmarks, ratios, and industry data

I have received affirmation from numerous nonprofit leaders that the benchmarks described herein are helpful and are among the most important for nonprofits to monitor and pursue for sound liquidity and financial position. Nonprofits may find other measurements useful in their financial operations. In some cases, comparisons of a nonprofit's data with industry data may be useful (if such information is available). In many cases, industry data may have limited usefulness, since nonprofits are as unique as the individuals who comprise them. For example, it might be interesting to know how a particular nonprofit stacks up against a peer group in the area of personnel expense as a percentage of the operating budget or annual giving per donor. However, individual nonprofits have widely varying philosophies about such matters as compensation philosophy and the socioeconomic demographics of a particular nonprofit will have a dramatic effect on per-donor giving.

Even if the peer group to which a nonprofit compares itself is extraordinarily homogeneous, the fact that a group of nonprofits, for example, spends four percent on average of its budget on travel costs means just that. It doesn't necessarily mean that such a spending level is appropriate for a particular nonprofit. Such a determination would be based on the philosophy, mission, and objectives of the particular nonprofit. The same even can be said about broad areas, such as personnel expense as a percentage of operating expenses. Individual practices and philosophies vary widely. Some nonprofits, for example, believe in engaging volunteers heavily and others espouse the approach of employing people to carry out most duties.

Accordingly, a nonprofit interested in tracking financial measurements and benchmarks may find the most useful information by comparing the nonprofit's own numbers over time. For example, a nonprofit may find it valuable to track the percentage of its operating expenses spent on personnel costs over a period of several years in order to determine whether the percentage is trending higher or lower.

Whatever methods or measurements are employed, nonprofit leaders should assess the tools and benchmarks that will be most relevant and helpful given their nonprofit's unique identity.

INVESTMENT MANAGEMENT

Nonprofits that maintain cash reserves sometimes choose to invest in marketable securities in order to pursue increased returns on their investments, especially given the low interest rates that are often paid by banks on deposit accounts. Nonprofits that maintain investment portfolios must take care to invest prudently.

THE UNIFORM PRUDENT MANAGEMENT OF INSTITUTIONAL FUNDS ACT

At the time this publication went to press, every state in the United States except Pennsylvania had adopted a version of the Uniform Prudent Management of Institutional Funds Act (UPMIFA), a model law developed by the Uniform Law Commission. UPMIFA establishes legal requirements for nonprofit organizations related to the investment and management of "institutional funds." The term "institutional funds" is defined very broadly and, for all practical purposes, includes virtually all cash and investments maintained by a nonprofit organization.

According to the Uniform Law Commission,

> UPMIFA requires investment "in good faith and with the care an ordinarily prudent person in a like position would exercise under similar circumstances." It requires prudence in incurring investment costs, authorizing "only costs that are appropriate and reasonable." Factors to be considered in investing are expanded to include, for example, the effects of inflation. UPMIFA emphasizes that investment decisions must be made in relation to the overall resources of the institution and its charitable purposes. No investment decision may be made in isolation, but must be made in light of the fund's entire portfolio, and as a part of an investment strategy "having risk and return objectives reasonably suited to the fund and to the institution." A charitable institution must diversify assets as an affirmative obligation unless "special circumstances" dictate otherwise. Assets must be reviewed within a reasonable time after they come into the possession of the institution in order to conform them to the investment strategy and objectives of the fund. Investment experts, whether in-house or hired for the purpose, are held to a standard of care consistent with that expertise.[1]

---

1 See tinyurl.com/UPMIFAInfo

Note that each state with an enacted version of UPMIFA may have modified or adapted the model law in ways that are unique to that state. Accordingly, when evaluating the provisions of UPMIFA for a nonprofit in a particular state, the nonprofit should consult that state's specific laws. The model version of UPMIFA includes the following general requirements, which are generally consistent among the states that have adopted UPMIFA, for the investment and management of any institutional fund:

1. In managing and investing an institutional fund, the following factors, if relevant, must be considered:
    a. General economic conditions;
    b. The possible effect of inflation or deflation;
    c. The expected tax consequences, if any, of investment decisions or strategies;
    d. The role that each investment or course of action plays within the overall investment portfolio of the fund;
    e. The expected total return from income and the appreciation of investments;
    f. Other resources of the institution;
    g. The needs of the institution and the fund to make distributions and to preserve capital; and
    h. An asset's special relationship or special value, if any, to the charitable purposes of the institution.
2. Management and investment decisions about an individual asset must be made not in isolation but rather in the context of the institutional fund's portfolio of investments as a whole and as a part of an overall investment strategy having risk and return objectives reasonably suited to the fund and to the institution.
3. Except as otherwise provided by law other than this [act], an institution may invest in any kind of property or type of investment consistent with this section.
4. An institution shall diversify the investments of an institutional fund unless the institution reasonably determines that, because of special circumstances, the purposes of the fund are better served without diversification.
5. Within a reasonable time after receiving property, an institution shall make and carry out decisions concerning the retention or disposition of the property or to rebalance a portfolio, in order to bring the institutional fund into compliance with the purposes, terms, and distribution requirements of the institution as necessary to meet other circumstances of the institution and the requirements of this [act].

6. A person that has special skills or expertise, or is selected in reliance upon the person's representation that the person has special skills or expertise, has a duty to use those skills or that expertise in managing and investing institutional funds.

INVESTMENT PHILOSOPHY

Before a nonprofit decides on the specific investments to be included in its portfolio, the nonprofit's leadership must first agree on a philosophy with respect to the nonprofit's investing activities. A nonprofit's investment philosophy should be expressed in general terms, should be in writing, and should be officially approved by the nonprofit's governing body.

In adopting an investment philosophy, the nonprofit's primary considerations are its investment objectives and its risk tolerance. For example, nonprofit leaders may express their desire for moderate growth and income potential together with low volatility and low risk of significant decreases in value. It is important for nonprofit leaders to clearly articulate their investment objectives and risk tolerance and to arrive at a clear consensus regarding these matters.

INVESTMENT POLICY

Once nonprofit leaders have adopted an appropriate statement reflecting the nonprofit's investment philosophy, the nonprofit should adopt a more specific document that describes in more detail the nature of the investments to be held by the nonprofit and the allocation of the nonprofit's investment assets to particular categories of investments. Such a document is commonly referred to as an investment policy.

In adopting an investment philosophy, the nonprofit's primary considerations are its investment objectives and its risk tolerance.

Unless the nonprofit has leaders with significant investment expertise participating directly in the process, the nonprofit may wish to engage the services of an investment advisor or consultant in developing an appropriate investment policy.

The investment policy should conform to the objectives and risk tolerance expressed by the nonprofit in its investment philosophy statement described above. The investment policy will apply the principles from the investment philosophy statement to specific assets—commonly, in the form of asset allocation parameters. For example, an investment policy statement may dictate the percentage of the nonprofit's investment portfolio to be invested in asset categories such as growth equities, value equities, government debt securities, corporate debt securities, real estate securities, commodities, international investments, and so on. It is also common for investment policy statements to provide more specificity in each of these categories. For example, the policy may provide for specific levels of investment in short-term, intermediate-term, and long-term debt securities. Once an investment policy is drafted, it should be approved by the nonprofit's governing body to ensure consistency with the nonprofit's investment objectives and risk tolerance.

In addition to addressing the matters described in the preceding paragraph, the nonprofit's investment policy should also include provisions designed to remind those responsible for the nonprofit's investments of the requirements of applicable law, such as UPMIFA (addressed previously in this chapter). Accordingly, some nonprofits include certain UPMIFA requirements in their investment policy document—a practice I recommend. Additionally, the nonprofit's investment policy document should be reviewed and approved by the nonprofit's legal counsel before it is adopted in its final form.

ASSET MANAGEMENT

A nonprofit must decide how it will manage and oversee the investment process. Some nonprofits form an investment committee to oversee the process. Others delegate the responsibility to a finance committee or its equivalent. Some nonprofits have their governing body (or board) oversee the process directly. If a nonprofit utilizes a committee to oversee the investment process, the committee's charter should clearly state the committee's role and reporting responsibilities. Regardless of whether a committee is used or not, the nonprofit's governing body (or board) should maintain an appropriate awareness and exercise appropriate oversight of the process.

The process of managing the individual investments maintained by a nonprofit in its portfolio requires significant and continuous attention in order to ensure that the portfolio is managed in conformity with applicable laws and in conformity with the nonprofit's investment philosophy and investment policy. If the nonprofit's investment policy requires investments to be allocated among various asset categories, the management process also includes ensuring that the portfolio is "rebalanced" from time to time to conform to the asset allocation model adopted in the investment policy.

Because of the legal implications and related risks associated with asset management, most nonprofits with significant investment portfolios engage external professional investment managers to oversee and manage their investment portfolios. Most nonprofits do not have the expertise or capacity in-house to manage a significant investment portfolio in conformity with applicable laws, well-developed statements of investment philosophy, and investment policy. For particularly large investment portfolios, a nonprofit may wish to engage the

> For particularly large investment portfolios, a nonprofit may wish to engage the services of more than one investment manager. Such an approach not only diversifies risk with respect to the investment management process, but also creates an opportunity to evaluate the performance of each manager against that of the other.

services of more than one investment manager. Such an approach not only diversifies risk with respect to the investment management process, but also creates an opportunity to evaluate the performance of each manager against that of the other.

When using an external investment manager, it is important for the nonprofit to periodically evaluate the manager's performance. One of the most effective ways of evaluating an investment manager's performance is to compare the total return of the individual investments with appropriate benchmarks for investment returns in the applicable categories of investment. For example, the parties may agree that an appropriate benchmark for evaluating the nonprofit's investment in domestic growth equity securities is the S&P 500 index. The benchmarks should be agreed upon in advance between nonprofit leaders and the investment manager, and results should be evaluated periodically. Given modern technology for investment performance reporting, such an analysis is typically available on a monthly basis, along with regular investment performance reports.

In addition to for-profit investment advisors and managers, some nonprofit organizations offer such services.

USE AND MANAGEMENT OF DEBT

Debt is like a chainsaw. It can be a very useful tool in specific circumstances, but it can also cause lethal injury if used unwisely. In the nonprofit arena, there are circumstances in which the use of debt financing can be helpful and wise and there are circumstances in which the use of debt financing is inappropriate and dangerous.

There are generally two circumstances in which the use of debt financing by a nonprofit may be appropriate. One is when a nonprofit needs financing to fund the acquisition, construction, improvement, or refinancing of its long-lived furniture, equipment, or facilities. The other is when a nonprofit needs temporary financing to cover short-term, seasonal variations in cash flow. Even in these two circumstances, the specific conditions must be appropriate for debt financing.

> Debt is like a chainsaw. It can be a very useful tool in specific circumstances, but it can also cause lethal injury if used unwisely.

There are many circumstances in which the use of debt financing by a nonprofit is unwise, inappropriate, and dangerous. It is *not* appropriate to use debt financing in the following circumstances:

> Because of the legal implications and related risks associated with asset management, most nonprofits with significant investment portfolios engage external professional investment managers to oversee and manage their investment portfolios.

- To finance operating costs or non-capital outlays. (A working capital line of credit may be useful if cash flows are truly seasonal and receipt of funds for repayment is reasonably assured. However, an unexpected downturn or shortfall in revenue is probably the worst possible reason to incur debt financing.)
- When cash flows are not growing or at least stable. (A nonprofit should never enter into debt financing if its cash flows are declining—even if current cash flows cover the required debt service. The nonprofit must determine the reasons for the downward trend and address that satisfactorily before it should consider debt financing.)
- When personal guarantees are required. (Requiring personal guarantees of nonprofit leaders in connection with nonprofit debt would be an extraordinary requirement in today's market. If a lender were to impose such a requirement, it is likely an indicator that either the borrower does not have satisfactory capacity to obtain a loan under ordinary market terms or the lender does not operate in conformity with common lending practices.)
- When the lender will not offer the nonprofit market rates and terms. (Above-market interest rates and highly restrictive terms are indicators that a lender perceives the nonprofit's credit risk as higher than normal. A higher than normal credit risk means, of course, a higher risk that the nonprofit may not be able to satisfactorily service its debt obligations.)

Working capital loans

Nonprofits with highly seasonal variations in cash flow sometimes utilize working capital loans to bridge the temporary gaps in cash flow in order to maintain stable financial operations. Working capital loans are often made in the form of lines of credit, which allow the nonprofit to draw and repay amounts with flexibility within the maximum limit approved by the bank. Working capital loans are typically made by lenders only to the most creditworthy borrowers, and only in scenarios where there is a history of seasonal or cyclical cash flows creating reasonable assurance that the amounts borrowed will be repaid in the future. As mentioned previously, working capital loans should never be utilized to fund unexpected downturns in revenue or operating expense shortfalls unless the nonprofit has specific and reliable reasons to believe that near-term cash flows will be adequate to allow the nonprofit to repay the debt.

Working capital loans may have specific maturity dates or, in some cases, they are due "on demand," which means that the bank may require repayment at its demand at any time. Working capital loans typically require minimum payments equal to the monthly interest charge on the outstanding balance. Principal payments are typically flexible until maturity. In some cases, lenders will require that a working capital line of credit be paid down to a zero balance for a minimum period of time at least once annually.

Furniture and equipment financing

Nonprofits sometimes use debt financing to acquire furniture and equipment with long-term lives. Examples may include major new electronic equipment, a new air-conditioning system, vehicles, and so on. Furniture and equipment loans are typically term loans with fixed interest rates and fixed payments that amortize the loan over a period of three to seven years. In evaluating whether to utilize debt financing to acquire such assets, a nonprofit should consider whether it has alternative means for funding the acquisition of those assets and whether it has adequate cash flows to service the payments that will be required by the new financing. If a nonprofit has a stable history of generating cash flows that are more than adequate to service such debt, then the use of furniture and equipment financing may be appropriate.

Mortgage financing

The most significant type of debt financing utilized by nonprofits in the United States is mortgage financing incurred for the purpose of acquiring, constructing, improving, or refinancing nonprofit facilities. When it comes to mortgage financing, lending professionals generally agree that the best candidates for borrowing are those nonprofits who need the financing to support larger facilities or new facilities driven by the nonprofit's growth. The need to provide for growth is arguably the "healthiest" reason a nonprofit may pursue new mortgage debt. In addition to borrowing to support growth-driven expansion, borrowing to refinance existing debt to achieve more favorable terms (especially a lower interest rate) can also be a healthy reason for a nonprofit to pursue a new mortgage. However, refinancing for the purpose of extending maturities and reducing payments is often not a healthy scenario.

The Five C's of Credit in Nonprofit Mortgage Financing

Lending institutions often refer to "the Four C's of Credit." Interestingly, while there is some commonality among those who cite the Four C's, different institutions cite different "C's," and some refer to five rather than four. The C's most commonly cited are: Character, Capacity, and Collateral.

Based on professional experience and communications with numerous nonprofit lenders over the years, I hereby advance The Five C's of Credit in Nonprofit Mortgage Financing as follows:

> **Character.** The integrity and acumen of nonprofit leaders, and the quality of the nonprofit's accounting books and records. Character also includes the quality of the nonprofit's governing body (board) and the manner in which the governing body exercises oversight with respect to the nonprofit's activities.
>
> **Cash flow.** A stable history of positive cash flow which clearly supports, in a well-documented manner, the nonprofit's ability to honor the proposed debt obligations.
>
> **Cash reserves.** Cash and investment balances sufficient to provide the nonprofit with flexibility and time to adapt in the event that the nonprofit experiences unexpected difficulty in servicing the debt from regular operating cash flows.
>
> **Collateral.** Assets underlying the debt which have a market value significantly in excess of the debt amount and which are pledged to satisfy the debt in the event that the nonprofit is unable to repay.
>
> **Contingency plan.** A plan that nonprofit leaders develop in advance addressing how it will adapt to ensure the nonprofit's ability to honor its debt obligations in the event of a sudden or unexpected downturn in revenue or other financial challenge.

Let's take a look at each of these Five C's in more detail.

Character

The starting point for a borrowing-and-lending relationship between a nonprofit and a financial institution is *trust*. The lender must believe that the nonprofit's leaders are people of integrity; that they are capable leaders; that they have an adequate command of their nonprofit's operations and financial condition; that the nonprofit's books and records are adequate, timely, and reliable; and that the nonprofit has a genuine intent and ability to honor the terms of any proposed debt agreement.

Additionally, the lender must have a sense that the nonprofit is well-governed. The governing body (board) of the nonprofit has a legal, fiduciary duty to exercise due care and prudence in the oversight of the nonprofit's activities—both financial and operational. Character in this context involves healthy, rigorous, and proactive engagement by the nonprofit's governing body to ensure that the nonprofit and its leaders operate within well-developed policies and parameters and that it stays "on mission" with respect to its activities. These responsibilities of the governing body must be carried out with appropriate independence and without improper conflicts of interest.

While it may seem that addressing the topic of character and integrity in the context of nonprofit leadership may be unnecessary, unfortunately that is not the case. Nonprofits in America have experienced numerous high-profile examples of failed integrity and morality by those who lead them.

Cash flow

When considering a mortgage loan, a lender is looking for documented *history* of the nonprofit's ability to make the proposed debt payments, *not* a commitment from the nonprofit that it will raise revenues or decrease expenses in the future in order to be able to make the payments. In making that assessment, lenders typically calculate a ratio commonly referred to as the "debt service coverage ratio (DSCR)." While lenders most assuredly assess the nonprofit's DSCR in the loan approval process, the nonprofit may not realize how this method of cash flow assessment is calculated. The DSCR is typically calculated as follows:

> Most recent year's change in net assets without donor restrictions + depreciation expense + interest expense
>
> *Divided by*
>
> Next year's required debt payments (principal and interest)

> **NOTE:** *Some details of the DSCR calculation vary from lender to lender and from nonprofit to nonprofit, based on specific facts and circumstances.*

The idea behind this ratio is to determine whether the cash available from operations is adequate to make the proposed debt payments. Some lenders will accept a DSCR as low as approximately 1.1. However, many lenders require a DSCR of 1.25 or higher. In my opinion, a healthy DSCR will be at least 1.25 and a strong DSCR will significantly exceed

1.25. Some lenders will stipulate as a requirement of the loan agreement that a minimum DSCR be maintained in each year that the loan is in place.

Cash reserves (for debt service)

As addressed previously in this chapter, I suggest that a nonprofit with long-term mortgage debt maintain healthy operating cash reserves as well as a cash debt service reserve equal to at least six months of required debt payments (principal and interest). The nonprofit will maintain a stronger financial position by having a debt service reserve equal to at least one year of required debt payments. The larger the nonprofit's debt service reserve balance, the more time the nonprofit will have in the event of an unexpected downturn in revenue or other financial challenge to adapt to the situation while still being able to make the required debt payments.

Some lenders will stipulate as a condition of making a mortgage loan that a nonprofit maintain a minimum balance in a cash debt service reserve account at all times while the loan is outstanding. While such a requirement of the lender may seem to have the advantage of forcing the nonprofit to maintain a debt service reserve as described in the preceding paragraph, when the debt service reserve requirement is a contractual part of the loan, the concept is a bit more complicated.

When a nonprofit maintains a debt service reserve on its own (without a contractual requirement), the nonprofit can actually use a portion of the debt service reserve, if necessary, to maintain consistent operating cash flows. However, when the debt service reserve is a contractual obligation in the loan agreement with the lender, the nonprofit cannot spend the reserve balance below the required minimum without triggering an event of default under the terms of the loan. For this reason, if a nonprofit has a contractually required minimum debt service reserve as part of its loan terms, the nonprofit should maintain an additional debt service reserve above and beyond the contractual minimum. This will ensure that the nonprofit has funds that it can actually use in the event they are needed without triggering an event of default under the terms of the loan.

A special word about the importance of cash reserves for debt service

A nonprofit that is building or acquiring new property using debt financing typically puts significant cash equity into the property to reduce the amount of debt needed and to establish an appropriate loan-to-value ratio. While having substantial equity in its real estate is an advantage, in my opinion, maintaining an adequate debt service reserve is a higher priority than increasing equity in the real estate. In other words, it may be more advantageous to put less cash equity into a property in order to maintain an adequate cash reserve for debt service, assuming that the resulting loan-to-value ratio is appropriate. An adequate debt service reserve can provide much-needed flexibility and can assist in continuing to make debt payments in the event of an unexpected adverse financial development. Equity in the property does not offer that advantage.

Collateral

Nonprofit mortgage lenders typically require collateral in the form of the nonprofit's real estate as a condition of making a real estate-related loan. Commonly, lenders require that the loan amount not exceed 70 percent of the market value of the real estate that collateralizes the loan. There are occasional exceptions. In some cases, lenders require the loan-to-value ratio to be even lower than 70 percent. The loan-to-value ratio measurement is typically made at the beginning of the loan relationship and is not typically re-evaluated during the term of the loan unless there are unusual circumstances. An independent appraisal of the nonprofit's real estate is typically required to corroborate the value of the property.

Regardless of whether a lender requires a maximum loan-to-value ratio, a borrowing nonprofit should avoid entering into a mortgage loan relationship where there is not adequate collateral to satisfy payment of the loan in the event that the nonprofit is unable to pay. In the event a nonprofit is unable to make its required debt payments and no other solution is available, the lender may be required to foreclose on the nonprofit's property. While foreclosure on a nonprofit's property is certainly an unfortunate event, the situation is made worse when the proceeds from foreclosure do not adequately cover the balance owed by the nonprofit to the bank. In such cases, a lender may pursue the nonprofit's other assets to make up the deficiency.

Contingency plan

Nonprofit leaders should develop a plan in advance addressing how it will adapt to ensure the nonprofit's ability to honor its debt obligations in the event of a sudden or unexpected downturn in revenue or other financial challenge. While no one enjoys thinking about what bad things can happen, prudence dictates that it is wise to prepare for unexpected developments and to have a plan.

Suppose, for example, that a high-profile nonprofit learns that its CEO has been engaged in moral misconduct and is then terminated from his position. Such a nonprofit may experience a significant decline in financial support. If the nonprofit has significant mortgage debt outstanding, such a development can create immediate and significant financial challenges. The nonprofit will need to adapt by reducing expenses and possibly in other ways. Unexpected developments can certainly come in forms other than the moral failure of a nonprofit's leader. Other possibilities include macroeconomic developments such as war, recession, or other calamities, or microeconomic developments such as the sudden and unexpected death or disability of the nonprofit's leader; an act of misconduct by a person serving the nonprofit involving a child, a counselee, or another person; and so on.

A nonprofit's contingency plan in this context need not be particularly detailed. It can be a helpful exercise to simply develop a list (in order of priority) of the expenses that would be cut in the event of a significant unexpected development that adversely affects the nonprofit's revenue stream.

A nonprofit often can insure its risk in the event of the unexpected death or disability of its CEO or any other leader whose death or disability could lead to a significant downturn in the nonprofit's revenues. Insurance providing this type of coverage is commonly referred to as "key-man" insurance. Key-man life insurance is readily available (and typically, at a fairly reasonable cost) in the marketplace, assuming that the nonprofit leader is in good health and is otherwise insurable. Key-man disability insurance provides coverage in the event that the nonprofit leader is no longer able to perform his or her customary services for the nonprofit. Disability insurance coverage may be available in the form of a lump-sum payment or a stream of monthly or annual payments. Availability and cost of disability insurance varies significantly. Insurance professionals often cite statistics stating that a person is more likely to become disabled early in life than to die. Nonprofit leaders should take these factors into consideration if they have significant mortgage debt and if the nonprofit's revenue stream could be significantly harmed by the unexpected death or disability of one or more of the nonprofit's leaders. In some cases, lenders will require a nonprofit to maintain key-man life insurance in a particular minimum amount during the term of a mortgage loan. In rare cases, the lender may require a nonprofit to submit a leadership succession plan.

MORTGAGE DEBT OPTIONS AND TERMS

Mortgages come in many varieties. In some cases, a nonprofit may have the opportunity to choose from among various options made available by the lender. Following is a discussion of some of the more significant options and terms that are commonly addressed in the nonprofit mortgage lending process:

Fixed or variable?

Long-term fixed rate nonprofit mortgages are a very rare breed in the bank lending marketplace—for all practical purposes, they are extinct. Nonprofits that are interested in a true, long-term fixed rate mortgage may wish to consider bond financing as an alternative to bank debt (bond financing is addressed in more detail on page 167). However, banks and other traditional lenders will often offer a nonprofit the option of a loan with a variable interest rate or a loan with an interest rate that is fixed for a period commonly ranging from three to five years (the actual number of years in this range for which a lender will fix the rate varies by lender and by scenario). Banks and other traditional lenders very rarely offer fixed interest rates for periods in excess of five years, but it does happen on occasion. For short-term fixed-rate loans, the loans typically either mature at the end of the fixed-rate term or they "reprice," meaning that a new interest rate is set at that time based on current market rates. A fairly common arrangement is a 10-year loan with an interest rate that is fixed for the first five years and is then adjusted to a new fixed rate (based on market conditions at that time) that applies to the second five-year period of the loan.

In deciding whether a variable rate is appropriate for a particular nonprofit, nonprofit leaders should assess their appetite for interest rate risk as well as their perception about the future of interest rates. In the years since the Great Recession began in late 2008, the vast majority of borrowers who have made assumptions about future interest rates have been wrong in their assumptions. Nonetheless, a loan with a variable interest rate does carry interest rate risk based on changing market conditions. In some cases, banks will offer a variable rate with a floor and a ceiling, meaning that the rate will not go below a particular percentage, nor will it exceed a particular percentage. Such arrangements can be helpful for a nonprofit in limiting its ultimate risk. In evaluating the possibility of a variable rate loan, the nonprofit should consider the history of the particular rate, including highs and lows.

Variable interest rates for nonprofit mortgages are based on an "index rate," which is typically either the bank's "prime rate," (sometimes referred to as the "base rate") or "LIBOR," the London Inter-Bank Offered Rate.[2] The bank's prime rate, while technically set by each bank, is generally the same as the prime rate used by banks across the United States, and is often the same as the prime rate published in *The Wall Street Journal* each business day. The prime rate changes periodically based on market conditions. LIBOR is a benchmark rate that some of the world's leading banks charge each other for short-term loans.[3] LIBOR typically

---

[2] Occasionally, lenders utilize a different variable-rate index, such as the Five-Year Treasury Constant Maturity Index, an index published by the Federal Reserve Board based on the average yield of a range of Treasury securities adjusted to the equivalent of a five-year maturity. (See bankrate.com.)
[3] Investopedia: investopedia.com/terms/l/libor.asp

changes much more frequently than the prime rate and can change daily. LIBOR is typically expressed in one-month, three-month, and six-month rates in the context of variable-interest-rate mortgages. LIBOR rates are published daily in *The Wall Street Journal* and numerous other sources.

When the prime rate is used as the index in a variable-rate mortgage, the most creditworthy borrowers can commonly borrow at the prime rate or less. Borrowers whose financial position or other attributes are not as strong may be quoted rates in excess of the prime rate.

When LIBOR is used, lenders commonly use the one-month LIBOR rate, and LIBOR-based variable nonprofit mortgage rates are typically stated as some percentage in excess of the LIBOR rate. I have seen variable rates as low as one-month LIBOR +1.5 percent for extraordinarily strong borrowers.

> **NOTE:** *At the time of this book's publication, the LIBOR index was under scrutiny by the banking community due to allegations of abuse and misuse in its calculation. The banking community is evaluating alternatives, including a new index that is now published, the Secured Overnight Financing Rate ("SOFR").*

A fixed interest rate loan offers the security of knowing the interest rate that will apply during the loan's term. Fixed-rate loans also offer protection from rising interest rates. Invariably, however, the fixed rate offered by a lender is significantly higher than the variable rate available at the inception of the loan. Accordingly, nonprofits must evaluate the pros and cons of these factors. A nonprofit may consider the fixed-rate option to be its best choice, since the interest rate will not increase during the term of the fixed rate, and the nonprofit believes that it can refinance the loan in the event that rates significantly decline. In recent years, however, lenders have more frequently begun to impose prepayment penalties in connection with fixed-rate loans. Sometimes, these prepayment penalties are substantial. As a result, a nonprofit with a fixed-rate loan that has a significant prepayment penalty may not be able to economically refinance the loan in the event interest rates decline significantly. While prepayment penalties for fixed-rate loans are more common than has historically been the case, they are, in my experience, still relatively uncommon. A nonprofit considering a fixed-rate loan should carefully review the loan documents for prepayment penalty provisions and should avoid such provisions if at all possible.

Hedging variable interest rate risk

In response to lenders' reluctance to offer long-term fixed-rate mortgages, and the desire by borrowers for such mortgages, the financial marketplace offers various financial instruments designed to help borrowers mitigate their interest rate risk while allowing lenders to continue making variable rate loans. These financial instruments are "hedging instruments," and they come in a variety of forms. The most common form of hedging instrument used by nonprofits in today's lending marketplace is an "interest rate swap" contract.

An interest rate swap contract ("swap") is an agreement between the borrower (the nonprofit) and an investment banking firm (typically affiliated with the lender) in which the investment banking firm agrees to accept fixed interest payments from the borrower and to make variable interest payments to the lender. In other words, the borrower "swaps" the variable rate actually written into the loan agreement with a fixed rate that is accepted by the investment banking firm. A swap contract is a separate agreement from the loan documents and, accordingly, does not necessarily tie directly to the terms of the loan. In many cases, however, a swap agreement is drafted to align with the terms of the loan, including payment dates and principal balances, so as to have the effect of creating a fixed rate of interest on what is actually a variable rate loan. The advantage of a swap agreement to the borrower is that the interest cost related to the loan is fixed for the duration of the swap. The duration of the swap is a negotiable item, and it may or may not align with the maturity date of the loan. In some cases, a lender may require that the terms of a swap align with those of the related loan. Swaps are available with a variety of terms and a nonprofit considering such an arrangement should discuss it thoroughly with its lender, its financial advisors, and its legal counsel.

Since an interest rate swap contract is a separate contractual agreement from the loan itself, the swap itself has a value at any given time. The value to the borrower (the nonprofit) may be positive or negative depending on current market conditions. From a practical perspective, what this means is that if the borrower wishes to terminate the swap at any time, the borrower will either pay the investment banking firm to terminate the arrangement or the borrower will receive money from the investment banking firm in exchange for terminating the arrangement. Borrowers must understand this attribute of a swap. In a declining interest rate environment, the value of a swap will decrease and may go negative—substantially negative, which would mean that the nonprofit would be required to pay a substantial sum in order to terminate the swap. In a rising interest rate environment, the value of a swap will increase and may be positive, which would mean that the nonprofit would receive money from the investment banking firm if it were to terminate the swap.

Swap agreements are complex documents and the detailed provisions are not likely to be well understood by people who do not practice substantially in the investment banking arena. Accordingly, if the amounts of money involved are substantial, a nonprofit that is considering terminating a swap agreement and, therefore, needs to know the true economic value of its swap agreement, may wish to obtain an opinion from an independent party as to the value of the swap as of a given date, whether positive or negative. There is a current market of professionals who offer such services. Sometimes, independent professionals determine swap values that are significantly different from those calculated and provided by the investment banking firm that is the nonprofit's counterparty to the swap agreement. In the event a nonprofit engages an independent professional to value its swap contract and the independent professional determines a value that is significantly more favorable to the nonprofit than the value provided by the investment banking firm, the nonprofit should consider negotiating the terms of termination of the swap contract with the investment banking firm—ideally with the assistance of the nonprofit's legal counsel.

During the Great Recession, as interest rates declined significantly and remained low for a sustained period of time, many nonprofits who entered into swap agreements regretted that decision. However, the future of interest rates remains uncertain and the market will determine the popularity of swap arrangements in the years ahead.

Loan covenants

Loan agreements virtually always contain certain conditions that the borrower agrees to meet or maintain during the term of the loan. These provisions are often referred to as "loan covenants." Loan covenants vary substantially from lender to lender and from loan to loan.

Financial covenants

One category of loan covenants frequently found in nonprofit loans is "financial covenants"—covenants stating that the nonprofit will maintain certain specific financial benchmarks during the term of the loan. The three most common financial covenants written into nonprofit loan agreements are: a minimum cash reserves covenant, a debt service coverage ratio covenant, and a debt-to-net assets covenant.

Minimum cash reserves covenant

As mentioned previously in "The Five C's of Credit in Nonprofit Mortgage Financing," some lenders will stipulate, as a condition of making a mortgage loan, that a nonprofit maintain a minimum balance in a cash debt service reserve account at all times while the loan is outstanding. The amount of the required reserves is a matter of professional judgment—discretion is applied by the lender and required reserves amounts are typically equal to several months of debt payments.

Important note about cash reserves covenants

While a cash reserves covenant imposed by the lender may seem to have the favorable effect of forcing the nonprofit to maintain a debt service reserve, when the debt service reserve requirement is a contractual part of the loan agreement, special consideration is required. When a nonprofit maintains a debt service reserve on its own (without a contractual requirement), the nonprofit can actually use a portion of the debt service reserve, if necessary, to maintain consistent operating cash flows. However, when the debt service reserve is a contractual requirement of the loan agreement, the nonprofit cannot spend the reserve balance below the required minimum without triggering an event of default under the terms of the loan—which, at a minimum, will require a waiver or approval by the lender. For this reason, if a nonprofit has a contractually required minimum debt service reserves covenant, the nonprofit should maintain an additional debt service reserve above and beyond the contractual minimum in order to ensure that the nonprofit has funds that it can actually use in the event that they are needed without triggering an event of default under the terms of the loan.

Debt service coverage covenant

As mentioned on page 155 in "The Five C's of Credit in Nonprofit Mortgage Financing," lenders will assess the nonprofit's debt service coverage ratio (DSCR) in the loan approval process, regardless of whether the DSCR is expressed as an ongoing covenant in the loan agreement. The DSCR is typically calculated as follows:

Most recent year's change in net assets without donor restrictions + depreciation expense + interest expense

Divided by

Next year's required debt payments (principal and interest)

NOTE: *Some details of the DSCR calculation vary from lender to lender and from nonprofit to nonprofit, based on specific facts and circumstances.*

The idea behind this ratio is to determine whether the cash available from operations is adequate to make the proposed debt payments. Some lenders will accept a DSCR as low as 1.1. However, many lenders require a DSCR of 1.25 or higher.

> ***Important note about DSCR covenants***
>
> *Given the fact that the DSCR calculation is made annually, is based on a particular year's cash flows, and does not take into consideration prior year cash flows or assets available to service debt, it is possible for a nonprofit to be in a very strong financial position and still violate a DSCR covenant. For example, assume that a nonprofit receives substantial unexpected contributions in a given year and does not spend any of those additional funds during that year. For the year in which the substantial contributions are received, the nonprofit is likely to have a very large DSCR—well within compliance of the loan covenant. Assume that in the following year, the nonprofit spends one half of the unexpected contribution funds on a special project, resulting in a net loss for that year (the funds were received in the prior year). Regardless of the fact that the nonprofit still has one half of the unexpected contributions in its accounts, the loss incurred during Year 2 could cause the nonprofit to violate a DSCR covenant in that year.*

While I, of course, encourage nonprofits to maintain a strong financial position, for the reasons described previously, I also strongly encourage nonprofits to avoid having DSCR covenants in their loan agreements if possible. In the event a nonprofit finds itself in potential violation of a DSCR covenant for reasons like those described previously, the nonprofit should pursue a waiver of the covenant from its lender in light of the unusual circumstances.

Debt-to-net assets covenant

The debt-to-net assets covenant is typically defined as the ratio of the nonprofit's debt or total liabilities to the nonprofit's net assets without donor restrictions balance as of each year-end. The idea behind this covenant is to ensure that the nonprofit's total debt or liabilities do not exceed the nonprofit's overall equity in its assets beyond a certain level. The debt-to-net assets ratio is typically expressed as a maximum and, if present, is typically in a range of 2.0 to 3.0.

Evaluating financial covenants in general

The lender may impose financial covenants other than those described previously. For any financial covenants that a lender proposes to be included in the loan agreement, a nonprofit should carefully evaluate the covenant requirements, definitions, measurement methods, and measurement dates and have reasonable assurance that the nonprofit will be able to comply with the requirements on an ongoing basis during the term of the loan. The nonprofit should run "what-if" scenarios to evaluate the likelihood of compliance with financial covenants in different situations.

Nonfinancial covenants

A nonprofit loan agreement may include a variety of nonfinancial covenants. Some of the more common nonfinancial covenants included in nonprofit loans are:

- a requirement that the nonprofit submit audited financial statements annually within a certain period after each year-end,
- a requirement that the nonprofit submit internally prepared interim financial reports (e.g., quarterly),
- a requirement that the nonprofit maintain its entire banking relationship with the lending bank (which requires moving the relationship if it is not already with the lending bank),
- a stipulation that the nonprofit will not incur any new debt without the lender's approval,
- a stipulation that the nonprofit will not enter into any new long-term lease agreements without the lender's approval,
- a limit on the amount of capital expenditures that the nonprofit can make without the lender's approval,
- a stipulation that the nonprofit will not make any significant change in the nature or scope of its operations without the lender's approval, and
- a stipulation that the nonprofit will maintain its federal tax-exempt status.

The importance of engaging legal counsel to assist with debt financing

Mortgages and other loan documents are complex contractual agreements with many terms and provisions that can have significant implications for a nonprofit. In addition to loan covenant provisions such as those described previously, loan documents typically contain numerous other legally significant provisions that can affect a nonprofit's costs or options in the future, depending on the circumstances that arise. It may be tempting for nonprofit leaders to view the many provisions in loan documents as simply "boilerplate" provisions that "are probably non-negotiable" or "are probably in all loan documents," and, thus, to pay little attention to them. Numerous nonprofits have taken such an approach, only to regret it later when circumstances arise that bring to light the dramatic significance of provisions that they had deemed to be "boilerplate."

Accordingly, nonprofits should have their own legal counsel review all mortgage and other loan documents before they sign to ensure that the nonprofit's interests are adequately considered. (While the lending institution may have legal counsel involved in the loan document preparation process, the bank's legal counsel does not represent the interests of the nonprofit.) Additionally, a nonprofit should never assume that *any* provision in a lender-prepared loan document is non-negotiable. Banks and other lending organizations frequently make changes to loan documents based on requests made by borrowers or their legal counsel.

TAX-EXEMPT FINANCING

It is possible in many states for certain types of charitable and educational nonprofit organizations to obtain tax-exempt financing for their facilities. While the details of these arrangements are outside the scope of this publication, I would like readers to be aware of this possibility. Nonprofits may wish to consider tax-exempt financing if they qualify. While tax-exempt financing is somewhat complex in nature, it typically offers interest rates that are *substantially* below those that are otherwise available to nonprofits in the marketplace.

> ***Author's Note:*** *I am aware of circumstances in which tax-exempt financing has saved nonprofit organizations hundreds of thousands of dollars per year in interest costs. Interested nonprofits should consult lenders and legal counsel with specific experience in tax-exempt financing for nonprofits.*

BOND FINANCING

As an alternative to financing provided by bankers and other traditional lenders, nonprofits sometimes turn to bond financing to provide funds for real property acquisition, construction, improvement, or refinancing. With bond financing, investors hold the nonprofit's debt. The nonprofit's bonds are sold to the investors either by the nonprofit directly or by a bond underwriting firm.

Bond financing is sometimes used in order to permit a nonprofit to establish a truly long-term fixed interest rate for its debt without a prepayment penalty. Bond financing is also used in some cases by nonprofits that are not able to obtain credit from traditional lenders in other ways.

Nonprofit bond issues are generally issued on either a "firm" underwriting or a "best efforts" basis. A firm underwriting is a bond issue in which the bond underwriter guarantees the sale of all of the bonds, ensuring that the nonprofit will receive the full proceeds of the bond issue, net of applicable costs. As the term implies, a best efforts bond issue is one in which "best efforts" are made to sell the bonds with no guarantee as to what portion of the bonds will be sold and the amount of proceeds the nonprofit will receive.

Issuing bonds is a complex legal process and should only be undertaken under the advice of highly experienced and competent legal counsel who is knowledgeable about federal and state securities law as well as nonprofit bond law. Because of the complexity involved in issuing bonds, there are typically substantial up-front costs associated with a nonprofit bond issue. The nonprofit must consider the advantages provided by a nonprofit bond issue as compared with traditional borrowing in light of the higher up-front costs.

10 Rules for Financial Health in a Nonprofit Private School

Having advised numerous nonprofit private schools on matters of financial health and having served as chairman of the board of a nonprofit private school for 20 years, I would like to offer some special commentary on financial health for nonprofit private schools. I have personally seen the observations I provide below work dramatically. As a person of faith, I believe that in some cases, God's providence was the primary reason for the success, and I believe that God blessed these practices.

1. **Ensure that the school's governing board is made up of wise people who share a passion for the excellence and success of the school**

    I am often asked what attributes make for excellent board members of a nonprofit organization. I always give the same answer—two things—genuine wisdom and a passion for the mission of the organization. I do not answer that question with responses that relate to the technical expertise of board members (e.g., trying to get a banker, a lawyer, an accountant, etc. on the board), their connections in the community, their ability to raise money, or anything else like that. An organization can hire professional expertise—and often better professional expertise with respect to the organization's specific needs than a volunteer board member will be able to provide.

The role of the board of a nonprofit private school is a critically important one. You want wise people on the board who truly care about the mission and success of your school. If your board members are genuinely wise, they will know when they need special outside expertise—and they will get it.

Don't try to operate an excellent nonprofit private school with a mediocre board. The result will be mediocre decisions, and often, poor financial health.

2. **Have a very clear sense of mission and purpose**

As I describe at length in Chapter 1 of this book, having a clear sense of mission and purpose is a fundamental starting point for organizational success, including financial health. I won't reiterate all the reasons that is true here, but read Chapter 1 and follow the guidance in it.

Don't fall victim to the easy, lazy way out by taking the position that your mission and purpose are obvious—after all, you are a school—and you do what schools do, right? Wrong. There are all kinds of questions that a wise board will ask itself in defining and articulating the specific mission and purpose of the school. Questions like:

- Are we primarily a college-prep school or something else?
- What will be our target market for students?
- If our school is faith-based, how will the faith element affect our admissions, curricula, employment, and conduct policies?
- What are our objectives with respect to academic performance of our students?

- What are our objectives with respect to the caliber and credentials of our administration, faculty, and staff?
- What are our objectives with respect to extracurricular activities?
- How will we make our school's activities positive and motivating for all involved?

The board and staff leadership of a well-governed school serious about excellence will ask questions like these and develop well-thought-out answers to them to light the path for the school directionally. The result should be a clearly articulated statement of mission and purpose that is not just tucked in a drawer somewhere—rather, the statement of mission and purpose should become the foundational basis for all programs, activities, and initiatives carried on by the school—as well as the guidepost for evaluating the school's success.

3. **Ensure that the school has truly excellent staff leadership**

John Maxwell has famously stated that everything rises and falls on leadership. Just like you can't expect to operate an excellent school with a mediocre board, you shouldn't expect to operate an excellent school with staff leaders who are not, themselves, excellent at their work. Like great board members, staff leaders (especially the head of school) must be wise and passionate about the mission of the school.

I could expound significantly (pages and pages) on what constitutes excellent staff leadership. Rather than do that here, I want to focus on two elements—financial expertise and making tough decisions.

First, the school's board should ensure that staff leadership collectively includes strong business and financial expertise in addition to appropriate educational leadership skills. The head of school may or may not be a strong business administrator (some schools emphasize educational credentials for the head of school), but somewhere in the top leadership staff mix must be strong business and financial expertise. Failure to ensure this is a ticket to continuous financial mediocrity and/or stress.

Second, the school's board and head of school must be willing to make tough decisions about school leaders. When a particular person is not able to perform with excellence in carrying out the school's programs, the board (in the event that the head of school is the one with the performance issue) or the head of school (with respect to all other staff positions) must make a change. This is not easy to do sometimes, but when it is the right thing to do, it is necessary for the benefit of the students and the school's long-term viability.

4. **Determine what it costs to operate a school with true excellence in the details**

   School leaders often underestimate (knowingly or unknowingly) what it really costs to operate a school that truly has the ability to carry out with excellence the mission and purpose described in Item 2. Be honest with yourselves in this process. Define excellence. Price it. And then include it in your cost estimates.

5. **Set tuition and fees at levels that cover the entire cost of operating the school with true excellence and a reasonable surplus**

   In his now out-of-print 1996 book entitled *From Candy Sales to Committed Donors,* Bruce Lockerbie advocated charging tuition and fees sufficient to cover the costs (determined in Item 4) to operate a non-profit private school with excellence. And operating a school with excellence financially means allowing for a reasonable operating surplus in the budget. (See more about operating surpluses and financial health in Chapters 1 and earlier in this chapter). His advice was revolutionary at the time. For some reason, many private schools were simply unwilling to charge tuition and fees sufficient to cover the actual costs of operating the school with excellence. In failing to do so, the schools created a highly stressful annual obligation to raise money in all kinds of conceivable ways (candy sales, gift wrap sales, magazine sales, banquets, etc.) literally just to pay the bills! And in years where such fundraising efforts were not adequately successful, the ramifications were significant and stressful.

Lockerbie's advice is as relevant today as it was in 1996. If a school is to operate in a financially healthy manner, it should charge tuition and fees sufficient to cover the costs—all the costs—of operating the school with true excellence in pursuit of its specific mission and purpose. Period.

6. **Establish a financial aid support program at levels appropriate for your school and its community**

Not everyone in your school's community will be able to afford your school's tuition and fees, no matter what level your school sets them at. Every school should determine the nature and extent of financial aid it plans to offer to families who cannot afford full tuition and fees.

The main questions each school must address in this arena are:

- How much financial aid will the school make available in total to families for each school year?
- How will the financial aid be funded? (Are there donated funds available for this purpose or will be financial aid be funded through the budget?) [Note that when financial aid is funded through the budget, full-paying families are effectively subsidizing the tuition of families who receive financial aid. My point in noting that is just to ensure awareness, not to imply that such an approach is wrong or problematic. In fact, such an approach is very common among nonprofit private schools.]
- What is the maximum amount of financial aid that the school will make available for any one student?
- How will the amount of financial aid for each student be determined? [Note—there are companies/organizations that specialize in

assisting schools in making such determinations based on income and other information provided by families that apply for financial aid.]

A well-administered financial aid program can help families that would not otherwise be able to participate in the school's program to do so—an important element for many schools desiring to serve their community.

7. **Budget and manage financial condition in a healthy manner**

Chapters 1 and this chapter provide extensive information about budgeting for and managing the financial health of a nonprofit organization. The guidance in those chapters applies to schools in the same manner as it does for other types of nonprofit organizations. Accordingly, I won't elaborate much here—with the exception of the notes that follow about ensuring that tuition and fees are collected when due.

a. **Ensure that tuition and fees are collected when due**

A particularly challenging area of financial operations for some schools is collecting tuition and fees when they are due. Of course, any well-governed school will have financial policies that require timely payment of tuition and fees as a condition of continuing to participate in the school's programs. But when Susie's parents don't pay her tuition on time, the decision to tell them that Susie can't attend classes anymore is understandably difficult and painful. No one wants to do that.

Because enforcing tuition payment policies is so painful, many schools take a path of lesser resistance and begin to let slow-payment and no-payment situations slide. When they do that, before you know it, the school has a receivables problem—and often a big one. And if the school becomes lax in its enforcement of payment policies, it can be sure that word will spread among families in the school. When that happens, there are two bad outcomes.

More families will stop making timely payments and families who make timely payments will become upset that students whose families are not paying continue to participate in school activities with impunity—a fact that they will call out as unfair.

School leaders must accept a hard truth. If, after applying appropriate available financial aid as described in Step 6, a student's family is unable to timely pay applicable tuition and fees, that student's family is not a financial fit for the school. School leaders must kindly and lovingly help the family understand that and gently help them transition to a school that is a better match.

Author's Note: I have seen financially well-off donors inform the school leadership that they want to know if any student is at risk of being dismissed from the school due to nonpayment. In some cases, depending on the facts, the donors make payments anonymously to cover the outstanding tuition and allow the student to continue to participate. A couple of thoughts about such well-intentioned arrangements. It is probably a good idea for the school not to reveal to the donors the identities of the specific students or families involved for privacy and confidentiality reasons, and such arrangements can be great if the problem causing nonpayment is a temporary one. If the problem is not a temporary one, the donor's payment of current balances due may just defer the issue rather than solve it.

In my capacity as an auditor and advisor to nonprofit private schools, I have seen some incredible examples of failure to enforce tuition payment policies. Some schools allow the problem to become so bad that the very existence of the school is threatened. I have literally seen schools with millions of dollars in past due tuition receivables. That is not OK. The good news is that I have also seen schools take my firm's advice, correct the situation, and experience dramatic financial turnarounds.

8. **Raise funds for special things**

   If a school operates with the financial plans described in Items 1-7, the school should not have to raise money to pay the bills. Accordingly, the school can raise money for special things. New things. Great things. Cool things. Like a new lab, or new computers, or a new gym, or a performing arts center, or a chapel, or any number of other great, new things.

   It is much easier to motivate donors to give to help a school acquire beneficial new assets to improve the school's programs than it is to get donors to give so that the school has enough money to pay the bills for regular operations. And even if a school is able to raise money annually that is necessary to pay operating expenses, doing so limits how much the school can raise in addition when the school needs to acquire special new assets.

9. **Actually operate the school with true excellence in the details**

   In Item 2, we address the need for a well-governed school to clearly define and articulate its mission and purpose. In doing so, the school defines what it considers to constitute excellence in its operations.

   As an appropriate follow-on to that exercise, the school should define what excellence looks like in the details, and develop "markers of excellence." Markers of excellence are measurable or observable attributes that indicate when excellence (as defined by the school's leadership) is achieved. As an example, assume that a school has as one element of its mission and purpose helping students gain acceptance to competitive colleges. A marker of excellence in this area might be that 80 percent or more of the students in each of the school's graduating classes are accepted for admission to the college of their first choice.

The school should develop and identify markers of excellence for each significant area of its operations.

Developing and identifying markers of excellence is not the stopping point. The school's leadership should monitor, measure, and evaluate how the school is doing in attaining the markers of excellence in each area of operations. Such assessments should be reported regularly to the school's staff leadership and board. And when the school is not attaining the desired results, the school's leadership should take appropriate action.

This is an ongoing, iterative process.

10. **Create "zip" in key areas for motivation and excitement**

A final word about operating a school in a financially healthy manner. Create some "zip." Some excitement. As regularly as possible. Make the kindergarten and first grade classes as cool as they can be. Have an awesome playground. Have a *really cool* mascot. Have members of your faculty and staff who genuinely love and care about the students and who show it. Have positive people interact regularly with the students. Don't allow negativity. Teach students how to love and care for others, including those who are different from themselves.

I believe that making school as positive and exciting as school can be is a worthwhile endeavor. Our kids are our future leaders. We need bright, motivated leaders in the future who have experienced positivity, love, and care. And maybe they will pass it on.

CHAPTER 7

Maintaining Sound Internal Control

A BIBLICAL EXAMPLE OF INTERNAL CONTROL

The Bible provides a clear example of internal control in 2 Corinthians 8:18–21:

> *And we are sending along with him the brother who is praised by all the churches for his service to the gospel. What is more, he was chosen by the churches to accompany us as we carry the offering, which we administer in order to honor the Lord himself and to show our eagerness to help. We want to avoid any criticism of the way we administer this liberal gift. For we are taking pains to do what is right, not only in the eyes of the Lord but also in the eyes of man.*

The passage above is an example of *dual control* (described in more detail later in this chapter) and also conveys an appropriate "tone at the top" expression of desire to operate with integrity in the context of nonprofit contributions.

THE CONCEPT OF INTERNAL CONTROL

The Committee of Sponsoring Organizations of the Treadway Commission (COSO) is the body generally recognized in the United States as the primary source of authority and guidance related to the topic of internal control. Guidance provided by COSO is used by financial institutions, publicly traded companies, government agencies, and many other types of organizations in establishing and maintaining systems of internal control. COSO is a joint initiative of the American Accounting Association, the American Institute of CPAs, Financial Executives International, The Association of Accountants and Financial Professionals in Business, and The Institute of Internal Auditors. COSO has developed an "integrated framework" for internal control which is updated periodically.

COSO defines internal control as:

> A process, effected by an entity's board of directors, management, and other personnel, designed to provide reasonable assurance regarding the achievement of objectives relating to operations, reporting, and compliance.

COSO's integrated framework for internal control states that internal control consists of five integrated components:

- *Control environment.* The control environment is the set of standards, processes, and structures that provide the basis for carrying out internal control across the organization.
- *Risk assessment.* Risk assessment involves a dynamic and iterative process for identifying and assessing risks to the achievement of objectives.
- *Control activities.* Control activities are the actions established through policies and procedures that help ensure management directives are carried out to mitigate risks to the achievement of objectives.
- *Information and communication.* Relevant and quality information must be communicated in a continual, iterative process of obtaining, providing, and sharing.
- *Monitoring activities.* Monitoring activities consist of ongoing and separate evaluations to ascertain whether each of the components of internal control is present and functioning.[1]

More information about COSO and its integrated framework for internal control is available at COSO.org.

PRACTICAL APPLICABILITY OF INTERNAL CONTROL FOR NONPROFITS

Following is a practical working definition of internal control with respect to a nonprofit's financial matters:

> *The system of checks and balances necessary to protect the nonprofit from intentional or unintentional acts that could cause a loss of the nonprofit's assets or that could result in misreporting of the nonprofit's financial information.*
> (Author's definition)

---

1 Committee of Sponsoring Organizations of the Treadway Commission, Internal Control—Integrated Framework, Executive Summary, May 2013, available at coso.org.

This chapter will focus on internal control matters that are most relevant and most commonly addressed by nonprofits in the United States. Accordingly, the focus here is on internal control matters related to:

- Safeguarding of assets, particularly in connection with cash transactions;
- Relevant and timely financial reporting; and
- Compliance with applicable laws and regulations.

"TONE AT THE TOP"

The COSO integrated framework addresses the **control environment** of an organization. The control environment includes an organization's culture and what COSO refers to as the "tone at the top." The idea is that an organization has a particular culture among its leaders with respect to issues related to internal control and similar matters. While many organizations have leaders that desire to operate with complete integrity and in compliance with applicable laws, not all organizations are blessed with such leaders. The tone at the top of an organization has a significant effect on the nature, extent, and quality of an organization's internal control.

If a nonprofit organization and its leaders do not have a genuine desire to operate with integrity and a desire to comply with applicable law, that nonprofit has a much more fundamental problem than its internal control. While in the minds of many the previous sentence may go without saying, the sad reality is that some nonprofits are led by people who do not share such ideals and who pay little respect to sound internal control, operating with financial integrity, and compliance with applicable law. For any nonprofit official reading this publication and addressing the topic of internal control in his or her nonprofit, the tone at the top is the starting point and it may also be the endpoint. **If your nonprofit is led by people who do not respect sound internal control, financial integrity, and legal compliance, you should find a different organization with which you can engage—and quickly.** The remainder of this chapter on internal control assumes the nonprofit's leaders have a genuine desire to operate with integrity.

ADEQUATE STAFFING AND FINANCIAL EXPERTISE: AN IMPORTANT PRIORITY

A nonprofit with the right attitude regarding financial integrity and compliance may still find internal control difficult if it does not have adequate staffing and financial expertise. In order for a nonprofit to maintain accurate financial records and implement appropriate safeguards, the nonprofit must have people with the knowledge and capacity to accomplish such objectives. Nonprofits sometimes struggle in this area—and many times, this struggle is caused by the nonprofit's unwillingness to incur the financial costs necessary to hire the right people and use the right outside help to maintain adequate capacity and expertise to address financial matters well.

Having adequate capacity in financial administration and oversight should be a high priority for any nonprofit. Nonprofit leaders who place a low priority on financial administration invariably find themselves dealing with frequent financial and administrative challenges—challenges that are often an impediment to the growth and influence of the organization. Nonprofit leaders who place a low priority on financial administration sometimes have a "blind spot" with respect to this issue, not understanding that having strong and sound financial administration is like having a strong and sound foundation for a building. With a strong foundation, a large building may be built with confidence. But if the foundation is thin and weak, the building may easily collapse. Rarely, if ever, does a large, growing, effective, and dynamic nonprofit operate successfully for a long period of time with a low priority on the quality of its financial administration.

Part of having adequate capacity in financial administration is having talented and knowledgeable accounting and finance staff. Nonprofits should be selective in hiring accounting and finance staff. Care should be taken to ensure that accounting and finance employees have the talent and ability to perform their duties with excellence. In addition to checking references, nonprofits should find other ways to evaluate the talents and abilities of prospective employees. If the nonprofit has a relationship with a knowledgeable CPA, the nonprofit may consider asking the CPA to interview a candidate for employment to discuss accounting matters. Another option is to require candidates to complete assessment exams for accounting and financial matters. Once hired, employees must be regularly evaluated to address the quality of their work. The nonprofit must address situations where employees are not performing in an excellent manner by requiring them to improve or by replacing them. Many nonprofits struggle in this area, taking the position that "grace and mercy" should be applied to justify retaining poorly performing employees. The experiences of highly effective nonprofits, however, consistently reveal that the "greater good" is to do what it takes to the best of our ability to administer the nonprofit with excellence.

SCREENING FINANCE AND ACCOUNTING EMPLOYEES

In addition to seeking finance and accounting employees with talent and ability, nonprofits must also ensure that their employees are people of high moral character. Nonprofits must

CHAPTER 7 | Maintaining Sound Internal Control

check references provided by prospective employees and volunteers for finance and accounting positions.

It is also essential to perform criminal background checks on all employees or volunteers who are involved in the financial administration of the nonprofit. However, background checks must be performed with screenings specifically related to the jobs and duties that the individual will perform if selected, due to federal antidiscrimination laws. Nonprofits should consult their legal counsel for advice regarding policies for obtaining and using criminal background checks in connection with employment decisions.

> **The theory behind obtaining a credit history report for prospective accounting and finance employees is that if an individual is experiencing significant financial challenges, he or she may be unusually tempted to engage in improper activities.**

Many employers obtain credit history reports for finance and accounting employees, in addition to criminal background checks. Such a practice is wise. The theory behind obtaining a credit history report for prospective accounting and finance employees is that if an individual is experiencing significant financial challenges, he or she may be unusually tempted to engage in improper activities. In determining whether to obtain credit history reports for its finance and accounting employees, a nonprofit should evaluate applicable law under the advice of its legal counsel. The laws of some states govern how credit history reports may be used by employers, and also mandate procedures that employers must follow in obtaining and using such reports.

> **Criminal and credit background checks should be periodically updated for existing employees.**

Criminal and credit background checks should be periodically updated for existing employees. A nonprofit may hire an employee with no criminal record, but unless the nonprofit periodically updates its background checks, the nonprofit may not be aware if an employee subsequently engages in criminal activity.

INSURANCE COVERAGE FOR EMPLOYEE DISHONESTY

A nonprofit should maintain adequate insurance coverage for the risk of employee theft or fraud. In determining an appropriate level of coverage, the nonprofit should take into consideration the cash balances it maintains in bank accounts, investment accounts, and similar assets. Typically, such coverage is relatively inexpensive and adds an element of protection against the risk of misappropriation or embezzlement.

Insurance coverage for employee dishonesty is not, however, a substitute for sound internal controls. Some nonprofit leaders may have the view that if the nonprofit has insurance coverage for employee dishonesty, it has little need to put significant internal controls in place. There are serious flaws in such logic. First, it is irresponsible to ignore a risk merely because the risk is insured. It is possible that an insurance company may challenge a claim made by a nonprofit that is irresponsible in maintaining basic internal control. Second, and perhaps more importantly, the nonprofit must realize that it can only make a claim against its insurance policy if it is aware that a loss has occurred. In a nonprofit where internal controls are inadequate, the nonprofit may experience significant losses without knowing the losses occurred. Finally, insurance coverage for employee dishonesty has limits. A significant loss that occurs over an extended period of time can easily exceed any reasonable level of insurance coverage.

> Some nonprofit leaders may have the view that if the nonprofit has insurance coverage for employee dishonesty, it has little need to put significant internal controls in place. There are serious flaws in such logic.

PROTECTING CASH TRANSACTIONS

Cash transactions are the most important area of internal control for the financial activity of nonprofits. Internal control over cash transactions may be defined as the processes and systems designed to reduce the risk that embezzlement or misappropriation could occur and not be detected in a timely manner.

Prevention or detection?

Not all misappropriation, embezzlement, or fraud can be prevented. While internal control should serve to reduce the risk that such activities could occur, it is impossible to design a practical system that can completely prevent such improper activities. Accordingly, internal control must be designed to reduce the risk that an impropriety could occur and not be detected in a timely manner.

For example, consider an accounts payable clerk who has access to a nonprofit's blank check stock for writing checks to vendors. Even if the accounts payable clerk is not an authorized signer on the nonprofit's bank account (which he/she should not be), he/she could create a check payable to himself/herself or to a fictitious vendor and forge the signature of one or more authorized signers. It would be very difficult to design a practical system that would completely prevent such a possibility. However, a sound internal control system should reduce the risk that the accounts payable clerk could perpetrate such a fraud without being detected in a timely manner.

It's not just the green paper with images of past presidents

At the outset, it is important to note that, for the purposes of this chapter, the term "cash" refers to money in any form, including currency, electronic transfers, checks, or any other form. Nonprofit leaders sometimes make the mistake of thinking that internal control is only important with respect to currency transactions.

For example, when addressing internal control over the receipt of donations and contributions, some nonprofit leaders take the position that since the vast majority of their donations and contributions come in the form of checks or electronic transfers, there is little need for concern about internal control. Few things could be further from the truth. Sadly, there are numerous ways that ill-intentioned people may convert checks to their own use or divert the destination of electronic transfers. Specific instructions on how such misappropriations can occur are beyond the scope of this chapter. Suffice it to say, however, that conversion of all forms of money to improper use is relatively simple in the absence of adequate internal control.

Does internal control represent a distrust of the individuals involved?

Nonprofits sometimes justify a lack of internal control based on the premise that the nonprofit employees, and others who are involved in financial administration, are trustworthy people. One would certainly hope that the nonprofit trusts the people it has vested with the responsibilities of financial administration. Imagine the alternative! Of course the nonprofit trusts its people! Maintaining sound internal control is not a practice based on distrust. During the Cold War, President Ronald Reagan was known for his expression, "Trust but verify," when addressing the global reduction in nuclear arms. The concept of "trust but verify" sums up a healthy view of internal control as it relates to the integrity of the nonprofit's finance and accounting team.

Nonprofit leaders are sometimes wary of implementing internal controls for fear that doing so will cause the people in charge of financial administration to perceive that the nonprofit does not trust them. If the people in charge of financial administration are actually financially savvy, not only will they not harbor that viewpoint, they will typically argue just the opposite. The fact that they are trustworthy is the reason that implementing sound internal control is welcome.

Internal control is for individual protection as well

Sound internal control not only serves to safeguard the assets of the nonprofit, it also serves to protect individuals from false accusations or suspicion.

EXAMPLE Mildred, the bookkeeper, has signatory authority over the nonprofit's checking account, keeps all the books and records, produces the financial reports, reconciles the bank account, and processes the organization's incoming donations for deposit alone. One day, someone accuses the nonprofit of mishandling donations and says that money has been taken from the donations and not accounted for.

What defense will Mildred have? Very little, if any.

On the other hand, if the nonprofit's practices required two people who are not bookkeepers for the nonprofit to accompany the donations at all times, through the point at which a deposit was fully prepared and a log or other record was made of the items in the deposit, Mildred would have a very strong defense. In reality, if such practices were followed, it is unlikely that such an accusation would even be made. In the absence of such practices, regardless of whether any improper conduct occurred, it will be difficult, if not impossible, for Mildred to avoid suspicion.

Lead us not into temptation

Sound internal control over cash transactions also reduces opportunity for people to engage in impropriety or embezzlement, due to the likelihood of being detected. Placing someone in a position in which they could perpetrate a fraud or embezzlement without detection is clearly unwise and represents poor fiscal management. Regardless of how trustworthy a nonprofit may consider its people, it should never place people in the path of temptation.

KEY PRINCIPLES OF INTERNAL CONTROL FOR CASH TRANSACTIONS

Specific internal controls related to cash transactions should be developed and maintained based on an understanding of certain key principles. Three primary applicable principles are:

- Segregation of duties with people and systems;
- Dual control; and
- Appropriate oversight and monitoring.

Segregation of duties: people

Certain duties with respect to cash transactions and related activities are not compatible and should not be carried out by one person. (For this purpose, members of the same family should be considered one person.) A lack of appropriate segregation of duties creates an environment in which there is a greater risk that misappropriation, embezzlement, or fraud could occur and not be detected in a timely manner.

As a general rule, it is ideal to separate duties that involve the following roles with respect to cash:

- *Authorization of cash disbursements.* The authorization to make cash disbursements involves the authority to commit the nonprofit to making expenditures, purchases, contractual commitments, or other similar actions. Authorization to make cash disbursements is usually vested in the top leadership of a nonprofit.
- *Custody or control over cash.* Custody over cash can be in the form of physical possession (e.g., handling of donations received during a fundraising event) or signatory authority over bank accounts, investment accounts, and other cash accounts.
- *Accounting responsibilities.* Accounting responsibilities include the responsibility to maintain the books and records of the nonprofit, including (but not limited to) the nonprofit's general ledger, contribution records, accounts payable, accounts receivable, payroll, financial statements, and other reports and financial records related to cash transactions.

While separating duties related to all three of the categories of responsibility described above is ideal, the size and makeup of many nonprofits sometimes makes it difficult to fully separate the responsibility for authorization of cash disbursements from control over cash. For example, a nonprofit's CFO or business administrator is often vested with the authority to approve or authorize spending commitments, purchases, and contractual commitments. The CFO is also often vested with signatory authority over the nonprofit's bank accounts. Such arrangements are common and do not necessarily present significant weaknesses in internal control, so long as other appropriate safeguards are in place. In reality, a nonprofit's CFO is typically in the best position to know whether a disbursement is proper and whether a check or other instrument authorizing the disbursement is appropriate.

While combining the duties of authorizing cash disbursements and signatory authority over cash accounts may be permissible in some circumstances, it is never permissible or acceptable to combine the duties of custody or control over cash with accounting responsibilities that involve cash transactions. For example, it is not appropriate for the nonprofit's primary accountant to have physical custody of cash or to have signatory authority over any of the nonprofit's bank accounts.

Segregation of duties: systems

In addition to applying the proper segregation of duties to the assigned roles of individuals, the nonprofit's financial accounting software system should be configured in a manner that requires adherence to the segregation principles described previously.

Properly configuring the financial accounting software system involves assigning user rights to individuals in a manner that aligns with their duties. User rights should permit employees to perform the duties to which they are assigned and should not permit them to perform other incompatible duties or functions. For example, a person responsible for handling incoming funds should not generally have the ability to enter or modify accounting data related to incoming funds or to general accounting. As another example, a person with signatory authority over the nonprofit's bank accounts should not have the ability to enter or modify accounting data related to expenses, disbursements, or to general accounting.

A detailed analysis of the topic of assigning and maintaining system user rights in a nonprofit's financial accounting software applications is beyond the scope of this chapter, but following are some key principles for nonprofits to consider in this important area:

1. An application that allows for multiple levels of user rights will have an "administrator" role, which is the role of assigning user rights to individual users.
2. The administrator role may also permit the master administrator to allow other users to have administrative rights—permitting them to also assign or change user rights. Having more than one user with administrative rights is generally not a good practice.
3. Ideally, the person with administrative rights (we will refer to this person as the "administrator") will be a person who has no financial authority, meaning no control or custody over assets (including no signatory authority) and no accounting or financial reporting responsibilities.
4. The person vested with the responsibility to determine how user rights should be assigned (we will refer to this person as the "authorizer") will be different from the administrator. The authorizer should be a person in a position of executive authority with knowledge about the financial operations of the nonprofit, but not a person with direct accounting or financial reporting responsibilities. The authorizer should not have user rights that permit the entry or modification of system data— the authorizer may have "read-only" access.
5. The authorizer will carefully consider the roles and duties of individual users and will authorize the assignment of individual user rights. The authorization should be

in writing and should be communicated to the administrator, who will physically implement the assignment of user rights pursuant to the instructions of the authorizer. The administrator and authorizer will retain the written authorization of user rights as an important record. Modifications to user rights must be approved by the authorizer in writing and communicated to the administrator in the same manner that applies to the assignment of user rights. The administrator and authorizer should retain records of user rights modifications as important records.

6. Some applications may allow for "profiles," which are bundles of user rights that are typically assigned to persons with a particular role. For example, some applications may have a user rights profile labeled "accountant" with user rights deemed by the application publisher to be appropriate for most accountants in an organization. An authorizer must take care with using pre-bundled profiles to ensure that all of the rights assigned to a particular person are appropriate. Software publishers may not adequately consider internal control matters in their creation of bundled user profile options, regardless of how they may be labeled.

7. Some financial software applications allow for user rights to include the ability to delete or modify a previously posted transaction or entry. Such a feature is dangerous and should never be permitted in a sound internal control environment. When assigning user rights, no user should have the ability to delete or modify an individual transaction, record, or entry once it is posted or entered into the system. (A previous mistake should be corrected by posting a new entry so that a proper record of the postings may be maintained.) The nonprofit's financial software application should maintain a permanent log or record of all activity, entries, or modifications.

8. Users should not have rights to perform functions within the system for which they are not assigned, regardless of whether such functions are incompatible with their duties or not. For example, the CFO or treasurer should not, normally, have rights that would permit data entry or data modification. It would be common and appropriate in most circumstances for such individuals to have "read-only" access.

9. The nonprofit's human resources processes should include removing a user's access rights to the system immediately upon termination.

10. As a matter of policy, all users should be advised to report to their supervisors any variations from the nonprofit's policies in this area or any other anomalies that may be cause for concern.

Dual control

The practice of dual control relates to having at least two unrelated people working together when handling "live" funds. A lack of dual control in circumstances where it is warranted creates an environment in which there is a greater risk that misappropriation, embezzlement, or fraud could occur and not be detected in a timely manner.

Most commonly, dual control is practiced in nonprofits in connection with the collection of contributions. Contributions may be collected through the mail, during a fundraising event, from donation collection receptacles, or by other means. Dual control may also be practiced when currency is used for operating purposes (e.g., on an international service trip, when carrying out disaster relief, or in similar circumstances).

> Properly configuring the financial accounting software system involves assigning user rights to individuals in a manner that aligns with their duties. User rights should permit employees to perform the duties to which they are assigned and should not permit them to perform other incompatible duties or functions.

Appropriate oversight and monitoring

In addition to the principles of segregation of duties and dual control, nonprofit leaders must engage in adequate oversight and monitoring of the nonprofit's financial affairs. That includes carefully reviewing financial reports, reconciliations, and other records. This responsibility also includes monitoring to verify that policies, procedures, and internal controls which are supposed to be in place are, indeed, in place and being carried out by those who are responsible. See Chapter 8 for more information about oversight and monitoring.

SPECIFIC INTERNAL CONTROLS OVER CASH TRANSACTIONS

Following are a number of recommended internal controls that should be applied to cash transaction activities. Cash transaction activities may be generally divided into three categories:

- Receipts (including storage);
- Disbursements; and
- Reconciliation.

Receipts

Physical collection

Cash receipts obtained by physical collection (from fundraising events, receptacles, mail, and so on) should be handled under dual control at all times, up through the point at which a deposit is prepared and a log is made of the items being deposited. The deposit documents and the log should be signed off by the two or more people who are handling and processing the funds. The log or detailed record of items deposited should be securely provided to separate persons with accounting responsibilities.

As a general rule, the people physically handling funds and preparing the deposit should be separate from the people who post deposits to the accounting records or to donor records. The use of electronic scanners to gather data from checks for the purpose of assisting with the posting of contributions to donor records, or for the purpose of depositing the funds in the bank, does not negate this principle or the need to exercise dual control throughout the process. Care should be taken to ensure that the nonprofit's process would not permit someone to misappropriate a check or currency while still having the contribution represented by that check or currency posted to a donor's contribution records. Proper reconciliation of amounts posted to donor records to amounts deposited will reduce such risks.

The concept of dual control should be applied from the very moment nonprofit officials have access to funds. For example, if donations are collected during a fundraising event, those who collect the funds should never physically be in a location where they cannot be seen by others. They should gather together in plain sight of the attendees, and then at least two of them should accompany the donations to the place where it is stored or further processed. If contributions are collected from receptacles, such receptacles should be locked and should only be accessed by two people working together. The keys to such receptacles should be stored in a manner that requires at least two people working together to retrieve them.

For cash receipts received by mail, such items should be segregated from other mail and processed under dual control.

As mentioned above, the people who physically collect and process cash receipts should be separate from those who have accounting responsibilities for the nonprofit.

In recent years, nonprofits have begun to add additional elements of physical security as part of the process of receiving and processing cash receipts. For example, some nonprofits use security guards, police officers, armored courier services, security surveillance cameras, and other safeguards that help reduce the risk of theft—or even robbery or burglary. Nonprofits are wise to consider such measures in light of the increasing frequency of crimes in this area. It is not difficult to understand how the nonprofit's people or funds could be vulnerable, if it is known that funds are processed in a certain location following a certain schedule and then transported predictably to a specific location. Many banks now offer armored car service pickups to facilitate deposits.

When processing checks for deposit, checks should be restrictively endorsed immediately upon their receipt. This is true even if the nonprofit uses electronic scanners and makes deposits through the "remote capture" services offered by its bank. Restrictively endorsing checks makes it more difficult for the checks to be misappropriated. The remote capture scanning service offered by some banks and software companies includes restrictive endorsement of the scanned checks as an automatic part of the process.

Storage

Deposits of cash receipts should be made immediately after funds are received and processed. When immediate deposit is not possible, funds should be stored in a safe and secure manner that requires dual control for access. For example, the nonprofit could use a safe that requires both a key and a combination to open it. No one person should have both a key and the combination to the safe. In recent years, safe manufacturers have added security features, such as biometric devices, to reduce the risk of unauthorized access. Regardless of the security features, a safe or other storage device should not permit one person to access it alone. Surveillance cameras that record activity can be placed at the door of the safe or vault or even inside the safe or vault as an additional measure of protection.

Electronic collection

In recent years, donors have increasingly adopted the practice of making contributions to their nonprofits electronically. Electronic contributions may be made through ACH transactions from their bank accounts or by credit or debit card transactions initiated on the user's device. Electronic collection of cash receipts greatly reduces the risk of misappropriation and fraud. It can also improve donor giving consistency! However, there are important considerations to keep in mind in safely accepting cash receipts electronically.

When a nonprofit utilizes a service provider, such as a merchant processing firm, to facilitate electronic transactions via the Internet, the nonprofit should take care to ensure that the service provider itself maintains appropriate internal controls and secu-

CHAPTER 7 | Maintaining Sound Internal Control

rity measures to conduct its activities. Practically, there is virtually no way to assess a service provider's controls other than to determine whether the service provider has obtained a report on its internal controls from an independent certified public accounting firm. The report that the nonprofit should seek from a service provider is referred to as a "SOC 1" report, and it should include an opinion on the effectiveness of the organization's internal control with respect to processing transactions. There are two types of SOC 1 reports—cleverly labeled "Type 1" and "Type 2." A Type 1 report does not provide an opinion on the effectiveness of the organization's internal control. A Type 2 report does. Nonprofits that engage in significant and material electronic transactions utilizing an online merchant processing firm should insist that their service provider produce a SOC 1 Type 2 report. The SOC 1 Type 2 report should contain a favorable opinion regarding the organization's internal control over the processing of transactions. Not all service providers in this arena obtain independent assessments of their internal control and therefore, not all service providers can produce the type of report described herein. Some service providers will bristle at such a demand. Nonprofit leaders are wise to seek a service provider that regularly obtains such a report and can provide it.

Deposits of cash receipts should be made immediately after funds are received and processed. When immediate deposit is not possible, funds should be stored in a safe and secure manner that requires dual control for access.

Note that the type of report described here is a report on the organization's internal control. Some service providers who do not have a SOC 1 report will point to the fact that they have Payment Card Industry Data Security Standards (PCI DSS) certification. These standards are mandatory for the payment card industry and relate to data security. While data security is important, internal control over electronic cash transactions involves much more than simple data security. PCI DSS credentials alone are not adequate to establish that an organization maintains effective internal control over its processing of transactions. The SOC 1 Type 2 report is intended to address the service provider's overall system of internal control for processing transactions.

Surveillance cameras that record activity can be placed at the door of the safe or vault or even inside the safe or vault as an additional measure of protection.

EXAMPLE A nonprofit used a service provider to process online contributions. Donors submitted their credit and debit card information along with information about the amounts they wished to contribute to the nonprofit. The nonprofit was contacted one day by a donor who stated that he had not received an acknowledgment for his online contributions to the nonprofit. Upon investigating the matter, the nonprofit determined that it had not received the online contributions the donor claimed to have made. Charges, however, were posted to the donor's credit card account. Upon further investigation, the nonprofit learned that several hundred thousand dollars of online contributions made by its donors had been diverted due to the inadequate internal controls and processes maintained by its service provider. [A true story.]

Electronic collection of cash receipts greatly reduces the risk of misappropriation and fraud. It can also improve donor giving consistency!

Other cautions about credit and debit card processing arrangements

When a nonprofit establishes an agreement with a debit or credit card processing organization, the nonprofit must advise the service provider of the destination bank account for the incoming funds. Nonprofits must ensure that the person authorized to enter into the agreement or to make changes to the agreement does not also have accounting responsibilities. The risk in this area relates to the possibility that a nonprofit official could designate an unauthorized account, such as his or her own, as the destination for processed funds. If the individual with the authority to make such changes also has accounting responsibilities, there is a greater risk that such a scheme might not be detected in a timely manner.

It is wise to maintain a separate bank account for the purpose of receiving deposits from merchant processing companies. A separate account can facilitate reconciliation to the records provided from the merchant processing firm. Additionally, monitoring of the separate account by an independent official can reduce the risk of impropriety by identifying unusual activity.

One other important point should be made regarding processing receipts from credit or debit card transactions. The ability to accept contributions or purchases made by debit or credit cards, whether online, by telephone, or in person, often carries with it the ability to issue credits or refunds to cardholders. The ability to issue a credit or refund to a cardholder is the same as the ability to disburse the nonprofit's funds. Accordingly, merchant processing account activity should be monitored by an independent official for the possibility of unauthorized credits issued to cardholders. For example, an employee working in the nonprofit bookstore might issue a credit to his own credit card account. More sophisticated merchant processing systems will only allow credits to accounts for which there has been a recent corresponding debit and only in an amount that does not exceed the corresponding debit. Nonprofits should question their service providers regarding such security measures and appropriately monitor account activity for impropriety.

Beware of the contribution refund scam—The Kind Fellow Who Made an Error in His Donation Amount May Be a Con Artist

A very kind but anxious fellow named Tom calls your finance office and informs your team that he just realized he accidentally submitted an electronic donation to your nonprofit in the amount of $5,000. He meant for it to be $50. He pleads for an immediate refund of the difference, since he is on a fixed income

Some service providers who do not have a SOC 1 report will point to the fact that they have Payment Card Industry Data Security Standards (PCI DSS) certification. These standards are mandatory for the payment card industry and relate to data security. While data security is important, internal control over electronic cash transactions involves much more than simple data security. PCI DSS credentials alone are not adequate to establish that an organization maintains effective internal control over its processing of transactions. The SOC 1 Type 2 report is intended to address the service provider's overall system of internal control for processing transactions.

and a $5,000 charge to his account would create a terrible hardship for him. Your team wants to help the poor chap immediately. You check the records for your online gifts and sure enough, there it is: an online ACH gift from Tom, a new donor, in the amount of $5,000. You quickly come to Tom's rescue and issue a refund of $4,950 to him through the ACH system. Now that you've saved the day, you can move on to more mundane things.

But two days later, you get a notice from your bank that the original $5,000 gift from Tom was rejected due to insufficient funds in his account. As a result, $5,000 is debited from your nonprofit's account as a chargeback. You try to call Tom and the number is no longer a working number. After you think about it for a couple of minutes, the reality begins to sink in…you got scammed. You issued a refund for $4,950 of a $5,000 contribution you never actually received.

The scenario described above is happening with increasing frequency to nonprofit organizations across the United States. There are variations on the specific approach.

Fraudsters attempt to steal funds by taking advantage of the lag time associated with bank processing of payments from deposit accounts (that is, the time between the date the transaction was made and the date it clears the banking system).

What to do
Refund requests for contributions should ring alarm bells. A refund of all or part of a charitable contribution is a very unusual occurrence. In fact, the very nature of a contribution involves the relinquishing of ownership and control over the gift. Nonprofits are not at liberty to simply refund contributions upon a donor's request. (Imagine a donor giving a large gift, the nonprofit using the gift to pay for a significant initiative, and the donor subsequently asking for a refund. If such practices were allowed, nonprofits couldn't properly function.)

It is true that if a donor accidentally gave more than he/she intended, a nonprofit may have a moral duty (if not a legal one) to rectify the situation. But only if it was genuinely an accident and only if the nonprofit ensures that it is not the victim of a scam in the process. A simple way to avoid being scammed in the manner described herein is to appoint a special team to handle any donation refund requests and train the team on these types of scams. The nonprofit should never issue a refund for an allegedly erroneous contribution until the nonprofit ensures that the funds originally given have fully cleared the banking system and are settled. Simple awareness and adhering to such a policy can prevent a nonprofit from being flimflammed.

Disbursements
Segregation of duties
One of the most important internal control principles that should be applied in the area of cash disbursements is that no one individual should have duties or authority that would permit him or her to initiate and complete a cash disbursement in its entirety. For example, the person who prepares checks for payment to vendors should not be an authorized signer on the nonprofit's bank account and vice versa. Authorized signers should not have access to blank check stock. Electronic disbursements from the nonprofit's bank account should require participation or approval by more than one individual. This principle reflects the concept of segregation of duties.

Controlled review of bank and credit card account activity
Another key rule that nonprofits should apply in the arena of cash disbursements is that a person with signatory authority should perform a controlled review of bank state-

ments or bank activity and credit card account activity to verify the propriety of all disbursements. Controlled review refers to a review of banking or credit card account activity performed in a manner that ensures that the reviewer is analyzing unaltered documentation.

An example of a controlled review is a review of bank or credit card statements received from the bank or credit card company that are still sealed in their original envelopes when delivered to the reviewer. Another example of a controlled review is a review of cash disbursements activity or charges online on the bank or credit card company's website. Both approaches permit the reviewer to analyze information directly as it comes from the bank or credit card company and reduces the risk that the reviewer analyzes altered or fraudulent documentation. The review should include an analysis of all canceled check images, as well as information about all other charges or debits (or reductions) in the nonprofit's bank account.

Don't forget PayPal

In performing a review of bank activity for the purpose of vetting disbursements, nonprofit leaders should consider all monetary accounts in which activity could be conducted, including those that may be "off the radar" accounts, such as PayPal accounts, virtual currency accounts, and so on. The existence and use of such accounts is on the rise. The nonprofit should have a policy governing the authorization, creation, and use of any accounts in which financial activity on behalf of the nonprofit is to be conducted.

Positive pay services

Another way that a nonprofit can reduce the risk of unauthorized disbursements is to utilize "positive pay" services offered by its bank—especially if the service includes "payee verification." With a bank's positive pay service, the bank only pays checks or debits that are preauthorized by the bank customer (the nonprofit). The nonprofit sends the bank an electronic file listing the checks that have been authorized for payment. The bank then compares checks that are presented to it for payment against the list provided by the nonprofit. If a check presented for payment does not match the file provided by the nonprofit, the bank reports it to the nonprofit as an exception, and the nonprofit then has an opportunity to determine whether the check is valid or not. Basic positive pay services typically do not include verification of the name of the payee—only the check number and the amount of the check.

The enhancement of payee verification reduces the risk of a fraudulent disbursement that may be recorded in the nonprofit's books as having been made to a payee who is different from the actual payee indicated on the check. In order to establish the greatest protection in using positive pay, the person reviewing and submitting the positive pay file to the bank should be someone who is knowledgeable about authorized vendors and disbursements and who is someone other than an accounts payable or other accounting person.

Cloud-based paperless accounts payable applications
As is more fully described in Chapter 2, in recent years cloud-based paperless accounts payable applications have become increasingly popular. An example of such a service is Bill.com. In addition to providing significant efficiencies, electronic accounts payable management systems generally facilitate improved internal control by requiring multiple individuals to provide approvals in connection with disbursements (assuming the application has been properly set up with segregated user rights).

For example, such an application offers "roles," such as the accountant role, with duties that align with the principle of segregation of duties. An accountant, for example, would not be permitted to execute a "pay" command.

Another feature that enhances internal control is that such systems do not produce physical checks to be signed by the nonprofit's employees and mailed or delivered from the nonprofit's office. Instead, disbursements are either made electronically through the ACH system or checks are actually prepared and mailed by the service provider directly to the vendors. Cloud-based paperless accounts payable management systems offer significant advantages over traditional paper-check-based systems. The applications integrate with a number of accounting software applications.

Application to payroll
While the internal control practices described previously are explained primarily in terms of disbursements to vendors, the same principles should apply with respect to payroll disbursements. Segregation of duties should apply in the area of payroll such that no one person is responsible for all phases of payroll processing.

For example, it would be inappropriate for a single person to maintain personnel records, to input information about pay rates into the payroll processing system, prepare the payroll, and authorize or make payroll disbursements without any other independent review. Even though vesting one person with the authority to perform all the duties would represent a lack of segregation of duties, such arrangements are common in nonprofits.

A relatively practical way to apply segregation of duties in the payroll arena is to require a controlled review of payroll information for each payroll after the fact. If an outside payroll service is used, the reviewer should obtain payroll information related to each payroll directly from the payroll service provider, either by receiving the information in an unopened package or by reviewing the information directly online. The reviewer should be a person who is knowledgeable about the nonprofit's employees and pay rates and should not be a member of the payroll staff or the accounting team. Such a review is designed to reduce risks that include, but are not limited to, unauthorized modification of pay rates and payment to fictitious employees.

Timely reconciliation

It should go without saying that a nonprofit's bank accounts and investment accounts should be reconciled in a timely manner after the end of each month (at a minimum). An ordinary bank account reconciliation should be performed by an appropriate member of the accounting team, and not by any person who has signing authority with respect to the accounts or other custody or control over the funds.

Review of reconciliation

Once account reconciliation is performed, sound internal control dictates that the reconciliation be reviewed by an appropriate official who does not have accounting responsibilities. Ideally, this official is a person with authority and knowledge about the nonprofit's financial activities—particularly disbursements.

One step further

To adequately close the loop of internal control with respect to cash and investment activity and the nonprofit's financial reporting, one final key step in the reconciliation process should be performed regularly by an appropriate high-level nonprofit official. That step is making a comparison of the cash and investment balances as determined by the reviewed reconciliations described previously, with the balances reported in financial reports provided to the nonprofit's financial oversight body (finance committee, board, and so on).

EXAMPLE Elm Street Nonprofit has two bank accounts and one investment account. The bookkeeper performs a monthly reconciliation of all three accounts. The original bank statements and reconciliations are provided to the treasurer, who reviews the reconciliations for propriety. The treasurer also compares the reconciled balances for all three accounts to the cash and investment balances reported in the financial reports provided to the finance committee. The treasurer signs off on a log indicating that he performs this step each month.

SAFEGUARDING OF ASSETS OTHER THAN CASH

Internal control encompasses safeguarding other types of assets in addition to cash. While internal controls over cash transactions likely warrant the most attention to detail in a nonprofit's system of internal control, controls related to other assets should be considered as well. If a nonprofit maintains significant assets of a type that may be vulnerable to theft, the nonprofit should consider applying appropriate internal control measures to protect the assets. Common examples of non-cash assets that may be particularly vulnerable to theft in a nonprofit would be:

- Food service inventories;
- Bookstore inventories; and
- Electronic and media equipment.

If such assets are significant, the nonprofit should apply accounting procedures to track the inflow and outflow of such items. The accounting records for such assets should be maintained by someone other than the people who have custody or control over the assets. Additionally, accounting team members can perform analytical procedures to identify anomalies in inventory levels or related items.

For electronic and media equipment or other similar assets used by the nonprofit in its operations, the nonprofit should consider maintaining an inventory record of such items that includes a description of the item, its cost, the date it was acquired, the location at which the asset is to be kept, and the name of the person or persons responsible for the asset.

Additional protection may be afforded by using serially numbered tags affixed to the assets, where the serial numbers correspond to entries in the asset inventory records. Periodic inspections should be made to ensure that the assets are still on hand and in their proper locations. Some nonprofits fail to maintain an inventory of their vulnerable non-cash assets because they believe that such an inventory must be maintained for all furniture, fixtures, and equipment. But that is not true. The nonprofit may choose to inventory only those items that it considers vulnerable, such as electronic or media equipment. Applying such an approach can make the task of maintaining inventory records for such items much more manageable.

RELEVANT AND TIMELY FINANCIAL REPORTING

In a healthy internal control environment, financial statements and reports are produced for nonprofit leadership on a regular and timely basis. The financial reports should be complete and correct, allowing nonprofit officials to review them and inquire about unexpected or unusual items. Timely production of relevant financial information facilitates a healthy review process and is essential in maintaining sound internal control. Sometimes, a nonprofit's finance or accounting team may get behind in its work and months may pass during which financial reports are not produced and reviewed. This is a most unhealthy scenario, and nonprofit leaders should take action to restore proper procedures when such events occur.

To enhance internal control and to facilitate a healthy review process, those who prepare financial reports should proactively highlight or otherwise identify and explain unusual items, fluctuations, and so on. In a healthy reporting process, members of the accounting team do not wait for questions that they know will or should be asked by those who will review the reports.

The financial reporting process, further described in Chapter 2, should be clearly defined to include:

- Specific financial reports;
- Specific due dates for the reports; and
- A defined distribution list for the reports.

COMPLIANCE WITH APPLICABLE LAWS AND REGULATIONS

With respect to laws and regulations generally, a nonprofit can employ practices to reduce the risk of noncompliance or legal controversy. Following are some healthy practices that can help reduce such risks:

- Hire and use legal counsel with significant experience in nonprofit law to review and address items, such as:
    - The nonprofit's governing documents (articles of incorporation and bylaws);
    - The nonprofit's board-approved policies (employment policies, child safety policies, transportation policies, and so on);
    - Significant contractual agreements (before they are executed); and
    - Other important documents.
- Conduct a "legal audit" in which an attorney significantly experienced in nonprofit law assesses the nonprofit's compliance with a variety of laws and regulations, and provides a report to the nonprofit's leadership on his or her findings.
- Hire knowledgeable, capable, and business-savvy people to lead the administrative operations of the nonprofit.
- Hire qualified tax counsel, such as a CPA firm or a law firm knowledgeable in the area of nonprofit tax law, to perform an assessment of the nonprofit's compliance with significant aspects of the tax laws. Such an assessment should be followed by a report to the nonprofit's leadership of the findings and recommendations of the tax counsel.

CHAPTER 8

Audits and Other Financial Accountability Activities

The term "audit" can—and does—mean many different things to different people in different contexts. For our purposes, the term "audit" and references to other accountability activities are used to refer to activities conducted or contracted by a nonprofit for the purposes of addressing:

- The reliability of financial statements or reports;
- Whether the nonprofit has vulnerabilities in internal controls, tax compliance, or legal matters; and
- Whether certain aspects of a nonprofit's operations are being carried out as intended or expected.

FINANCIAL ACCOUNTABILITY

Financial accountability should be of utmost interest to any nonprofit and its leaders. The highest and best reason for a nonprofit to have an external audit is to facilitate the nonprofit's financial integrity and accountability, and to increase the likelihood that significant internal control deficiencies, tax compliance vulnerabilities, or similar matters will come to the attention of the nonprofit's leadership.

INDEPENDENT ACCREDITATION—A VERIFIABLE DEMONSTRATION OF ACCOUNTABILITY

Nonprofits in America, particularly larger ones, are increasingly pursuing independent accreditation as a means for verifiably demonstrating a commitment to accountability and financial integrity.

Some nonprofit organizations (such as schools) are subject to accreditation requirements based on the nature of their operations. Requirements of sector accreditation bodies may or may not focus significantly on matters of financial integrity.

The Better Business Bureau's (BBB) Wise Giving Alliance is a national accrediting body for nonprofit organizations. BBB Wise Giving Alliance produces evaluative reports on charities based on 20 BBB Standards for Charity Accountability that address four areas: governance, results reporting, finances, and truthful and transparent communications. More information about BBB Wise Giving Alliance is available at give.org.

> Nonprofits in America, particularly larger ones, are increasingly pursuing independent accreditation as a means for verifiably demonstrating a commitment to accountability and financial integrity.

The largest and most prominent independent accrediting body for evangelical churches and Christian ministries in America in this area is ECFA. ECFA is a national nonprofit, tax-exempt organization that accredits churches and ministries in the areas of financial integrity and governance. ECFA-accredited member churches and ministries must comply with ECFA's Seven Standards of Responsible Stewardship. Information about ECFA and the Seven Standards is available at ecfa.org.

External and internal audits

Nonprofits tend to utilize internal and external audits and other accountability processes in ways that correlate to the size of the nonprofit. Smaller nonprofits tend to utilize informal internal accountability processes performed by members of the nonprofit's governing body, its finance committee, or by volunteers. Larger nonprofits (annual revenues exceeding $2 million) commonly engage external auditors. Very large nonprofit organizations (annual revenues in excess of $50 million) often engage external auditors as well as maintaining a regular, formal internal audit function by employing an internal auditor on staff or contracting with a vendor for formal internal audit services.

External audits and other CPA-performed engagements

Nonprofits may have external audits performed as a condition of acquiring a loan. Lending institutions often require audited financial statements for larger loans. A nonprofit that has an external audit performed solely for the purpose of complying with a contractual obligation required by a lender may see little value in the audit beyond the nonprofit's contractual obligation.

Only Certified Public Accountants (CPAs) and CPA firms are licensed under state law throughout the United States to render opinions and provide certain other services with respect to an organization's financial statements. It is a violation of state law for anyone other than a CPA or a CPA firm to provide assurance or attestation with respect to an organization's financial statements. Nonprofits should be careful when seeking an external audit to ensure that the person or firm being engaged is licensed or legally authorized to practice as a CPA or CPA firm.

The highest quality external audits for nonprofits are those provided by independent CPAs or CPA firms with extensive and reputable experience serving nonprofit organizations. Firms with such experience should be able to help the nonprofit identify issues that are common to the nonprofit sector and warrant attention.

In addition to independent external audits, CPA firms offer other levels of service with respect to a nonprofit's financial statements and/or operating activities. The primary levels of engagement and the relative value and usefulness of each is described below.

AUDIT

An audit is the highest level of assurance a CPA firm can provide with respect to a nonprofit's financial statements. Audited financial statements provide the nonprofit's governing body with the auditor's opinion as to whether the financial statements are presented fairly, in all material respects, in conformity with the method of accounting utilized. The opinion offers reasonable but not absolute assurance with respect to the financial statements to which it applies.

In an audit, the CPA firm should obtain an understanding of the organization's internal control and assess the risk of material misstatement in the financial statements. The firm should also corroborate the amounts and disclosures included in the financial statements by obtaining audit evidence through inquiry, physical inspection, observation, third-party confirmations, examination, analytical procedures, and other procedures.

A properly performed audit should result in the following reports, at a minimum:

- An opinion on the financial statements;
- Financial statements and related disclosures;
- A report addressing any material weaknesses or significant deficiencies in internal control identified by the CPA firm in performing the engagement *(a nonprofit should request its auditor to issue a report addressing internal control regardless of whether the auditor identifies material weaknesses or significant deficiencies in the course of the audit)*; and

- A report to those charged with oversight of the nonprofit regarding certain matters related to the audit process itself, such as the independence of the auditors, sensitive items in the financial statements, and difficulties performing the engagement.

> If the CPA firm performing the audit has extensive experience addressing tax and operational matters for nonprofits, the CPA firm may utilize the audit process to identify other vulnerabilities, such as tax compliance risks, or opportunities, such as tax exemptions not fully utilized by the nonprofit. When a firm provides such value-added commentary to a nonprofit for which it is performing an audit, the overall value received by the nonprofit in an audit process is further enhanced.

Commentary

A well-performed audit conducted by a CPA firm with extensive reputable experience serving nonprofit organizations should yield significant value to a nonprofit and its leaders. An audit results in an opinion on the financial statements by the CPA, providing reasonable assurance that the financial statements are fairly stated (assuming the audit test work supports such a conclusion). No other level of engagement provides a comparable level of assurance regarding the nonprofit's financial statements. The other levels of engagement described in the pages that follow are substantially less in scope than an audit.

Additionally, in an audit, the CPA is required to obtain an understanding of the nonprofit's internal control and assess the risk of material misstatements, including the risk of fraud, in the financial statements to the extent necessary to perform the audit. In the event that the auditor identifies material weaknesses or significant deficiencies in the nonprofit's internal control, the auditor is required to report such matters to the nonprofit's leadership. The auditor's report addressing internal control can be one of the most valuable products of the independent external audit process. A well-performed audit that identifies weaknesses in a nonprofit's internal controls can help the nonprofit improve its systems, processes, and protocols to reduce the risk of improprieties and financial misstatements in the future.

Finally, if the CPA firm performing the audit has extensive experience addressing tax and operational matters for nonprofits, the CPA firm may utilize the audit process to identify other vulnerabilities, such as tax compliance risks, or opportunities, such as tax exemptions not fully utilized by the nonprofit. When a firm provides such value-added commentary to a nonprofit for which it is performing an audit, the overall value received by the nonprofit in an audit process is further enhanced.

While an independent external audit provides the most value to the nonprofit of all of the types of engagements a CPA firm may provide, an audit is also typically the costliest type of engagement. Accordingly, nonprofits considering having an independent external audit must weigh the value of the services to be received with the overall cost. For this reason, it is more common for larger nonprofits (typically, those with annual revenues of $2 million or more) to have independent external audits than it is for smaller nonprofits to do so.

See a sample audit report on page 214.

REVIEW

Financial statements reviewed by a CPA provide the nonprofit's governing body with comfort that the CPA is not aware of any material modifications that should be made to the financial statements for the statements to be in conformity with the financial reporting framework utilized. A review is substantially less in scope than an audit and does not require obtaining an understanding of internal control, assessing the risk of fraud, or testing the nonprofit's records.

In a review engagement, the CPA firm performs procedures (primarily analytical procedures and inquiries) that will provide a reasonable basis for obtaining limited assurance that there are no material modifications that should be made to the financial statements.

A properly performed review should result in the following reports:

- A review report expressing limited assurance on the financial statements.
- Financial statements and related disclosures.

Note that a review does not result in a report addressing internal control, since a CPA firm performing a review is not required to obtain an understanding of internal control as part of conducting the engagement.

Commentary

A review of a nonprofit's financial statements has limited value. A review is often obtained by a nonprofit in scenarios where the nonprofit is contractually required to obtain either a review or an audit of its financial statements and the nonprofit does not wish to incur the cost of an audit. A review provides the nonprofit's governing body with "limited assurance" regarding the reliability of the financial statements. The CPA firm conducting a review is not required to obtain an understanding of the nonprofit's internal control, nor is the CPA firm required to perform any specific tests of the underlying documentation supporting the nonprofit's financial statements. As a result, a review engagement typically does not involve any report to the nonprofit with respect to its internal control, tax compliance matters, or other potential operational risks or vulnerabilities. If a nonprofit wishes to engage a CPA firm for the purpose of obtaining assurance with respect to the financial statements and to obtain information about weaknesses in the nonprofit's internal control, a review engagement is not adequate. A nonprofit should carefully evaluate the value being received before entering into an engagement to have a review of its financial statements.

See a sample review report on page 215.

COMPILATION

A compilation represents *the most basic level of service* a CPA firm may provide that includes a report with respect to a nonprofit's financial statements. In a compilation engagement, the CPA assists management in presenting financial information in the form of financial statements without undertaking to obtain or provide any assurance with respect to the financial statements. In a compilation, the CPA firm is required to have an understanding of the industry in which the client operates, obtain knowledge about the client, read the financial statements, and consider whether the financial statements appear appropriate in form and free from obvious material errors.

A compilation does not contemplate performing inquiry, analytical procedures, or other procedures ordinarily performed in a review; or obtaining an understanding of the organization's internal control, assessing fraud risk, or testing of accounting records ordinarily performed in an audit. Compiled financial statements may be prepared without disclosures (notes to the financial statements). The compilation report provides no assurance whatsoever with respect to the financial statements.

A properly performed compilation typically results in the following reports:

- A compilation report expressing no assurance on the financial statements.
- Financial statements and (if applicable) related disclosures.

Commentary

A compilation is the *simplest and lowest cost engagement option* involving a nonprofit's financial statements in which a report is issued by a CPA firm. A compilation can be vernacularly described within the accounting profession as taking the client's financial information, without checking or testing it, and putting it into the format of proper financial statements. That description, while simple, reasonably summarizes the nature of a compilation engagement. Typically, the CPA firm assists the nonprofit in preparing financial statements in the format required for the particular method of accounting used. The CPA firm uses the nonprofit's financial information to do so, but the firm does not test the information as it would in an audit, nor does it perform analytical procedures and inquiries as it would in a review. While it is true that a compilation results in a report from the CPA, the report specifically states that the CPA provides no assurance with respect to the financial statements.

There are multiple reasons that nonprofits may engage CPA firms to perform compilations of their financial statements. In many cases, the reason revolves around the lack of ability or capacity of the nonprofit's staff to prepare proper financial statements in conformity with an applicable method of accounting. By engaging a CPA firm to perform a compilation, the nonprofit essentially contracts with the CPA firm to prepare the nonprofit's financial statements in a proper format. The compiled financial statements may be used for internal purposes, which may include financial reporting to the nonprofit's donors. Sometimes, a compilation of the nonprofit's financial statements is obtained in response to a requirement by the nonprofit's lender as a condition of making a loan to the nonprofit. (A compilation may be an acceptable level of financial statement engagement for a lender when the loan amount is small. Typically, the larger the loan amount, the higher the level of financial statement engagement a lender may require.)

Given the fact that a CPA firm provides no assurance with respect to the financial statements in a compilation engagement, a nonprofit should not expect or depend on a compilation engagement to address the reliability or accuracy of the nonprofit's financial statements. The nonprofit most certainly should not have the impression that a compilation engagement will help the nonprofit identify any internal control deficiencies that may exist, tax compliance risks that may exist, or other vulnerabilities. While a compilation may serve a useful purpose, such as one or more of those described previously, its value is severely limited—a fact nonprofits should take into consideration when considering such an engagement.

See a sample compilation report on page 216.

OUTSOURCED ACCOUNTING SERVICES (WITH OR WITHOUT COMPILATION)

A nonprofit also may outsource its accounting and financial reporting processes to an accounting firm. In outsourced accounting arrangements, the accounting firm takes on the role normally performed by the nonprofit's internal accounting staff. Various service providers offer various forms of outsourced accounting. Historically, outsourced accounting services tended to be in the form of after-the-fact bookkeeping services. In recent years, some accounting firms have begun to offer live or real-time outsourced accounting services in which the accounting firm takes on the role of day-to-day processing of transactions and accounting records. Depending on state law, it may be possible for some service providers that are not CPA firms to provide certain outsourced accounting services. In some states, such services may not be referred to as "accounting" services unless they are provided by a CPA firm. Nonprofits interested in engaging a firm other than a CPA firm to provide outsourced accounting services should ensure that the firm is properly licensed to provide the required services.

If outsourced accounting services are provided by a CPA firm, such services may (by mutual agreement) include the production of financial statements with a compilation report by the CPA firm. Depending on the nature of the services provided by the CPA firm, the CPA firm may not be independent with respect to the nonprofit. Professional standards governing the accounting profession permit a CPA firm to issue a compilation report with respect to an organization's financial statements, even if the CPA firm is not independent with respect to the organization. In such cases, the lack of independence must be disclosed in the compilation report.

Commentary

Nonprofits wishing to simplify their internal responsibilities for financial administration may find that outsourcing the accounting function to a CPA firm or other service provider allows nonprofit leaders to focus more on mission and program-related activities and less on administrative matters. In some cases, the cost of such an arrangement may be less than if the nonprofit were to perform the services internally. If a nonprofit does outsource its accounting and internal financial reporting responsibilities and can also benefit from a compilation report on its financial statements, the nonprofit can engage a CPA firm to perform the outsourced services and include a compilation of the appropriate financial statements. Such an arrangement may be appropriate in cases where a lender or other third party requires compiled financial statements.

AGREED-UPON PROCEDURES

Another type of engagement for which a nonprofit may involve a CPA firm is an agreed-upon procedures engagement. As the term implies, the CPA performs certain procedures agreed upon by the client through an agreement specifically describing the procedures to be performed. A nonprofit may engage a CPA to perform procedures that are important to the nonprofit for some reason or that help the nonprofit assess its practices in certain areas. Professional standards provide significant freedom for the CPA in designing an agreed-upon procedures engagement.

The CPA firm performing the agreed-upon procedures will provide a report of the results of the procedures performed. Professional standards governing the accounting profession provide, however, that the reported results are to represent the objective outcomes of the procedures performed. The CPA firm does not provide an opinion regarding the procedures performed or regarding the items or matters that are subjected to the procedures. For example, it would be inappropriate under professional standards for a CPA to include in an agreed-upon procedures report language such as, "therefore, we believe the cash balance as of December 31 is reasonable," or "accordingly, the procedures related to reconciling contributions revenue are being correctly followed by the nonprofit's staff." An example of appropriate language in an agreed-upon procedures report related to year-end cash balances follows:

> *We inspected the original bank statement as of December 31, 20XX, and compared the ending balance per the bank statement to the balance per bank on the nonprofit's bank reconciliation report as of the same date without exception. We identified deposits in transit on the nonprofit's bank reconciliation as of December 31 individually in excess of $1,000 and traced the items to the nonprofit's original January bank statement, noting that all items cleared the bank within the first five days of January without exception. Further, we identified debits to the nonprofit's bank account as reported in the first 10 days of January on the nonprofit's original January bank statement, and traced those in excess of $500 to the nonprofit's December 31 reconciliation report, without exception.*
>
> *[Note that the language in the example provided above does not include qualitative assessments with respect to the procedures performed. For example, the CPA does not use the words "reasonable" or "opinion" in this language. He or she merely describes the procedures performed and objectively states that they were performed "without exception." Had there been exceptions, the CPA would specifically describe the exceptions noted. An agreed-upon procedures engagement does not result in an assessment of the quality of an item nor an opinion with respect to it.]*

Following are examples of procedures that a nonprofit may agree with a CPA firm to perform in connection with the nonprofit's financial operations. (Note that these are merely a couple of examples. The nonprofit and the CPA may agree to a variety of procedures provided that they can be performed objectively and reported on objectively. Specific dates and other parameters, or their basis of selection, must be described in order for the CPA to perform the procedures objectively.)

- Compare the cash balance per bank as reported in the original bank statement to the balance used by the nonprofit in performing its year-end bank account reconciliation. Trace deposits in transit reported on the nonprofit's bank account reconciliation in excess of a certain amount to clearing the bank within a certain number of days as noted on the original bank statement for the following month. Trace debits clearing in the original bank statement for the first 10 days of the following month to the outstanding debits reported by the nonprofit in its year-end bank reconciliation report. Describe any exceptions that are identified.
- For three separate months randomly selected by the CPA, compare the amounts recognized as contributions revenue in the nonprofit's general ledger with the amounts included in the nonprofit's donor contribution database for the same period. Identify the reason and basis provided by the nonprofit's staff for any difference in excess of $1,000 for a particular month and report same.

Commentary

Given the constraints that apply to an agreed-upon procedures engagement under the professional standards that govern the accounting profession, the process of planning and specifically tailoring an agreed-upon procedures engagement to meet the particular needs of a nonprofit can be intricate and tedious. Further, since an agreed-upon procedures engagement results in an objective report describing the specific outcomes of the procedures and not an opinion or other qualitative assessment, the report may have limited value for the nonprofit. For example, if procedures such as those described above were performed for a nonprofit and the CPA firm identified two deposits in transit that did not clear within the specified time and three debits that did not appear as outstanding debits on the nonprofit's bank reconciliation, the agreed-upon procedures report would simply note that fact, along with the amounts and other descriptive information regarding the items identified. An agreed-upon procedures engagement does not provide assurance regarding the items tested, nor does it involve making corrections to the nonprofit's accounting records or financial statements.

Agreed-upon procedures engagements may be useful when a nonprofit has certain elements or practices for which it wishes to have independently performed procedures to address or test. In reality, such situations are rare.

Nonprofits should also be careful to address whether the CPA firm has the experience necessary to plan and perform the agreed-upon procedures engagement properly. For example, while the professional standards prohibit a CPA firm from making qualitative statements or providing an opinion with respect to procedures performed in an agreed-upon procedures engagement, some CPA firms unwittingly violate the standards and issue reports using terms such as "reasonable," "in our opinion," or other similar verbiage.

ADVISORY SERVICES

A nonprofit may also consider engaging a firm to provide advisory services with respect to certain aspects of its financial operations. Advisory services engagements provided by CPA firms may take many forms, but they generally involve a formal agreement to provide advice to the nonprofit with respect to a particular area of the nonprofit's financial operations. Examples of areas for which the nonprofit may wish to engage a CPA firm to provide advisory services include, but are not limited to, the following:

- Internal control matters;
- Tax compliance matters;
- Efficiencies in financial operations;
- Accounting treatment for certain transaction types;
- Business-oriented commentary on proposed transactions;
- Risk management; and
- Board governance.

Along these lines, some nonprofits choose to engage law firms to provide what is sometimes referred to as a "legal audit." The nature of such engagements will vary, but they generally involve an assessment by the law firm of the nonprofit's compliance with, and risks associated with, various aspects of the law.

Commentary

A good, regular, and proactive working relationship with a CPA firm and a law firm can be a great source of help to nonprofit leaders as they address business, financial, risk, and legal matters. Such working relationships are common among larger nonprofits that use their professional advisors as sounding boards in a proactive manner to facilitate and reduce the risk associated with significant new transactions, initiatives, and policy matters.

INTERNAL AUDITS

Internal audits and similar activities may be conducted in a variety of ways. In some cases, a nonprofit's board members, finance committee members, or their equivalent perform the tasks. In other cases, volunteer supporters of the nonprofit perform the duties. In larger settings, the nonprofit may contract an individual or a firm to perform procedures, and in very large nonprofit organizations, an internal auditor may be employed by the nonprofit.

The purposes of internal audits often vary significantly from the purpose of an external audit. As noted, external audits are primarily focused on addressing the reliability of the nonprofit's financial statements. Internal audits, however, may be designed to address either financial or operational matters. For example, an internal audit may be performed to assess a nonprofit's compliance with its own operational policies in areas such as internal control, human resources, child safety, transportation safety, or other areas of significant interest (and potential risk) to the nonprofit.

Regardless of who leads and carries out an internal audit process for a nonprofit, certain attributes should exist with respect to any internal audit activity in order for the activity to be useful and credible:

- An internal audit process should be overseen by a person or group [the oversight body] that is independent with respect to the issues being addressed.
- The person or group performing the internal audit procedures and issuing the related reports [the internal auditor] should also be independent with respect to the issues being addressed.
- The internal auditor should report directly to the oversight body and not to the nonprofit's management. While the internal auditor will certainly interact with the nonprofit's management and employees in performing audit procedures, the internal auditor must issue and present reports directly to the oversight body in order for an internal audit process to maintain credibility.

KEY POINT If an internal auditor is an employee of the nonprofit, he or she is subject to the nonprofit's applicable employment and other policies. With respect to such matters, an employee-internal auditor is subject to the authority of the nonprofit's management, so long as management's oversight does not interfere with, or impede the objectivity of, the internal auditor's work and reporting responsibilities.

- The oversight body should establish and formally approve specific objectives of the internal audit process, the methodologies to be used, and the timing and nature of the reports to be issued.
- The internal auditor should conduct the internal audit procedures and prepare the related reports pursuant to the objectives and methodologies approved by the oversight body described in the preceding sentence.
- The internal auditor's reports should provide an objective description of the internal auditor's findings. The quality and credibility of an internal auditor's reports can be severely compromised when the internal auditor's report goes beyond reporting objective findings to drawing personal conclusions or making subjective statements of opinion regarding the matters subject to the audit.

EXAMPLE An internal auditor notes in his report that he observed certain children's classrooms being supervised by only one adult in violation of the nonprofit's two-adult protocol. This note, in and of itself, is objective. However, if the internal auditor also adds a subjective statement such as, "These violations jeopardized the safety of our nonprofit's children," or "The teachers responsible for these violations should be disciplined," the credibility and objectivity of the internal auditor's report would be compromised. Further, such statements could increase the nonprofit's legal risks.

Standard Audit Report

REPORT OF INDEPENDENT AUDITOR

The Governing Body
Elm City Nonprofit, Inc.
City, State

We have audited the accompanying financial statements of Elm City Nonprofit, Inc. ("the Nonprofit"), which consist of the statement of financial position as of December 31, 20XX, and the related statements of activities, functional expenses, and cash flows for the year then ended, and the related notes to the financial statements.

Management's Responsibility for the Financial Statements
Management is responsible for the preparation and fair presentation of these financial statements in accordance with accounting principles generally accepted in the United States of America; this includes the design, implementation, and maintenance of internal control relevant to the preparation and fair presentation of financial statements that are free from material misstatement, whether due to fraud or error.

Auditor's Responsibility
Our responsibility is to express an opinion on these financial statements based on our audit. We conducted our audit in accordance with auditing standards generally accepted in the United States of America. Those standards require that we plan and perform the audit to obtain reasonable assurance about whether the financial statements are free from material misstatement.

An audit involves performing procedures to obtain audit evidence about the amounts and disclosures in the financial statements. The procedures selected depend on the auditor's judgment, including the assessment of the risks of material misstatement of the financial statements, whether due to fraud or error. In making those risk assessments, the auditor considers internal control relevant to the Nonprofit's preparation and fair presentation of the financial statements in order to design audit procedures that are appropriate in the circumstances, but not for the purpose of expressing an opinion on the effectiveness of the Nonprofit's internal control. Accordingly, we express no such opinion. An audit also includes evaluating the appropriateness of accounting policies used and the reasonableness of significant accounting estimates made by management, as well as evaluating the overall presentation of the financial statements.

We believe that the audit evidence we have obtained is sufficient and appropriate to provide a basis for our audit opinion.

Opinion
In our opinion, the financial statements referred to above present fairly, in all material respects, the financial position of Elm City Nonprofit, Inc. as of December 31, 20XX, the changes in its net assets, and its cash flows for the year then ended in accordance with accounting principles generally accepted in the United States of America.

SIGNATURE
City, State
Month Day, 20XX

Standard Review Report

REVIEW REPORT OF INDEPENDENT ACCOUNTANT

The Governing Body
Elm City Nonprofit, Inc.
City, State

We have reviewed the accompanying financial statements of Elm City Nonprofit, Inc. ("the Nonprofit"), which consist of the statement of financial position as of December 31, 20XX, and the related statements of activities, functional expenses, and cash flows for the year then ended, and the related notes to the financial statements. A review includes primarily applying analytical procedures to management's financial data and making inquiries of management. A review is substantially less in scope than an audit, the objective of which is the expression of an opinion regarding the financial statements as a whole. Accordingly, we do not express such an opinion.

Management's Responsibility for the Financial Statements
Management is responsible for the preparation and fair presentation of these financial statements in accordance with accounting principles generally accepted in the United States of America; this includes the design, implementation, and maintenance of internal control relevant to the preparation and fair presentation of financial statements that are free from material misstatement whether due to fraud or error.

Accountant's Responsibility
Our responsibility is to conduct the review engagement in accordance with Statements on Standards for Accounting and Review Services promulgated by the Accounting and Review Services Committee of the AICPA. Those standards require us to perform procedures to obtain limited assurance as a basis for reporting whether we are aware of any material modifications that should be made to the financial statements for them to be in accordance with accounting principles generally accepted in the United States of America. We believe that the results of our procedures provide a reasonable basis for our conclusion.

Accountant's Conclusion
Based on our review, we are not aware of any material modifications that should be made to the accompanying financial statements in order for them to be in accordance with accounting principles generally accepted in the United States of America.

SIGNATURE
City, State
Month Day, 20XX

Standard Compilation Report

COMPILATION REPORT OF INDEPENDENT ACCOUNTANT

The Governing Body
Elm City Nonprofit, Inc.
City, State

Management is responsible for the accompanying financial statements of Elm City Nonprofit, Inc. ("the Nonprofit"), which consist of the statement of financial position as of December 31, 20XX, and the related statements of activities, functional expenses, and cash flows for the year then ended, and the related notes to the financial statements in accordance with accounting principles generally accepted in the United States of America. We have performed a compilation engagement in accordance with Statements on Standards for Accounting and Review Services promulgated by the Accounting and Review Services Committee of the AICPA. We did not audit or review the financial statements nor were we required to perform any procedures to verify the accuracy or completeness of the information provided by management. Accordingly, we do not express an opinion, a conclusion, nor provide any form of assurance on these financial statements.

SIGNATURE
City, State
Month Day, 20XX

CHAPTER 9

Tax Compliance

This chapter provides concise and summarized information about a number of key areas of tax compliance that are relevant for nonprofits and their leaders. For information about how tax laws apply to a particular nonprofit's situation, nonprofit leaders should consult a tax advisor with significant experience in the arena of nonprofit taxation.

The guidance provided in this chapter, and in this book more generally, is applicable to 501(c)(3) organizations that are classified as "public charities" under US federal income tax law, and not "private foundations." A public charity is generally a 501(c)(3) organization that is broadly publicly supported, as compared with a private foundation, which is typically funded by one person, one family, one company, or a small group of benefactors. There are substantial differences in federal tax law applicable to private foundations as compared to public charities. For example, while public charities are generally permitted to engage in a limited amount of lobbying as described later in this chapter, private foundations are generally prohibited under federal tax law from engaging in any amount of lobbying (with very limited exceptions).

Additionally, the guidance in this chapter, and in this book more generally, is applicable to 501(c)(3) public charities other than churches and certain church-related organizations. While churches are generally public charities for purposes of US federal income tax law, certain aspects of tax law apply uniquely to churches and certain church-related organizations as compared to other types of public charities. I address tax laws applicable to churches and certain church-related organizations in my book *Church Finance*.

Nonprofit organizations enjoy various exemptions from federal, state, and local taxes. Charitable, religious, educational, scientific, or literary organizations described in Section 501(c)(3) of the Internal Revenue Code qualify for federal income tax exemption and enjoy a status that permits contributions to them to be deducted by donors for federal income tax purposes. Many federally tax-exempt organizations also have exemptions from state income taxes, state sales taxes, property taxes, and other taxes, depending on the facts and the laws in their jurisdictions. A nonprofit organization's tax exemptions are highly valuable and should be protected.

One might assume that a nonprofit, tax-exempt organization has little to be concerned with in the tax arena. In reality, it's not quite that simple. The compliance requirements to qualify for and maintain tax exemption must be heeded. In some cases, the exemptions require a renewal application process which must be monitored. Additionally, even though nonprofits may have exemptions from certain taxes, there are often other taxes which can and do apply. For example, virtually all nonprofit organizations that have employees are subject to the employer's Social Security and Medicare tax on employee wages. Additionally, a nonprofit organization that engages in certain types of business activities unrelated to its exempt purposes may be subject to federal and state income taxes. And there are other types of taxes that can apply as well. So, there is more than meets the eye when it comes to nonprofits and tax compliance.

WHAT TAX COMPLIANCE MATTERS SHOULD BE ON THE RADAR OF NONPROFIT LEADERS?

While the list below is not intended to be exhaustive, it represents key areas of tax compliance relevant to nonprofit leaders in the United States. A brief description related to each is provided further below.

Federal
1. Federal tax exemption recognition for nonprofits
2. Organization
3. Operations
4. Private inurement, excess benefit transactions, and private benefit
5. Political campaign intervention
6. Lobbying
7. Violation of public policy
8. Unrelated business income
9. Payroll taxes
10. Form 990
11. IRS examinations

State and local
1. State income tax exemption
2. State and local sales tax
3. State and local property tax

FEDERAL TAX EXEMPTION RECOGNITION FOR NONPROFITS

Nonprofit charitable, religious, educational, scientific, and literary organizations other than churches and certain church-related organizations must generally apply to the IRS for recognition of their federal tax-exempt status in order to be exempt from federal income tax as a 501(c)(3) organization.

501(c)(3) status is important, as it not only confers a general exemption from federal income tax on the organization, it is also the status that permits contributions by donors to the organization to be tax deductible under federal tax law for income tax purposes. Federal 501(c)(3) status is also often a requirement for exemption from various state and local taxes.

For reasons that are obvious, nonprofit leaders should protect the tax-exempt status of their nonprofit.

ORGANIZATION

As a condition of federal tax exemption, 501(c)(3) organizations are required to be "organized" exclusively for one or more exempt purposes—charitable, religious, educational, scientific, or literary. Being organized exclusively for one or more exempt purposes means that the governing documents of the organization (typically articles of incorporation and bylaws) must contain certain language exclusively dedicating the organization to such purposes.

OPERATIONS

501(c)(3) organizations are required to be operated exclusively for exempt purposes. As this requirement has been applied and interpreted, it means that an exempt organization may not be operated for any substantial nonexempt purpose. This is not an abundantly clear area of the law, and it is often misunderstood. The most commonly relevant areas of application for this requirement are excessive unrelated business activity (described in Chapter 4) and operation for private benefit rather than public benefit (described further on the next page).

Recordkeeping

One very important aspect of operating for exempt purposes is maintaining proper records. IRS Publication 4221-PC, *Compliance Guide for 501(c)(3) Public Charities*, states, "In general, a public charity must maintain books and records to show that it complies with tax rules. ... If an organization does not keep required records, it may not be able to show that it qualifies for tax-exempt status... ."

The records kept by a nonprofit should document the income and expenses of the nonprofit, the nature and sources of income, the nature and purpose of expenses, and information supporting the position that the nonprofit's financial activities are conducted for exempt purposes. The records should include source documents such as receipts and bank records where appropriate in addition to bookkeeping records. Specific documentation requirements exist in certain areas, such as for expenses incurred for travel, meals, hospitality, and other similar activities.

PRIVATE INUREMENT, EXCESS BENEFIT TRANSACTIONS, AND PRIVATE BENEFIT

A nonprofit, like other 501(c)(3) organizations, must serve a public interest, rather than a private one, in order to establish and maintain its federal tax-exempt status. While nonprofit leaders and their advisors are generally aware of the "private inurement" prohibition and the prohibition of "excess benefit transactions" in federal tax law for 501(c)(3) organizations, there is less awareness and understanding of the prohibition of substantial "private benefit." While some people, on occasion, use the terms interchangeably, they are not interchangeable. There are important distinctions between the private inurement prohibition (and the related excess benefit transactions prohibition) and the substantial private benefit prohibition. A little-known aspect of the substantial private benefit prohibition is the fact that an organization may be in violation of the substantial private benefit prohibition even if its transactions are at "fair value" terms or involve unrelated parties.

Private inurement and excess benefit transactions

Prior to 1996, if a nonprofit 501(c)(3) organization paid excessive compensation to its leaders or otherwise allowed its earnings to benefit private individuals (actions referred to as "private inurement"), the Internal Revenue Service (IRS) had only one enforcement tool available—revoking the organization's tax-exempt status. While revocation was appropriate in egregious cases, the measure was considered inappropriately harsh in many other situations. Revocation was also often viewed as an improper response in many cases, since it penalized the organization and, indirectly, the people who benefit from its charitable, religious, or educational mission, rather than the individuals who received the prohibited benefits or those who approved them.

In an effort to provide the IRS with more appropriate and effective options to administer the law, Congress adopted "intermediate sanctions" as part of the Taxpayer Bill of Rights in 1996. Now found in Section 4958 of the Internal Revenue Code, the intermediate sanctions law imposes very significant excise tax penalties on individuals who receive an excess benefit from a 501(c)(3) organization, as well as organizational leaders who knowingly approve excess benefits.

An "excess benefit transaction" occurs when a 501(c)(3) organization makes a payment or provides an economic benefit to an organizational leader in which the payment or the value of the benefit exceeds the value of what the organization receives from the leader in exchange (including performance of services). Excessive or unreasonable compensation is an example of an excess benefit transaction. The amount by which a payment or benefit exceeds the value of what the organization receives in exchange is referred to as the "excess benefit amount."

Under current law, if a nonprofit leader (referred to in the law as a "disqualified person"), or a person or entity with certain types of relationships to a nonprofit leader, receives an excess benefit, a two-tier penalty structure applies to that leader (or person or entity). First, a penalty of 25 percent of the excess benefit amount applies. Additionally, the leader must "correct" the excess benefit (generally by returning the value of the excess benefit to the nonprofit organization) within a specified timeframe. In the event that the excess benefit is not corrected in a timely manner, a second-tier penalty, equal to 200 percent of the excess benefit amount, applies to the leader.

While nonprofit leaders and their advisors are generally aware of the "private inurement" prohibition and the prohibition of "excess benefit transactions" in federal tax law for 501(c)(3) organizations, there is less awareness and understanding of the prohibition of substantial "private benefit." While some people, on occasion, use the terms interchangeably, they are not interchangeable.

Also under current law, nonprofit officers, board members, or their equivalent (referred to in the law as "organization managers") who knowingly approve an excess benefit transaction are individually subject to excise tax penalties as well—10 percent of the excess benefit amount, up to $20,000 for each excess benefit transaction.

The IRS may revoke the exempt status of an organization that engages in private inurement. However, Treasury Regulations provide that the IRS will consider the facts and circumstances of a violation and consider the significance and frequency of violations to determine whether revocation is appropriate.

Key elements of the private inurement and excess benefit transactions prohibitions

Private inurement or excess benefit transactions generally involve certain elements:

1. **The transaction or arrangement must be between the organization and one of its insiders or leaders.** As a general rule, it is not possible to engage in private inurement or an excess benefit transaction with a non-leader employee or with a party who is unrelated to the organization. Code Section 4958 specifically defines "disqualified persons" as organizational leaders and parties related to them (e.g., their family members or businesses in which they have a significant ownership interest). Similarly, case law with respect to the private inurement prohibition has generally held that a party must be an "insider" to the organization for the rule to apply.
2. **The transaction must involve the 501(c)(3) organization transferring more value to the related party than the organization receives in exchange.** Private inurement or excess benefit transactions do not generally exist when the terms of a transaction between a 501(c)(3) organization and a related party are at fair value, or if the organization receives more value than the other party in a transaction. For example, if an organization rents a building for use in its operations from one of its board members and pays the board member fair market rental value for use of the property, the transaction would not ordinarily constitute an excess benefit transaction or private inurement.

Examples of private inurement and excess benefit transactions in a nonprofit

- Paying compensation to a CEO in excess of that which is reasonable (See Chapter 5)
- Purchasing property from a nonprofit board member and paying more for the property than it is worth
- Hiring a construction company owned by the son of the CEO to build a building for the nonprofit and paying more than fair market value for the construction
- Selling a vehicle to the CEO for less than it is worth and not treating the difference as taxable compensation
- Allowing the CEO to use an office in the nonprofit to operate a side business without paying fair market rent to the nonprofit
- Paying the travel expenses of the CEO without requiring proper documentation (as required by federal tax law) and not treating the payments as taxable compensation to the CEO

Private benefit

Private inurement is a subset of private benefit.

Federal tax regulations provide that an organization is not organized or operated exclusively for exempt purposes unless it serves a public, rather than private, interest. Thus, even if an organization has many activities that further exempt purposes, exemption may be precluded if it serves a private interest. Federal courts have ruled that the presence of private benefit, *if substantial in nature*, will destroy the exemption regardless of an organization's other charitable purposes or activities.[1]

The reason private benefit must rise to a "substantial" level in order to be problematic is very simple. All business and financial transactions confer some element of private benefit on one or more parties. Private benefit exists any time a party benefits from a transaction with a nonprofit 501(c)(3) organization. For example, when a nonprofit hires an unrelated vendor at fair market value to provide maintenance services for the nonprofit's facilities, an element of private benefit occurs because the arrangement benefits the vendor. Payment of compensation by a nonprofit to its employees provides some private benefit to the employees. Accordingly, some amount of private benefit is inherent in the operations of any nonprofit.

A 501(c)(3) organization crosses the line in the area of private benefit when such a benefit is *substantial*. As the IRS stated in its 1990 training materials for IRS agents, "In the charitable area, some private benefit may be unavoidable. The trick is to know when enough is enough."[2]

The IRS has also stated in its training materials that private benefit generally constitutes a benefit that is provided to a person or group other than the "charitable class" of people who are the ordinary beneficiaries of the organization's exempt activities (such as the needy, sick, homeless, spiritually lacking, and so on).[3]

Cases addressing private benefit have generally found that when an organization's activities substantially benefit people or groups other than a "charitable class," an organization does not qualify for 501(c)(3) exemption. An example is a nonprofit organization formed to promote interest and appreciation in classical music. When the IRS learned that a local for-profit radio station stood to benefit significantly from the organization's activities, the IRS denied

---

1 See IRS EO CPE Text, 2001, "Private Benefit Under IRC 501(c)(3)" by Andrew Megosh, Lary Scollick, Mary Jo Salins and Cheryl Chasin.
2 IRS EO CPE Text, 1990, Overview of Inurement/Private Benefit Issues in IRC 501(c)(3).
3 See IRS EO CPE Text, 2001, "Private Benefit Under IRC 501(c)(3)" by Andrew Megosh, Lary Scollick, Mary Jo Salins and Cheryl Chasin.

501(c)(3) status to the organization—even though the people who controlled the nonprofit organization were unrelated to the for-profit radio station.

Examples of substantial private benefit in a nonprofit

- A nonprofit engages in numerous very costly international humanitarian relief mission trips. The nonprofit requires that all travel arrangements for such trips must be booked through one local travel agency—a for-profit business owned by one of the nonprofit's major donors.
- A large nonprofit refers many people every year for counseling services. The nonprofit requires that all counseling referrals be made to a local for-profit counseling agency—one that is owned by a friend of the nonprofit's CEO.

Confusion surrounding the concept of private benefit and helping people in need

Serving a "charitable class" of people, such as the needy, those who are victims of a disaster or tragedy, the sick, etc. is clearly a valid exempt purpose for nonprofits and other 501(c)(3) organizations, if such activity is administered correctly.

Nonprofit leaders can quickly discern whether a transaction or arrangement properly benefits appropriate individuals or parties. Here are three examples to help leaders understand the types of permissible arrangements they can establish:

EXAMPLE The Wilson family lives in a community served by Elm Nonprofit—a local charitable relief organization serving the poor. A devastating home fire destroys most of the Wilson family's belongings and severely injures two of the family's three children. No member of the Wilson family is employed by the nonprofit or related to any leader of the nonprofit. The Wilson family's homeowner's insurance policy did not cover all of its losses, nor did their insurance cover the non-medical costs associated with meeting the needs of the injured children. Many people involved in serving Elm Nonprofit want to help. The nonprofit's board decides to open a fund to meet the family's needs and allows people to give to the fund. The nonprofit obtains documentation supporting the amount of the Wilson family's needs and ensures that the assistance it provides the family does not exceed the documented need. The nonprofit informs its donors that any excess amounts contributed to the family's fund will be transferred to the nonprofit's general benevolence fund.

Does this activity by the nonprofit represent a violation of the private inurement, excess benefit transaction, or substantial private benefit prohibition?

No. Since the Wilsons are not leaders of the nonprofit or related to leaders of the nonprofit, it is not possible for any arrangement between the nonprofit and the Wilson family to constitute private inurement or an excess benefit transaction. Since people in need are part of the "charitable class" served by the nonprofit, the assistance provided by the nonprofit does not constitute substantial private benefit.

EXAMPLE Assume the same facts as above, except that instead of the nonprofit establishing a fund to help the Wilson family, a few constituents of the nonprofit offer to give money to the nonprofit to help the Wilson family. The nonprofit constituents want to help anonymously by giving through the nonprofit. The givers realize they are not entitled to a charitable contribution deduction for their gifts because they are, in essence, gifts to the Wilson family and not to the nonprofit. The nonprofit is willing to accommodate the gifts for the Wilson family. The nonprofit accepts the gifts from the givers and transfers the funds to the Wilson family. In doing so, the nonprofit obtains documentation of the Wilson family's demonstrated financial need and ensures that the amount transferred does not exceed the need.

Does this activity by the nonprofit represent a violation of the private inurement, excess benefit transaction, or substantial private benefit prohibition?

No. Since the Wilsons are not leaders of the nonprofit or related to leaders of the nonprofit, it is not possible for any arrangement between the nonprofit and the Wilson family to constitute private inurement or an excess benefit transaction. Since people in need are part of the "charitable class" served by the nonprofit, the nonprofit's involvement does not constitute substantial private benefit. In fact, since the overall arrangement really represents a gift from the givers to the Wilson family, the nonprofit's assets are not significantly involved in the arrangement.

EXAMPLE One of the volunteer groups serving Elm Nonprofit learns that Sadie, the granddaughter of one of its group members, needs leg braces and her family cannot afford them. The volunteer group decides to host a chicken dinner at the nonprofit's headquarters to raise money for Sadie's leg braces. The volunteer group gives the event's net proceeds to Sadie's family to help pay for the braces. Sadie has no relationship to the nonprofit other than the fact that her grandmother is a member of the volunteer group.

Does this activity by the nonprofit represent a violation of the private inurement, excess benefit transaction, or substantial private benefit prohibition?

No. Since Sadie is not a leader of the nonprofit or related to leaders of the nonprofit, it is not possible for any arrangement between the nonprofit and Sadie's family to constitute private inurement or an excess benefit transaction. Since Sadie is part of the "charitable class" served by the nonprofit (the needy), the nonprofit's involvement does not constitute substantial private benefit. In this case, the small and isolated nature of the activity to aid this person also strongly supports this conclusion.

Sadly, nonprofit leaders occasionally receive poor advice with respect to arrangements like the ones used in the Wilson family and Sadie examples above, causing them to stop the nonprofit or volunteer group from conducting the activities to help.

> There is no evidence that any nonprofit has ever lost its federal tax-exempt status for providing reasonable help—including financial help—to people in genuine need who are not leaders of the nonprofit. And without regard to that fact, imagine the public relations nightmare the IRS or any other regulatory agency would face if it revoked a nonprofit's exempt status for helping such people. That is not a realistic possibility.

There is no evidence that any nonprofit has ever lost its federal tax-exempt status for providing reasonable help—including financial help—to people in genuine need who are not leaders of the nonprofit. And without regard to that fact, imagine the public relations nightmare the IRS or any other regulatory agency would face if it revoked a nonprofit's exempt status for helping such people. That is not a realistic possibility.

POLITICAL CAMPAIGN INTERVENTION

501(c)(3) organizations are prohibited from endorsing or opposing any candidate (or group of candidates, such as a political party) in an election campaign for political office. Individual leaders of the nonprofit, operating in their individual capacity and not in the capacity of a nonprofit leader, are not subject to this prohibition.

The lines of demarcation in this area are far from clear. The IRS has taken the position that a nonprofit leader endorsing or opposing a candidate during an official nonprofit function (such as a nonprofit's program meeting or fundraising event) or in an official nonprofit publication (such as a newsletter) is a violation of this prohibition, even if the nonprofit leader states that he/she is speaking in his/her own capacity and not on behalf of the nonprofit. The IRS has also taken the position that expressing views on social or moral issues could violate this prohibition on campaign intervention depending on when, where, and how such expressions are made.

In reality, because of the legal quagmire surrounding this issue, it is an area of law with very little current enforcement as it relates to nonprofits.

> 501(c)(3) organizations are prohibited from endorsing or opposing any candidate (or group of candidates, such as a political party) in an election campaign for political office.

For information on the IRS's guidance and positions in this area, good resources are IRS Publication 1828 and Revenue Ruling 2007-41.

For an in-depth analysis of the challenges that exist in this area of the law and suggested solutions, see the report by the Commission on Accountability and Policy for Religious Organizations, entitled *Government Regulation of Political Speech by Religious and Other 501(c)(3) Organizations—Why the Status Quo Is Untenable and Proposed Solutions*, issued in 2013, available at religiouspolicycommission.org.

LOBBYING

501(c)(3) public charities are not permitted to engage in a "substantial" amount of lobbying (attempting to influence any legislative body with respect to the adoption or rejection of specific legislation).

For this purpose, specific legislation means an identified proposal, bill, proposed ordinance, referendum, or similar item. Addressing a general principle or issue does not constitute attempting to influence specific legislation. Communicating with members of Congress, a state legislature, a county commission, or a city council about proposed legislation would constitute lobbying. A CEO urging the nonprofit's constituents to contact legislators about specific legislation would constitute lobbying. Urging nonprofit constituents to vote a certain way on a ballot referendum is also lobbying, as the voting public is deemed to be the "legislative body" when it comes to ballot referenda. But if a CEO shares with a member of Congress his or her concerns about a particular moral issue, without attempting to influence specific legislation, such a communication would not constitute lobbying.

Unlike the case with political campaign intervention, which, according to the law, is absolutely prohibited, a nonprofit is not prohibited from engaging in lobbying. Rather, the law states that lobbying cannot be more than an "insubstantial part" of a nonprofit's activities. Neither the law nor the regulations provide clear guidance as to how much lobbying activity would cause a nonprofit to cross the line (but see information in the next paragraph about the election available under Internal Revenue Code Section 501(h)). A nonprofit that very rarely, and in a limited manner, engages in lobbying activity is likely safe. If a nonprofit were to wish to engage in lobbying activity at more than a negligible level, it should do so only under the advice of experienced nonprofit tax counsel.

For 501(c)(3) public charities other than churches and certain church-related organizations, an election is available under Section 501(h) of the Internal Revenue Code that allows the organization to have identifiable boundaries in the arena of lobbying. Section 501(h) of the Code, enacted in 1976, allows section 501(c)(3) public charities to elect to have their lobbying activities measured in terms of dollars spent on lobbying rather than being subject to the more nebulous "no substantial part" limitation. An organization that makes the election may make lobbying expenditures within specified dollar limits. If an electing organization's lobbying expenditures are within the permissible dollar limits, the organization is in compliance. If the organization's lobbying expenditures exceed the permissible limits, the organization must pay a federal excise tax on expenditures in excess of the limit in any given year. If the organization's lobbying expenditures normally are more than 150 percent of the permissible limits, the organization's tax-exempt status as a section 501(c)(3) organization will be revoked.

VIOLATION OF PUBLIC POLICY

While not explicitly stated in Section 501(c)(3) of the Internal Revenue Code, the IRS and federal courts have taken the position that operating in a manner that violates public policy precludes an organization from exemption under Section 501(c)(3). For example, an organization that plans to provide financial assistance to the poor and which plans to obtain its funding by robbing banks or selling drugs illegally would not qualify for exemption.

In the 1960s and 1970s, concerns arose about nonprofit private schools forming for purposes of racial segregation and operating in a racially discriminatory manner. During that time,

CHAPTER 9 | Tax Compliance

the IRS issued guidance taking the position that operating in a racially discriminatory manner violates public policy and would be a basis for denial or revocation of exempt status under Section 501(c)(3). The IRS's guidance in this area culminated in the issuance of Revenue Procedure 75-50 (issued in 1975 and still in effect with minor modification), a very detailed guide outlining racial nondiscrimination requirements for nonprofit private schools. Revenue Procedure 75-50 applies to preschools, K-12 schools, and colleges, including those operated by nonprofits. It sets forth specific requirements including a policy that must be in place, required communications of the policy, records that must be kept regarding racial composition of the student body and employees, and more. Pursuant to Revenue Procedure 75-50, nonprofits that operate private schools are required to report on their compliance with Revenue Procedure 75-50 either as part of their annual Form 990 filed with the IRS (see guidance later in this chapter on Form 990) or, for organizations not required to file Form 990, via filing Form 5578 annually.

In 1983, the US Supreme Court affirmed the IRS policy of revoking an organization's exempt status for violating public policy (particularly in the context of racial discrimination) when it upheld the IRS's revocation of the 501(c)(3) status of Bob Jones University for engaging in racially discriminatory practices.

UNRELATED BUSINESS INCOME

An extensive description of federal tax law in the area of unrelated business income is provided in Chapter 4, beginning on page 98.

Key points are:

- If a nonprofit generates income from certain activities not substantially related to one or more of their exempt purposes, it may be required to file federal and state income tax returns and pay federal and state income tax on such income.
- If a nonprofit engages in an excessive amount of unrelated business activity, the nonprofit's 501(c)(3) federal tax exemption could be in jeopardy.

PAYROLL TAXES

Of all the areas of tax compliance applicable to a nonprofit, arguably the one with the highest level of risk is payroll tax compliance. The reason is very simple. For a nonprofit with employees, payroll taxes are a recurring, pervasive aspect of financial operations. And the implications of noncompliance are major.

Nonprofit financial leaders must ensure that the nonprofit complies with federal and state payroll tax laws and regulations. Failure to comply with payroll tax requirements can result in extremely severe penalties. In some circumstances, severe penalties can apply to the individuals who are responsible for payroll tax compliance, including those who have an oversight role with respect to such compliance. For example, in many instances, the IRS has assessed substantial penalties against individuals who were involved in or aware of an organization's decision not to remit payroll taxes due to the government in a timely manner. In fact, willful failure to remit payroll taxes to the government that have been withheld from employees' pay is a crime—a felony.

The following are the most important elements of payroll tax compliance that a nonprofit finance leader should ensure are covered:

- The nonprofit does not treat workers as independent contractors (thus, not withholding payroll taxes) when the workers meet the criteria for classification as employees under federal tax law.
- Applicable payroll taxes are properly withheld from employees' pay as required by federal law and (if applicable) state law.
- Payroll taxes are properly and completely paid in to the appropriate tax authorities within the timeframes required by law. (Note that for many employers, payroll taxes are due within a matter of a few days from the time they are withheld from an employee's pay).
- Payroll tax returns are accurately filed in a timely manner.

Because of the significant risks associated with noncompliance with payroll tax law, and my observations of numerous scenarios in which nonprofits have found themselves with serious payroll tax violations, I support nonprofits using highly reputable payroll processing companies with a demonstrated track record of sound internal controls. Highly reputable companies such as ADP and Paychex (and others) offer advantages to employers in the compliance process, including:

CHAPTER 9 | Tax Compliance

- Payroll taxes are withheld from employee's pay as part of the regular payroll process,
- As part of the payroll processing exercise, the employer's portion of payroll taxes is required to be remitted to the processing company along with the gross wages being paid to employees,
- The payroll taxes withheld from employees' pay and the employer's portion of payroll taxes are automatically deposited by the payroll processing company within the prescribed timeframes,

In many instances, the IRS has assessed substantial penalties against individuals who were involved in or aware of an organization's decision not to remit payroll taxes due to the government in a timely manner. In fact, willful failure to remit payroll taxes to the government that have been withheld from employees' pay is a crime—a felony.

- Payroll tax returns are automatically prepared and filed by the processing company by the required due dates, and
- Penalties for any failure to comply with the due dates for depositing tax payments or filing proper returns will generally be covered by the processing company if the error is on their part.

Here are some additional facts to keep in mind about payroll processing companies:

- There are numerous examples of employers, including nonprofits, using payroll processing companies that failed to comply with legal requirements. In many such cases, the employer paid the payroll taxes to the provider, but the provider did not remit the taxes to the proper tax authorities. In such cases, the IRS will look to the employer to pay the taxes, regardless of the fact that the employer may have already paid them to the payroll processing company. The results are often severe penalties and significant financial stress for the employer. It is not worth the risk to use a payroll processing company without a strong reputation and track record of compliance.
- The fees charged by highly reputable payroll processing companies are often not significant in relation to the service they provide and the risks they help cover. One reason is that one way payroll processing companies make money is that they earn interest on the "float" on the money paid to them by employers between the time it is remitted to them and the time they either remit it to employees or to the government. For example, if your nonprofit processes a payroll with a payroll processing company, assume that you remit the gross wages and employer payroll taxes to the payroll processing company in the amount of $100,000 on Wednesday. The payroll company deposits the pay into employees' accounts on Friday and remits the payroll taxes by

their due date, which is the following Wednesday. During the time between the date you submitted the payroll and the date that the company pays all of the money out as required, it is holding your funds on your behalf. The agreement you have with the company allows it to earn interest on that money during those few days. That may not seem like much time for a company to earn interest. But, if you consider how many employers' money a large payroll processing company is holding at any one time, the amount of money the payroll company has on deposit earning interest is very large.

Helpful resources

For helpful information about the specifics of payroll tax compliance, I recommend the following resources:

- IRS Publication 15 (also known as Circular E), *Employer's Tax Guide*
- IRS Publication 15-A, *Employer's Supplemental Tax Guide*
- IRS Publication 15-B, *Employer's Tax Guide to Fringe Benefits*

FORM 990

For a nonprofit organization required to file it, no document the organization produces is likely to have more potential to affect the organization, its donors, and its other stakeholders than IRS Form 990.

Form 990 is an annual information return that must generally be filed with the Internal Revenue Service by most tax-exempt organizations, including 501(c)(3) public charities (other than churches and certain church-related organizations). Small nonprofits (those with annual revenues normally less than $200,000 and assets less than $500,000) are permitted to file a somewhat abbreviated version of Form 990 (Form 990-EZ), and very small organizations (those with annual revenues normally not more than $50,000) must file a simple notice with the IRS electronically each year.

The purpose and use of Form 990

The primary purpose of Form 990 is to report information about an organization's activities to the Internal Revenue Service. The IRS uses the information to assess the organization's compliance with applicable laws and to identify issues that may require further attention. Information provided by an organization on Form 990 may be the basis for an IRS inquiry or examination.

Form 990 is required to be made available for public inspection by the filing organization and by the IRS. The IRS provides copies of all Forms 990 that it receives to the nonprofit organization GuideStar, which in turn, makes the forms public on the GuideStar.org website shortly after they are filed with the IRS.

In addition to being used by the IRS, information in Form 990 is used by a variety of other parties in multiple ways:

- The public and the media use Form 990 to access information about an organization's activities to form a perception of the organization. The perception can affect media coverage of the organization and giving decisions by the public. Typically, the media and members of the public have the highest level of interest in the Form 990 disclosures about compensation of the organization's leaders and business transactions with related parties.
- Charity "watchdog" groups use information in Form 990 to evaluate and rate nonprofit organizations. The most well-known example is Charity Navigator, an organization that rates 501(c)(3) charities using a "star" system based heavily on an organization's financial information and practices as described in Form 990. Grant-funding organizations and donors are sometimes influenced by the ratings of charitable organizations by such watchdog groups. Charity watchdog groups tend to focus heavily on organizations' overhead expenses, fundraising expenses, executive compensation and benefits, and related party transactions.
- Nonprofit organizations that solicit contributions are often required to submit a copy of their annual Form 990 to state government officials in connection with state charitable solicitation registration. As a result, the Form 990 often becomes accessible to the public within the applicable state agency's records in addition to being publicly available through the IRS or on the GuideStar website.

The depth and breadth of Form 990

In addition to requiring exhaustive financial information, Form 990 requires organizations to disclose significant information about their governance procedures and policies, governing documents, relationships with their organizational leaders and with third parties, and much more.

Part I of Form 990 includes inquiries into the following:

- Number of independent voting members of the governing body

- Number of non-independent voting members of the governing body
- Number of employees
- Number of volunteers
- Total unrelated business income
- Revenue in the form of contributions and grants
- Program service revenue
- Investment income
- Expenses in the form of grants
- Benefits to or for members
- Salaries
- Fundraising fees

Part III of Form 990 asks the filing organization to describe its:

- Mission
- Largest three "Program Service Accomplishments" (in terms of expenses)
- Total expenses

Part VI of Form 990, entitled "Governance, Management, and Disclosure," is a detailed inquiry into the organization's governance and management.

Part VII of Form 990 requires reporting on:

- Compensation of officers
- Compensation of directors
- Compensation of trustees
- Compensation of key employees
- Highest compensated employees
- Compensation of independent contractors

A number of additional schedules may also apply, depending on the filing organization's activities, including schedules detailing information about:

- The identity of the organization's largest donors;
- Lobbying activities;
- Activities conducted outside the United States;
- Grants and other assistance made;

CHAPTER 9 | Tax Compliance

- Compensation for certain officers, directors, individual trustees, key employees, and highest compensated employees;
- Certain compensation practices;
- Financial transactions or arrangements between the organization and related parties; and
- Much more.

To say that Form 990 requires detailed reporting about an organization's activities is a significant understatement. Even the summary provided does not begin to adequately describe the depth and breadth of the information required to be disclosed on Form 990.

Form 990 also presents an opportunity to share positive information

The highly public nature of Form 990 provides filing organizations with free publicity—and therewith an opportunity to present positive information about the organization and its activities. Some of the questions in Form 990 present unique opportunities to share information about the organization's mission and purpose, the positive impact of its activities, and the effectiveness of its programs. Nonprofit organizations should use these opportunities well.

The sobering implications of filing an incorrect or incomplete Form 990

Form 990 is signed by an organization's officer "under penalties of perjury." Federal law allows the IRS to assess significant penalties on an organization and/or its leaders for providing incorrect or incomplete information in Form 990. Additionally, it is a federal criminal offense to knowingly submit false information on Form 990 to the Internal Revenue Service. Given the expansive amount of information and the exhaustive number of questions on Form 990 and its related schedules, the potential for providing incorrect information is significant.

When Form 990 is provided by an organization to state agencies in connection with charitable solicitation registration, state-level requirements for truthfulness typically apply. Most states have laws that prohibit an organization from providing false or misleading information in connection with fundraising solicitations made within the state. State government officials may apply such statutes to an organization soliciting funds in the state if the state learns that information in Form 990 submitted to the state is incorrect or incomplete.

Review of Form 990 by the organization's governing body (board)

Best practices dictate that a copy of Form 990 should be provided to the organization's governing body (e.g., board of directors) for review prior to filing with the IRS. In fact, a question on the Form 990 asks whether the organization provides a copy of the completed form to all members of its governing body before filing it. The form also requires the organization to describe the process used by the organization to review the Form 990. There are good reasons for an organization's board members to review the Form 990, including the fact that doing so helps the board maintain an awareness of important details and aspects of the organization's operations. If any board member reviewing the form has questions or concerns about its content, he/she should address those matters with the board chair and the CEO promptly.

IRS EXAMINATIONS

With the exception of special, protective rules that apply to churches and conventions or associations of churches, the IRS can generally initiate an examination of the federal tax and information returns filed by a nonprofit organization at any time for any reason or no reason.

In an IRS examination, IRS agents are generally afforded wide latitude in their ability to request records and information necessary to address an organization's compliance with applicable federal tax laws.

An IRS examination is not an exercise to be taken lightly. In the event an IRS agent identifies areas of noncompliance by an organization which he/she deems to be significant, the implications can be serious and costly.

The importance of representation by tax counsel in an IRS inquiry or examination

In the event a nonprofit receives notice from the IRS indicating the commencement of an examination, it is wise to engage tax counsel (an attorney or CPA) with significant experience in nonprofit tax law to assist and represent the nonprofit in the matter.

In my opinion, it is unwise for nonprofit officials to represent the nonprofit themselves in dealing with an IRS inquiry or examination. One main basis for this position is that by allowing tax counsel to represent the nonprofit, a "buffer" exists between the IRS and nonprofit officials. Experienced tax counsel will insist (which is appropriate) that the IRS conduct its inquiry or examination in accordance with the law. Tax counsel can appropriately limit the manner in which the IRS gathers information, can appropriately limit the nature of inquiries of nonprofit officials, can require that the IRS submit all questions and requests for records in writing, and can otherwise assist in the proper handling of the process.

I am personally and specifically aware of instances in which nonprofit leaders decided to represent their organizations in IRS examinations themselves—as opposed to engaging highly experienced tax counsel—with very bad results. In one case in particular of which I am aware, the organization's leaders thought that the organization was well-prepared for the examination; represented the organization in the examination themselves; and then spent a massive amount of time and money (on lawyers and others) defending the organization against a possible revocation of its exempt status by the IRS—a scenario that quite possibly could have been avoided had the organization been represented by highly experienced tax counsel in the examination.

In my opinion, it is unwise for nonprofit officials to represent the nonprofit themselves in dealing with an IRS inquiry or examination.

STATE INCOME TAX EXEMPTION

Exemption from federal income tax may or may not result in automatic exemption from income tax under applicable state law. Every state's laws are unique. A few states do not have a corporate income tax. For those that do, the laws of many bestow income tax exemption automatically to a nonprofit based on its federal exemption. For example, in the state of Florida, an organization exempt from federal income tax and described in any part of Section 501(c) of the Internal Revenue Code is automatically exempt from Florida's corporate income tax (other than for unrelated business income). In the state of California, however, nonprofits are specifically required to apply for and obtain an "exempt determination or acknowledgment letter" from the State of California Franchise Tax Board in order to be exempt from California's corporate income tax.

Exemption from federal income tax may or may not result in automatic exemption from income tax under applicable state law. Every state's laws are unique.

As a general rule, states do not require nonprofits to file any state information returns disclosing their overall financial activities. Many states do impose a state-level income tax and a state income tax return filing requirement on nonprofits and other federally exempt organizations that generate income from one or more unrelated business activities (described previously in this chapter and more extensively in Chapter 4.)

The importance of evaluating applicable state law

Nonprofits should evaluate the income tax exemption requirements of any state in which they operate to determine the requirements for exemption from state income tax. As stated above, exemption is not always automatic.

STATE AND LOCAL SALES AND USE TAX

Many states impose a sales tax on purchases of certain goods or services that occur within the state, and a use tax on the value of certain items brought into the state. A state sales or use tax may be labeled differently, depending on the state. For example, Arizona law refers to a "transaction privilege tax," which is the equivalent of a sales tax. States that impose a sales tax or its equivalent generally require the sellers of items subject to tax to collect the tax from buyers at the time of the sale and remit it to the state.

The importance of evaluating applicable state law

State laws vary significantly in terms of exemptions for nonprofits in the arena of sales and use taxes. In Florida, for example, 501(c)(3) organizations are exempt from sales tax on items they purchase (after applying for and obtaining a certificate of exemption) and certain, limited types of nonprofit organizations are exempt from the typical requirement to collect sales tax on items they sell. Georgia, on the other hand, has very limited sales tax exemption for purchases made by nonprofits. Arizona has no general sales tax exemption for items purchased by nonprofits but does exempt certain sales by nonprofits.

It is almost universally true that if a state's law offers an exemption from its sales tax for nonprofits, an organization eligible for the exemption is required to apply for and receive an exemption certificate. The primary reason for such a requirement is that sellers who would otherwise be required to collect sales tax on a transaction must have evidence that a buyer is exempt in order to avoid liability for failing to collect the tax.

Nonprofits should evaluate applicable state law in any states in which they operate to determine the applicability of sales tax and possible exemptions. It is important to remember that if a nonprofit sells items (e.g., in a bookstore or thrift shop), the nonprofit must determine whether it is required to collect and remit sales taxes on the items it sells. The same can be true when the nonprofit rents or leases property to others. Failure to collect and remit sales taxes when required can result in significant penalties and interest in addition to the taxes due. State revenue authorities generally have the right to collect such taxes from sellers even if they were not collected from the buyers who should have paid the tax at the time of the transaction. And state tax authorities can generally initiate a sales tax examination of a nonprofit at will.

A recent US Supreme Court case held that a state may impose the requirement on a seller to collect sales tax on sales to parties in a state, even if the seller has no physical presence in the state. Accordingly, nonprofits that sell items should address possible sales tax com-

> Nonprofit leaders sometimes confuse the principles of sales tax law and federal income tax law with respect to unrelated business income. For example, nonprofit leaders sometimes think that if the sale of an item by the nonprofit is substantially related to the nonprofit's exempt purpose, it is exempt from sales tax and the nonprofit has no obligation to collect and remit sales tax on the sales of such items. State sales tax law and federal income tax law for unrelated business income are two completely different topics.

pliance requirements in any states into which they sell.

A word of clarity—sales tax laws have nothing to do with the federal tax laws for unrelated business income.

Nonprofit leaders sometimes confuse the principles of sales tax law and federal income tax law with respect to unrelated business income. For example, nonprofit leaders sometimes think that if the sale of an item by the nonprofit is substantially related to the nonprofit's exempt purpose, it is exempt from sales tax and the nonprofit has no obligation to collect and remit sales tax on the sales of such items. State sales tax law and federal income tax law for unrelated business income are two completely different topics. As a specific example, a nonprofit art museum may sell books on early American art in its gift shop—an activity that may be substantially related to the museum's exempt purposes—and thus, not an unrelated business activity for federal income tax purposes. But regardless of the federal income tax treatment of such activity, state law in the nonprofit's state may impose a sales tax on the sales of such books as well as a requirement that a seller collect the sales tax from buyers and remit it to the state. If the state has no exemption from such a requirement for nonprofits, the nonprofit must collect and remit the sales tax on the sales of the books, even though the sales of the books are exempt from federal income tax.

STATE AND LOCAL PROPERTY TAX

State property taxes are generally administered at the county or municipal level, but the laws governing exemption from property taxes typically apply at the state level. State laws exempting property owned by nonprofits from property tax are common, but they vary significantly in the specifics. For example, some states require property to be used *exclusively* for exempt purposes in order to qualify for exemption and others require that property must be used *primarily* for exempt purposes. Some states allow a partial property tax exemption for property used partially, but not exclusively, for exempt purposes; and other states will deny a property tax exemption completely for *any* non-exempt use. Some states narrowly define exempt use and others broadly define it. Some states impose limits on exemptions for ancillary property (e.g., residences for security or custodial staff) and others impose no such limits. Some states allow an exemption for property that nonprofits are preparing to accommodate exempt use (e.g., where the property is vacant but plans are underway to construct a building on it to be used for exempt-purpose activities) and others allow an exemption only if the property is actually in active use for an exempt purpose.

Property tax exemptions are determined not only state-by-state, but property-by-property. The key elements of state property tax exemption laws are:

- ownership of the property by an exempt organization and
- use of the property for exempt purposes (as defined in each state's laws).

In recent years, state and local property tax authorities in many areas have become more aggressive in denying or revoking property tax exemptions for nonprofits. In applying for or appealing to retain an exemption, nonprofit leaders must understand the specific requirements of their state's laws and regulations. Court cases may also be an important source of information in this area, as legal controversies over property tax exemptions are common.

Don't overlook personal property

Many states impose a tax on personal property (furniture, fixtures, and equipment) in addition to taxes on real property. The criteria for exemption from taxes on personal property are often similar to exemption requirements for real property. Overlooking the need to pursue exemption from personal property taxes could subject a nonprofit to liability for such taxes. In some jurisdictions, nonprofits are required to file returns related to their personal property, even if it is exempt from tax. Such filing requirements exist to allow the tax authorities to measure and record the value of the property that is exempt from taxation.

Applications required

It is almost universally true that obtaining an exemption from property tax (whether on real or personal property) requires filing an application with and receiving approval from the appropriate tax authority. In pursuing property tax exemption, nonprofits should pay careful attention to the application requirements, including due dates and documentation that must be submitted with the application.

CHAPTER 10

Governance and Policies

Well-governed organizations will operate pursuant to a hierarchy of governing and policy documents. Such documents establish the parameters within which the organization, its board, and its staff leaders are to operate and are indispensable in establishing stability.

The legal hierarchy of governing and policy documents is not a matter of opinion or debate, but rather a matter of law. If a conflict exists among two or more documents in the hierarchy, the higher-level document trumps the others.

The hierarchy of documents is as follows:

- Law (federal, state, and local)
- Articles of incorporation
- Bylaws
- Policies (adopted by the board)
- Procedures (adopted by management)

Law

The laws of the state in which the organization was incorporated establish the ultimate legal framework within which the organization must operate. Every state has such laws. Portions of state nonprofit corporation law apply regardless of the provisions in the organization's articles of incorporation or bylaws. For example, Florida Statutes Section 617.0833 prohibits loans by a Florida nonprofit corporation to its officers, directors, and certain other related parties, regardless of whether the organization's articles of incorporation or bylaws permit such loans.

Other portions of state nonprofit corporation law provide authority regarding certain matters but defer to the organization's articles of incorporation or bylaws if they contain conflicting provisions. For example, Section 108.15(b) of the Illinois General Not For Profit Corporation Act states, "The act of the majority of the directors present at a meeting at which a quorum is present shall be the act of the board of directors, unless the act of a greater number is required by the articles of incorporation or the bylaws."

Since each state has unique laws covering employment, charitable solicitation, and other matters, nonprofit corporations incorporated in one state but operating in one or more other states should consult their legal counsel to determine which state laws apply or control. Additionally, local laws (often called "ordinances") should also be considered in the jurisdictions in which the organization operates.

Nonprofit organizations obtain their federal tax-exempt status through federal tax law, which dictates various criteria for obtaining and maintaining tax-exempt status. Tax-exempt organizations must take care to ensure compliance with applicable federal tax law in order to avoid losing their exemption. A detailed analysis of tax law compliance requirements is outside the scope of this book. However, as described in Chapter 9, the board should ensure that the organization proactively assesses the organization's compliance with applicable tax laws. Of course, compliance with other aspects of federal law is important as well.

Articles of incorporation

The articles of incorporation (sometimes referred to as the "charter") of a nonprofit corporation is the document that gives legal life to the organization. A corporation is a legal entity created by filing articles of incorporation with the appropriate state agency. The articles of incorporation are the highest-ranking governing document of the organization. Because the original document is filed with the state agency, amendments to the articles of incorporation must also be filed with the state agency. An organization's articles of incorporation and related amendments are generally public documents.

The articles of incorporation must contain certain minimum provisions under state law—typically the name and initial address of the organization, purpose language, an indication as to whether the organization has members, the names of initial board members, and the like. Additionally, a nonprofit organization that is or plans to be exempt from federal income tax as a charitable, religious, or educational organization described in Section 501(c)(3) of the Internal Revenue Code must include in its articles of incorporation certain provisions limiting the activities of the organization to those permitted for such exempt organizations.

It is permissible for an organization to include in the articles any amount of detail it wishes regarding the organization's governance. However, since all amendments to the articles must be filed with the appropriate state agency, it is common practice to make the articles of incorporation rather minimal in content and to include the organization's more detailed governance provisions in the bylaws, which are easier to amend and are not required to be filed

CHAPTER 10 | Governance and Policies

with the state agency. Accordingly, the articles of incorporation rarely include specific provisions related to financial operations.

A nonprofit organization should consult legal counsel with significant nonprofit experience when drafting its original articles of incorporation or any amendments to them.

Bylaws

The bylaws of an organization typically contain the specific governance provisions of the organization. Typical provisions in an organization's bylaws include, but are not limited to:

- Qualifications of members and process for joining (for organizations that have members);
- Qualifications for board members and terms of office;
- Process for the election and removal of board members and for filling board vacancies;
- Corporate officer titles, duties, responsibilities, election, removal, and terms of office;
- Information about the conduct of meetings, including quorum requirements and voting requirements (which may include supermajority voting requirements for certain matters);
- Indemnification of board members and officers with respect to liability stemming from the performance of their duties for the organization;
- The organization's fiscal year; and
- Requirements for amendment of the articles of incorporation and bylaws.

The organization should consult highly competent legal counsel for the drafting or amendment of its bylaws.

Policies

The nomenclature used in the area of "policies" varies dramatically in practice, so let's address that from the outset. The term "policies" can mean any number of things, including board resolutions, board-approved policy documents, management-approved documents, and more. Some distinguish between "board policies" and "management policies."

I prefer to distinguish between the guiding documents approved by the board and those approved by management by referring to board-approved documents as "policies" and management-approved documents as "procedures." No clear right or wrong approach to nomenclature exists, but it is essential to distinguish between the two in some clear and appropriate manner.

For example, the board of a nonprofit adoption agency may establish a policy requiring that prospective employees who would serve in the financial operations area of the organization complete a criminal background check and have no record of felonies or crimes that would be a concern in connection with the proposed duties. The CEO may establish a procedure further clarifying the policy by requiring that the background check be national in scope and defining the specific types of criminal violations that are not acceptable for prospective financial employees. It is important that the distinction be made between the board's policy and the CEO's procedure so that, if the CEO wants to modify the list of unacceptable crimes, it is clear that he/she may do so without board approval, so long as the new procedure still complies with the board's policy.

An organization's governing body (board) is responsible for adopting and maintaining such policies as it believes are necessary and appropriate to establish parameters for the orderly operation of the organization. It is not necessary or advisable for the board's policies to replicate provisions that are included in the articles of incorporation or the bylaws, since doing so raises the risk that the documents will get out of sync at some point. The board should adopt only those policies that are truly necessary for the legal and orderly operation of the organization.

Procedures

Management-adopted procedures represent guidance for the organization's staff under the leadership of the top staff leader (president, CEO, etc.). Procedures adopted by management should not conflict with board-approved policies or the organization's governing documents (articles of incorporation and bylaws). In fact, such procedures should typically address specific aspects of implementing the organization's board-approved policies or governing documents.

The importance of legal counsel

The board should ensure that highly competent legal counsel reviews all of the organization's governing and policy documents and advises the board regarding their propriety. Such a review should be conducted periodically to address changes that are made in the documents over time as well as changes that occur in the legal environment. Counsel should be involved in drafting and advising the board on any significant new policy considered by the board for adoption.

Confusion surrounding legal requirements for policies

Other than the requirements of state law and federal tax law for nonprofit organizations to include certain provisions in the articles of incorporation and bylaws as a condition for incorporation or tax exemption, there are rarely other legal requirements for nonprofit organizations to have specific board-approved policies. Much misinformation is communicated in this area of nonprofit governance and much confusion exists as a result. The two primary sources of misinformation in this area are:

- Those who state or imply that the *Sarbanes-Oxley Act*, which applies to publicly traded companies, somehow applies in a similar fashion to nonprofit organizations; and
- The IRS.

Sarbanes-Oxley

Confusion often stems from the invalid assertion or implication in some nonprofit publications or other media that the *Sarbanes-Oxley Act* passed by Congress to govern the affairs of publicly traded companies somehow applies to nonprofit organizations in the same manner that it applies to publicly traded companies. **It does not.** Notwithstanding that fact, the nonprofit community is still rife with publications and consultants stating or implying otherwise. A simple Google search of the term "nonprofit" together with "Sarbanes-Oxley" will reap a mother lode of "resources" on the topic, along with litanies of recommendations regarding various policies that nonprofits "should" adopt.

It is true that two provisions of *Sarbanes-Oxley* apply to nonprofits—but the reason they do is because they apply to everyone in America! Those two provisions relate to:

1. Retaliating against a "whistleblower"—someone who reports illegal activity; and
2. Destroying, altering, or falsifying documents that are the subject of a federal proceeding.

Even with respect to these two provisions of the *Sarbanes-Oxley Act*, there is no requirement that nonprofits have certain policies in place. The Act simply makes it a federal crime to violate the whistleblower and record retention provisions of the law.

The IRS and policy requirements

The IRS is another source of rampant confusion regarding policy requirements for nonprofit organizations. After concluding that poor board governance was at the root of virtually all high-profile financial scandals that arose in the nonprofit sector in the past several decades, the IRS decided in the mid-2000s that nonprofit organizations should be pressured into adopting certain governance policies and practices.

In 2008, the IRS radically modified the annual federal information form that most nonprofits file (Form 990—described in Chapter 9) to include numerous questions about whether the filing organization has adopted a variety of policies or practices related to its governance. The IRS added such questions to the form notwithstanding the fact that federal tax law contains no requirements for an organization to adopt such policies or practices as a condition of maintaining tax-exempt status.

As a result, a nonprofit organization filing Form 990 must now answer questions in this publicly disseminated form such as:

- The number of the organization's board members who are "independent" (the IRS arbitrarily devised its own definition of independence for this purpose);
- Whether the organization has a conflicts-of-interest policy governing transactions between the organization and its insiders;
- Whether the organization has a whistleblower policy;
- Whether the organization has a record retention policy;
- Whether the organization's board reviews the Form 990;
- Whether the organization follows specific procedures in establishing executive compensation;
- Whether the organization has a policy covering executive expense reimbursements; and
- Whether the organization has a gift acceptance policy.

By adding such questions to the Form 990, the IRS knowingly created an environment of pressure for nonprofit organizations to adopt policies and practices that would allow them to answer "Yes!" Answering "yes" helps organizations avoid appearing to be recalcitrant. Many advisors in the nonprofit sector, myself included, believe that "no" answers to such questions increase the risk of an IRS examination.

In late 2009, the IRS announced that it would have its examination agents ask numerous questions about an organization's governance practices in every examination of nonprofit organizations for a period of time. Among the numerous issues the agents were to address is the attendance record of individual board members at board meetings! The IRS's apparent reason for obtaining such information during examinations is to document what it believes is the correlation between poor board governance and noncompliance with federal tax law.

As a result of the IRS's pressure, most large and respected nonprofit organizations have adopted policies and practices of the types addressed in the Form 990. Such policies, if drafted carefully in a manner that is appropriate for the organization, can be helpful, but they are not a requirement for tax exemption.

Familiarity and compliance with governing and policy documents

Every board member should read and be familiar with the organization's articles of incorporation, bylaws, and board-approved policies. Those documents provide the framework within which the board and management are to conduct their business. The board should ensure that the organization operates in compliance with its governing and policy documents. Failure to do so will likely result in a disorderly operating environment and can create significant legal problems for the organization and its leaders.

SOURCES FOR SAMPLE POLICIES

In adopting language for a particular policy, nonprofits should consult legal counsel experienced in nonprofit law to ensure that the policy language is appropriate for the nonprofit. Sample policies can be helpful as educational resources, but no nonprofit should simply adopt a sample policy as their own without carefully evaluating its provisions and modifying or replacing it as necessary and appropriate for the nonprofit's unique circumstances. The sample policies provided in this book are provided only for educational and informational purposes and should only be used as such.

In addition to the sample policies provided in this book, nonprofit leaders may wish to consult the following resources for sample nonprofit policies:

- BoardSource (boardsource.org)
- The National Council of Nonprofits (councilofnonprofits.org)
- ECFA (ecfa.org)

What financial policies should a nonprofit have?

In determining whether a nonprofit's board should adopt a particular policy, the nonprofit should consider several factors. Among them are:

- Whether the policy would be helpful in ensuring compliance with the law;

- Whether the policy could help protect the nonprofit or its constituents;
- Whether the policy will enhance the effectiveness of the nonprofit in carrying out its mission and purpose; and
- Whether the policy fosters confidence and trust on the part of constituents or donors.

Philosophically, some nonprofits strive to minimize the number of formal policies they adopt. Once a policy is adopted, it requires monitoring and maintenance—to ensure that the policy is complied with and that the policy is kept up to date. Additionally, an argument can be made that the more policies a nonprofit has, and the more specific those policies are, the greater the risk of failure to comply with those policies. From a risk management perspective, having a policy in place and failing to comply with it can sometimes create more exposure to liability than if the nonprofit did not adopt the policy in the first place.

Many key areas of day-to-day financial operations can be governed by staff-developed procedures without the need for board-adopted policies. For example, procedures for reimbursing business expenses, specific internal control practices, and procedures for managing accounts receivable collections can typically be adequately addressed by staff-developed procedures.

I suggest that financial policies for nonprofits can be categorized into two groups:

- Policies that every nonprofit should probably have, and
- Policies that nonprofits should have if certain factors are present.

POLICIES THAT EVERY NONPROFIT SHOULD PROBABLY HAVE

Budget administration policy. Given the significance of the budgeting process for a nonprofit, provisions for approval and administration of a nonprofit's budget are often a component of the nonprofit's bylaws. Whether in the bylaws or in a separate policy approved by the board, a nonprofit should have an authoritative document governing the approval and administration of its budgets. A well-written policy will address approval and administration of the nonprofit's budgets for operations, capital expenditures, debt principal reduction, and possibly auxiliary activities. Among other important provisions, the policy should specifically set the process for addressing and approving budget overages. Sample budget policy provisions are provided in Chapter 1.

Conflicts-of-interest policy. A conflicts-of-interest policy addresses scenarios in which a person on the governing body (board) or otherwise in a position of leadership may benefit financially from a business arrangement or transaction involving the nonprofit. That can happen, for example, if the nonprofit buys goods or services from a nonprofit leader, from his/her company, from one or more of his/her family members, or from any of their companies. Other examples include selling items to one or more of these related parties, renting property to or from a related party, etc.

For good reason, federal tax law restricts the terms of certain transactions between tax-exempt nonprofits and their leaders (or parties related to their leaders). Violations of federal tax law in this area can have dire consequences—not only for the nonprofit but for the individuals involved in the transactions and the individuals who approve the transactions. (See Chapter 9 for more information about this important area of tax compliance.) Additionally, state nonprofit corporation laws also typically provide for adverse consequences if a nonprofit corporation engages in an improper transaction with a related party. Further, transactions between a nonprofit and its "insiders" can easily result in greater public scrutiny for the nonprofit and adverse public relations.

Sometimes, a related party transaction may be economically advantageous to a nonprofit (for example, if a board member sells property to the nonprofit for less than its value in order for the nonprofit to build a necessary new facility). Even when a related party transaction is economically advantageous on its face, the nonprofit should consider whether public perception of the transaction will be positive.

A well-drafted conflicts-of-interest policy prescribes how a nonprofit and its leaders are to address potential business arrangements in order to ensure that they are proper and in the best interests of the nonprofit.

A sample conflicts-of-interest policy is provided in Appendix A.

Executive compensation-setting policy. Compensation arrangements for a nonprofit's top leaders have characteristics similar to the related party business transactions addressed above in the description of conflicts of interest. A leader should never be involved in the decision-making process with respect to his or her own compensation. As with related party business transactions, federal tax law sets forth parameters for permissible executive compensation by tax-exempt nonprofits. As with other types of related party transactions, violations in the arena of executive compensation can have dire consequences.

A well-drafted executive compensation policy prescribes the process for setting executive compensation and documenting the process, along with the data supporting the decision.

A sample executive compensation-setting policy is provided in Appendix B.

Dishonesty, fraud, and whistleblower protection policy. While it might seem to go without saying, in today's culture it is a good idea to have a policy that specifically prohibits illegal activity, fraud, and other financial improprieties. Such a policy removes any doubt about whether such conduct in a nonprofit is permissible. A dishonesty, fraud, and whistleblower protection policy both prohibits improper activity and prescribes the process by which an employee can report apparent improprieties. It also establishes the manner in which a nonprofit addresses such reports. A provision of the Sarbanes-Oxley federal law prohibits retaliation by employers against workers ("whistleblowers") for reporting certain improprieties. A well-drafted policy will help a nonprofit avoid violating this law.

A sample policy on dishonesty, fraud, and whistleblower protection is provided in Appendix C.

Document retention policy. The federal Sarbanes-Oxley law includes provisions prohibiting the destruction or falsification of documents subject to certain federal proceedings. Additionally, federal tax law and other laws allow regulatory authorities to examine the records of nonprofits for various reasons (compliance with employment law, employee benefits law, etc.). Such laws also require nonprofits to maintain appropriate records related to compliance with the laws. It is important for nonprofits to maintain records that may be required to be produced in the event of an IRS or other regulatory examination. Attorneys generally advise nonprofits to adopt a document retention policy prescribing the types of records to be maintained and the duration of time that they will be maintained. In some cases, attorneys specifically advise that such policies require destruction of documents after the applicable retention period.

A sample document retention and destruction policy is provided in Chapter 2.

Donor privacy policy. In the current era of pervasive spam emails and data breaches, donors are increasingly interested in knowing how their data will be used and protected once it is provided to the nonprofit. It is considered a best practice in the nonprofit sector to have a donor privacy policy and to make that policy readily available to donors. Key elements of a donor privacy policy include informing the donor as to what kinds of information is gathered, how the information is used, whether it will be shared with others and under what terms, and how the donor may opt out of certain aspects of the nonprofit's use of the data. Donor privacy policies are, by their nature, specific to the nonprofit and its use of donor and member information. For example, some nonprofits publish membership directories or similar resources and others do not.

ECFA provides a sample donor privacy policy, which it refers to as a "Sample Giver Privacy Policy" as follows (used by permission):

Sample Giver Privacy Policy

XYZ Organization is committed to respecting the privacy of our givers. We have developed this privacy policy to ensure our givers that giver information will not be shared with any third party.

Awareness. XYZ Organization provides this Giver Privacy Policy to make you aware of our privacy policy, and to inform you of the way your information is used. We also provide you with the opportunity to remove your name from our distribution list if you desire to do so.

Information collected. Here are the types of giver information that we collect and maintain:

Contact information: name, organization, complete address, phone number, email address

Payment information: credit card number and expiration date, and billing information

Shipping information: name, organization, complete address

Information concerning how you heard about XYZ Organization

Information you wish to share: questions, comments, suggestions

Your request to receive periodic updates; e.g., upon individual request, we will send periodic communications related to specific fundraising appeals and newsletters.

How information is used. XYZ Organization uses your information to understand your needs and provide you with better service. Specifically, we use your information to help you complete a transaction, to communicate back to you, and to update you on the organization's activities. Credit card numbers are used only for donation or payment processing and are not retained for other purposes. We use the comments you offer to provide you with information requested, and we consider carefully each recommendation as to how we might improve communication.

No sharing of personal information. XYZ Organization will not sell, rent, or lease your personal information to other parties. We assure you that the identity of all our givers will be kept confidential. Use of giver information will be limited to the internal purposes of XYZ Organization and only to further the program activities and purposes of XYZ Organization.

Removing your name from our communications. It is not our desire to send unwanted communications to our givers. Please contact us if you wish to be removed from our distribution list.

Contact us. If you have comments or questions about our giver privacy policy, please send us an email at info@XYZorganization.org or call us at (800) 123-4567.

Policy requiring board approval for the issuance of debt and other financial obligations. Many nonprofits have provisions in the bylaws that require the board (or sometimes, the organization's membership, if applicable) to approve issuance of any debt above a certain threshold or entering into any contractual obligation (e.g., a lease) to make ongoing payments in excess of a certain threshold. That is a good practice. An alternative to having such a provision in the bylaws is for the board to adopt a policy with such requirements. A bylaws provision or policy requirement could be worded along these lines (of course, the provisions should be tailored to the governance model of the particular nonprofit):

> Board approval is required for the issuance of any debt instrument with a principal amount in excess of $_____; for permitting any encumbrance, mortgage, or lien on any property or asset of the nonprofit; or for entering into any contractual commitment not included in a board-approved budget to make ongoing payments (e.g., lease payments) totaling more than $_____. [If the board wishes to require a supermajority of the members of the board to approve such commitments, such a requirement should be included in the bylaws or policy. For example, the board may wish for such com-

mitments to be approved by at least 75 percent of the board members currently holding office, as opposed to simply a majority of board members present at a meeting at which there is a quorum.]

POLICIES THAT NONPROFITS SHOULD HAVE IF CERTAIN FACTORS ARE PRESENT

Gift acceptance policy. A gift acceptance policy addresses a nonprofit's practices for evaluating atypical gifts. Examples would be gifts accompanied by naming rights restrictions (e.g., that a particular building be named after the donor), gifts with restrictions not accommodated by existing restricted funds, gifts of real estate, gifts of personal property, gifts of ownership interests in privately held businesses, gifts of stock in foreign entities, etc. The policy should address what parties or groups in the nonprofit have authority to evaluate and accept gifts covered by the policy and the factors or criteria to be considered in making such decisions.

A gift acceptance policy is appropriate for nonprofits that receive atypical gifts with some frequency. Even nonprofits that rarely receive such gifts may benefit from such a policy.

A sample gift acceptance policy is provided in Chapter 3.

Executive expense reimbursement policy. A well-drafted expense reimbursement policy will describe who is covered by the policy, parameters for expenses that will be paid or reimbursed by the nonprofit, and documentation requirements. For example, some nonprofits adopt policies prohibiting payment or reimbursement for alcohol, first class travel, room service, movies, or other items. Whether a nonprofit formally adopts such a policy or not, it should, of course, maintain practices that comply with applicable tax law.

Other policies. The policies described above are not intended to constitute an exhaustive list of financial policies that may be appropriate for a nonprofit's board to adopt. Depending on the specific circumstances, additional policies may be helpful...or even necessary. Other policies that may be considered include, but are not limited to:

- **Any policies required as a matter of law.** The nonprofit's legal counsel can help determine what specific policies may be required as a matter of law. (For example, federal tax law requires private, nonprofit, tax-exempt schools, including those operated by nonprofits, to adopt and apply a policy of racial nondiscrimination.)

- **Policy for spending restricted funds.** In order to avoid misunderstandings and possible conflicts, nonprofits that receive significant contributions restricted for particular purposes may benefit from a policy that clearly delineates who in the nonprofit has the authority to spend the restricted funds.
- **Investment policy.** Nonprofits with significant investment portfolios should have an investment policy clearly describing the nonprofit's investment risk tolerance and specific parameters for investment portfolio allocation. Nonprofits should ensure that, among other things, their investment policy and practices are in conformity with applicable state law. Investment policies are, by their nature, specific to the nonprofit, its risk tolerance, and its investment objectives. See Chapter 6 for more specific information about developing and documenting an investment philosophy and an investment policy.
- **Joint venture policy.** For nonprofits that engage in joint venture activities with for-profit companies, a joint venture policy may be necessary to ensure compliance with applicable tax law. Nonprofits considering entering into joint venture arrangements should do so only under the advice of appropriately experienced legal and tax counsel.

CHAPTER 11

Risk Management

Now more than ever before, nonprofit leaders must recognize the importance of risk management as an inherent part of organizational oversight and leadership. But what does proper risk management look like, and whose responsibility is it? Many nonprofit governing bodies (boards) assume that the nonprofit leadership staff have the bases covered and board involvement is often limited to reacting to flare-ups. Such an approach to risk management is problematic and dangerous for multiple reasons.

The members of leadership staff in a nonprofit are typically consumed with day-to-day operating activities and decisions—the "tyranny of the urgent." As a result, they frequently do not have or take the time to step back and proactively assess and address risks organization-wide. If that is the case, and the board is operating under the assumption that leadership staff has risk management covered, the nonprofit may be a ticking time-bomb for obvious reasons.

A COLLABORATIVE APPROACH INVOLVING BOTH THE BOARD AND STAFF

A key area of responsibility for the board is to ensure that the nonprofit maintains an adequate approach to risk management. While the actual conduct of risk management activities is the responsibility of leadership staff under the authority of the president or CEO, the board should evaluate the nonprofit's risk management strategy since the board has ultimate responsibility for oversight.

An effective risk management plan is a holistic one—one that addresses risk in all aspects of the nonprofit's activities. The risk management plan should also be proactive rather than reactive—identifying risks before they become liabilities and taking appropriate steps to mitigate them.

ALL RISKS ARE FINANCIAL RISKS

All organizational risks carry a financial component. For example, the risk that a nonprofit's building could be damaged by fire is both a physical risk and a financial risk. Noncompliance with applicable laws can also have financial implications. Even the risk of adverse public relations can have a financial impact—adverse public perception about a nonprofit can negatively affect financial support by donors. Having an appropriate approach to overall risk management will help the organization mitigate financial risks.

The board or its appropriate committee should work with the CEO to ensure on an organization-wide basis that:

- Risks are identified and assessed as to likelihood of occurrence and severity;
- Risks are prioritized;
- Leadership staff has determined the extent to which identified risks have been mitigated; and
- Appropriate steps are taken to reduce identified risks to acceptable levels.

PRACTICAL APPLICATION OF RISK MANAGEMENT STEPS

Practically applying the risk management steps described above is a relatively straightforward exercise. Let's look at each element more closely.

Identify the risks

In brainstorming discussions and meetings that involve key leaders and staff members from every operational area of the nonprofit, nonprofit leaders should identify the key types of risks that the nonprofit faces in every area of operations. Nonprofit leaders can use the list provided later in this chapter as a starting point for such discussions. In identifying risks, it is important to be specific about their description. Specificity in identifying and describing a risk is a key element necessary for properly mitigating it. As an example, a vague description of a risk such as "transportation safety" would be of little value in determining how to mitigate the risk. However, describing a risk as "causing an accident by texting while driving during a nonprofit activity" would certainly help nonprofit leaders as they seek to determine appropriate ways to mitigate the risk.

Assess the risks

Nonprofit leaders should take the risks identified in the first step and assess the magnitude of each identified risk. The magnitude of a risk is the combination of the probability of its occurrence and the severity of the impact if it were to occur. We can assign a quantification to our assessments of probability and impact of an identified risk. I suggest quantifying both probability and impact on a scale of 1 to 5, with 1 being lowest and 5 being highest. We can then plot the assessed components of probability and impact on a graph. We can use the combined assessment of likelihood and impact to prioritize identified risks.

EXAMPLE We know that sadly, the risk of child molestation is a pervasive risk for nonprofits that serve minors (children). We also know that the impact of an incident of child molestation involving a nonprofit or its leaders would be extremely severe. A nonprofit's leaders quantify the probability of child molestation risk at level 4 (on a scale of 1 to 5). The nonprofit's leaders quantify their assessment of the impact of child molestation risk at level 5. The nonprofit's leaders plot the combined assessed levels of probability and impact on a graph, noting that the plot point is at the upper right corner of the graph. Such a placement on the graph indicates that the risk of child molestation is one of very high priority. The nonprofit's leaders would perform the same exercise for other identified risks. The nonprofit's leaders may, for example, assess the risk of an accident being caused by an employee while driving and texting with a probability of 3 and an impact of 4.

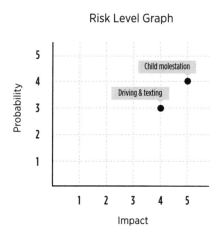

Prioritize the risks

Once risks have been assessed using an approach along the lines described above, nonprofit leaders should pursue risk mitigation on a priority basis. Risks assessed with the highest magnitude (combination of probability and impact) should be addressed first, and the list of identified and assessed risks can be pursued in priority order. Whether the nonprofit uses a quantification and graphing method like the one described above or some other method, the key point is that risks should be prioritized and the risks with the highest likelihood and potential for damage should be addressed first.

Determine the extent to which the risk being addressed has already been mitigated

As nonprofit leaders pursue mitigation of a particular risk that has been assessed and prioritized, the first step is to understand the extent to which the risk has already been addressed and mitigated. Nonprofit leaders should identify appropriate mitigation strategies for the risk (using experts, resources on the topic, and other appropriate points of reference). Nonprofit leaders should then determine the extent to which such mitigation strategies are already in place. A very important point to keep in mind here is that there may be a difference between what the nonprofit leaders believe has been implemented and what is actually happening. This can be true even if a nonprofit has a policy regarding a particular risk. Accordingly, in determining the extent to which mitigation strategies are in place, nonprofit leaders should "kick some tires"—that is, they should inspect and observe the practices that they believe are in place to confirm that they are in place and that they are being followed consistently.

> **EXAMPLE** Elm Private School has a policy directing that, to the extent practicable, at least two unrelated adults are to be present in classrooms where children are present for school activities. In addressing the extent to which appropriate risk mitigation strategies for child molestation are already in place, school leaders assume that the two-adult policy is being followed by workers consistently. The school leaders are unaware that the policy is regularly violated by a leader of the middle school program. Inspection or observation of the practices across the various programs of the school would [hopefully] help nonprofit leaders realize that the policy is not consistently followed.

Take appropriate steps to reduce the risk to an acceptable level

Any deficiencies that are identified between what the nonprofit believes are appropriate mitigation strategies to reduce the identified risk to an acceptable level and the strategies already in place should be addressed and corrected.

PREVENTIVE ACTION IS THE FIRST STEP—INSURANCE IS SECONDARY

Reducing risk by implementing preventive measures is, of course, a first step in risk mitigation. But implementing preventive measures is only one layer of risk management and it is different from insuring against risks. As part of its role in overseeing the adequacy of risk mitigation, the nonprofit's board should ensure that the nonprofit maintains appropriate insurance coverage with respect to applicable risk areas. (See the section later in this chapter on "Insurance coverage" for more information about the types of insurance commonly utilized by nonprofits.)

RISK MANAGEMENT IS AN ONGOING, RECURRING PROCESS

Proper risk management is not a once-and-done exercise. As time passes, circumstances change, people come and go, laws change, and the nature of risk changes. Accordingly, the multistep process of risk management is an ongoing, recurring, iterative process. Discussions about risk management and evaluation of the nonprofit's risks should be a standing agenda item for nonprofit leaders.

AREAS OF RISK TO CONSIDER

In addressing the nonprofit's overall risks, some key risk areas that warrant attention include, but are not limited to, the areas described below. Each area of risk listed is accompanied by a brief description and/or commentary. The description or commentary provided for each topic is not intended to be a thorough explanation—it is simply an overview in keeping with the purpose and scope of this book. Nonprofit leaders are not expected to be experts in the areas, but they are expected to take reasonable and appropriate steps to ensure that the risk areas are satisfactorily addressed. Accomplishing that objective may involve engaging specialists in certain fields who can provide their expert commentary to the organization in the appropriate areas. One way or another, the nonprofit board and leadership staff should determine that the risk areas (and any others that are applicable) are addressed to their reasonable satisfaction.

Corporate structure

Many nonprofits operate within one legal entity—typically a not-for-profit corporation. That one corporation typically conducts all of the activities of the nonprofit (including those that have more inherent risk than others) and owns all of the assets of the nonprofit (real estate, investments, cash, etc.). In today's litigious society, a nonprofit that owns significant assets and that conducts risk-generating activities should consider whether a one-entity legal structure is appropriate for risk mitigation purposes. Utilization of a multiple-entity structure could potentially help a nonprofit mitigate its financial risks—risks such as the loss of substantial assets due to an unreasonable or unfair "runaway jury" award in litigation that is not adequately covered by the nonprofit's insurance policies.

I, of course, do not advocate that any nonprofit shirk its appropriate legal and financial liability. But whether the award determined by a court or jury is fair or appropriate can be an entirely different matter. For example, if (God forbid) something bad happens to a child while on a trip with a nonprofit, is a liability of $10,000 reasonable? What about $1 million? Or what about $10 million? $50 million? In 2013, a student on a summer study trip with a Connecticut preparatory school was awarded $42 million by a jury in connection with a debilitating disease from a tick bite sustained during the trip. Whether the school had some legal responsibility and liability is one question. Whether that responsibility and liability should include a $42 million financial liability is a very different question. There is nothing unethical or improper about wisely structuring a nonprofit's corporate structure to limit exposure to liability. An attorney on the finance committee of an organization I served once stated the he believed it might be negligent for an organization's leaders not to consider corporate structure as a prudent risk management strategy.

A nonprofit wishing to avail itself of a multiple-entity structure should do so under the advice of excellent legal and tax counsel with specific experience in this area. It is important to preserve tax exemptions (federal, state, and local) for the entities involved as part of a corporate structure modification, and the rules for doing so are highly technical.

Some attorneys take the position that a multiple-entity structure is not effective in limiting exposure of a nonprofit's assets in the event of a liability claim that occurs in a related entity. I have worked in this area extensively with nonprofits across the country, together with highly respected attorneys from multiple high-profile law firms. The vast majority of attorneys with whom I have worked believe a multiple-entity structure can be an effective tool for risk mitigation when implemented properly. One attorney summed up his perspective noting that state laws allow corporations to have subsidiary corporations and limited liability companies for the very purpose of limiting liability. My firm and I have provided tax counsel to numerous nonprofits that have, under the advice of their legal counsel, adopted multiple-entity structures as part of an overall risk mitigation strategy.

No attorney will guarantee that a particular multiple-entity structure is "bullet-proof." But proper utilization of a multiple-entity structure may reduce an entity's exposure to loss in some situations. One prominent attorney described a multiple-entity structure as a "flying duck," which may be less prone to loss of assets than a "sitting duck."

Tax compliance
Compliance with applicable federal and other tax laws is a critical element of overall risk management. Chapter 9 addresses the topic of tax compliance specifically.

General legal compliance
Compliance with applicable law is, of course, a fundamentally important element of risk management for a nonprofit. Areas of law for which noncompliance can have significant implications include, but are not limited to:

- Laws addressing the legal manner of governance of the nonprofit
- Compliance with the nonprofit's own governing documents (articles of incorporation and bylaws)
- Compliance with key contractual agreements
    - Significant vendor contracts
    - Significant customer contracts
    - Significant loan agreements (including financial covenants)
- Human resources (labor, wage, healthcare, and employee benefits laws)
- Healthcare privacy laws
- Copyright law
- Laws governing the handling of donor-restricted funds
- Laws governing investment practices by nonprofit organizations
- Laws governing charitable solicitation and fundraising practices
- Laws governing the reporting of actual or suspected child abuse
- Zoning and land use laws
- Laws governing nondiscrimination in public accommodations
- Building codes

Nonprofits can assess their risks in these areas by consulting with legal experts specifically experienced in the applicable areas of law. Some law firms offer proactive assessment services sometimes referred to as "legal audits" that can help identify legal compliance issues that warrant attention.

Child molestation risk

For nonprofits that serve children, child molestation risk warrants special attention due to the severity of the damages that can occur. In recent years, an increasing number of high-liability claims have been made against nonprofits due to actual or alleged child molestation. Claims of that type can be devastating not only to the victims but also to a nonprofit and its leadership, both reputationally and financially. Multiple Catholic dioceses in the United States have filed for bankruptcy protection in connection with child molestation claims. The US Boy Scouts organization has also been subjected to numerous allegations and lawsuits in this area.   Many other nonprofits have experienced major claims. The board of a nonprofit should carefully evaluate the nature of the risks as well as prevention strategies and insurance coverage maintained by the nonprofit. Published resources are available on this topic. (See suggested references at the end of this chapter.)

Data security

Bad guys are continuously inventing new ways to attack and/or obtain sensitive data from people, government, businesses, and nonprofits. As technological capabilities continue to increase, and we live in an increasingly connected world, every nonprofit must consider the security of its sensitive data and employ reasonable steps to protect it. Failure to protect sensitive data can have legal, financial, and public relations ramifications, and in extreme situations, can jeopardize a nonprofit's ability to function. The board of a nonprofit should assess whether its leadership staff is adequately addressing risks related to data security.

Insurance coverage

One significant aspect of risk management includes ensuring that the nonprofit has appropriate insurance coverage for its significant risks. The evaluation of insurance coverage should include consultation with both legal counsel and highly experienced insurance agents. Specific coverage types to evaluate should include, but not be limited to:

- Property and casualty (for fire, theft, flood, earthquakes, sinkholes, vandalism, data loss, etc.);
- Business interruption;
- Data security, including cybersecurity;
- Employee theft;
- General liability;
- Sexual misconduct (including child molestation);
- Director and officer liability;
- Employment practices (for claims of discrimination, wrongful termination, sexual harassment, and other such matters related to employment practices);
- Fiduciary liability (for claims by employees related to the administration of employee benefit plans, particularly retirement plans); and
- "Key-man" life or disability (for financial remuneration to the nonprofit in the event of the death or disability of a key leader—useful where the nonprofit could be adversely affected financially in the event of such an occurrence).

Nonprofit leaders should discuss with their legal counsel and insurance agents whether they have risk exposures that may warrant other types of coverage.

Internal financial controls

A fundamental element of financial risk management involves ensuring that the nonprofit has an adequate and appropriate internal control structure in place with respect to financial activities. A detailed description of the topic of internal control is provided in Chapter 7.

Physical safety

A risk area of much more prominence today than in the past is that of physical safety. Physical safety risks can arise in many ways, including safety hazards in a nonprofit's facilities, transportation, and even violent confrontations (workplace violence, active shooters, etc.). A nonprofit's board should work with the CEO to ensure that the nonprofit has identified what it believes to be its significant risks in the area of physical safety and that it has implemented appropriate and reasonable safeguards to mitigate those risks where feasible. Since physical safety risks can take so many different forms, a nonprofit should consider engaging the services of experts to assist them in addressing particular risk areas. For example, a nonprofit that operates a school may wish to engage the services of local law enforcement authorities, or even a specialized consultant, with respect to the matter of school campus safety. A nonprofit with significant transportation activities may wish to engage a transportation safety consultant. Engaging and relying on the advice of experts in particularly high-risk areas can not only reduce physical safety risks, but can also help the nonprofit mount a legal defense in the event it is sued by a plaintiff claiming that the nonprofit was negligent.

Leadership succession

Many well-run and well-governed nonprofits suffer missionally and financially when a talented and charismatic leader retires or otherwise leaves the employment of the nonprofit. When such a departure comes suddenly and unexpectedly, the impact can be particularly severe. The topic of leadership succession can be uncomfortable for nonprofit leaders and boards to discuss. As with the topic of estate planning, many people simply don't like thinking about or discussing what will happen when they are no longer around. The same can be true when discussing the ultimate departure of a top leader from a nonprofit. However, a nonprofit's board must realize that, in many cases, the departure of a gifted leader with no succession plan creates a significant risk for the nonprofit—a risk that warrants attention.

Adequately addressing the issue of leadership succession does not necessarily mean picking the successor. A solid leadership succession plan may include designating with clarity who would serve as the acting leader in the event of the sudden and unexpected departure by the existing leader, together with a specific plan for how the next leader will be selected. Having a temporary contingent leadership plan in place, together with a well-thought-out process for selecting the next leader may be all that is needed. Without such measures in place, the departure of a top nonprofit leader can result in a period of confusion—and even heated disagreement—among board members and others at a time when the nonprofit is in a very vulnerable state. And it can significantly extend the amount of time required to identify and employ the next leader. Good planning by the nonprofit's board can prevent such a result.

Public relations

Controversial, adverse, high-profile publicity can be an unexpected and unwelcome guest for any nonprofit. Sometimes, a bad situation becomes worse because of how it is handled. When a nonprofit finds itself having to deal with adverse publicity, handling it properly is critical.

Imagine a tragedy of a child being severely injured in an accident while riding in a van provided by a nonprofit organization. The media pounces, seeking commentary from anyone who will comment. A television news station interviews a member of the nonprofit's staff who has no role whatsoever with respect to the organization's transportation operations. The staff member states that she has heard that there were some safety concerns about some of the vans, but doesn't know whether that had a role in the tragedy that occurred. That staff member's comments become a featured part of the news story broadcast about the incident.

Clearly, in the example described in the preceding paragraph, the staff member interviewed should not be making stray comments about matters of which he or she has no direct knowledge. Such comments could be damaging to the nonprofit. The risk of such stray commentary can be reduced significantly by implementing an appropriate media communications/public relations policy. Such a policy should clearly state who is authorized to speak to the media on behalf of the nonprofit and should prohibit others from doing so. The policy should be well-known to the nonprofit's employees.

Additionally, when and if a crisis occurs, a nonprofit may benefit significantly from the counsel of a public relations firm. It can be an added element of stress for the nonprofit to have to identify and hire such a firm in the middle of a crisis. If the nonprofit can proactively identify and establish a relationship with a public relations firm with which it is comfortable, that firm can jump right in to help in the unfortunate event that a crisis warrants public relations assistance.

ADDITIONAL RESOURCES

Some additional sources of information that may be helpful to nonprofits in addressing overall risk management include:

Nonprofit Risk Management Center

(nonprofitrisk.org)

Reducing the Risk: A Child Sexual Abuse Awareness Program

(reducingtherisk.com)

APPENDIX A

Sample Conflicts-of-Interest Policy

1. **Purpose.** The purpose of the conflicts-of-interest policy is to protect the Corporation's interest when it is contemplating entering into a transaction or arrangement that might benefit the private interest of an officer or director of the Corporation, or any other party that is a "disqualified person" as defined in federal income tax law. This policy is intended to supplement, but not replace, any applicable state laws governing conflicts of interest applicable to nonprofit corporations.

2. **Definitions.**

    (a) **Interested person.**

    (1) **General rule.** Any person who is a "disqualified person" within the meaning of Treas. Reg. §53.4958-3 is an "interested person" for purposes of this policy. Thus, any person who is, or during the preceding 5 years was, in a position to exercise substantial influence over the affairs of the Corporation is an "interested person." If an individual or entity is an interested person with respect to the Corporation or any entity affiliated with the Corporation, he or she is an interested person with respect to all affiliated entities.

    (2) **Particular persons.** Any person who is, or who was during the past 5 years, a director, principal officer, or member of a committee with board delegated powers, and who has a direct or indirect financial interest, as defined below, is an "interested person." In addition, the spouse, ancestors, siblings, and descendants (and spouse of any ancestor, sibling, or descendant) of any such person is an interested person. Finally, any business, trust, or estate, at least 35 percent of which is owned by one or more interested persons, is itself an interested person. Other factors, e.g., being the founder of the Corporation, a substantial contributor to the Corporation, or a key executive who is not an officer, will also

be taken into account in determining whether an individual or entity is an interested person.

(b) **Financial interest.** A person has a financial interest if the person has, directly or indirectly, through business, investment or family:

(1) an ownership or investment interest in any entity with which the Corporation has a transaction or arrangement;

(2) a compensation arrangement with the Corporation or with any entity or individual with which the Corporation has a transaction or arrangement; or

(3) a potential ownership or investment interest in, or compensation arrangement with, any entity or individual with which the Corporation is negotiating a transaction or arrangement.

(c) **Compensation** includes direct and indirect remuneration, as well as gifts or favors that are substantial in nature.

3. **Procedures.**

(a) **Duty to disclose.** In connection with any actual or possible conflict of interest, an interested person must disclose the existence and nature of his or her financial interest, and must be given the opportunity to disclose all material facts, to the directors and members of committees with board delegated powers that are considering the proposed transaction or arrangement.

(b) **Determining whether a conflict of interest exists.** After disclosure of the financial interest and all material facts, and after any discussion with the interested person, he/she shall leave the governing board or committee meeting while the determination of a conflict of interest is discussed and voted upon. The remaining board or committee members shall decide if a conflict of interest exists.

(c) **Procedures for addressing the conflict of interest.**

(1) An interested person may make a presentation at the board or committee meeting, but after the presentation, he or she shall leave the meeting during

the discussion of and the vote on the transaction or arrangement that results in the conflict of interest.

(2) The chairperson of the board or committee shall, if appropriate, appoint a disinterested person or committee to investigate alternatives to the proposed transaction or arrangement.

(3) After exercising due diligence, the board or committee shall determine whether the Corporation can obtain a more advantageous transaction or arrangement with reasonable efforts from a person or entity that would not give rise to a conflict of interest.

(4) If a more advantageous transaction or arrangement is not reasonably attainable under circumstances that would not give rise to a conflict of interest, the board or committee shall determine by a majority vote of the disinterested directors or committee members whether the transaction or arrangement is in the Corporation's best interest and for its own benefit, and whether the transaction is fair and reasonable to the Corporation. The board or committee shall make its decision as to whether to enter into the transaction or arrangement in conformity with such determination.

(5) Each agreement with an interested person shall contain an appropriate provision permitting the agreement to be modified or terminated in the event that the Internal Revenue Service determines that any transaction that is the subject of the agreement is an excess benefit transaction within the meaning of §4958 of the Internal Revenue Code.

(6) For purposes of this policy, a disinterested person is one who is not an interested person with respect to the transaction, who is not in an employment or other financial relationship with any disqualified person with respect to the transaction, and who does not have any other material financial interest that may be affected by the transaction.

(d) **Violations of the conflicts-of-interest policy.**

(1) If the board or committee has reasonable cause to believe that a member has failed to disclose actual or possible conflicts of interest, it shall inform the mem-

ber of the basis for such belief and afford the member an opportunity to explain the alleged failure to disclose.

(2) If, after hearing the response of the member and making such further investigation as may be warranted in the circumstances, the board or committee determines that the member has in fact failed to disclose an actual or possible conflict of interest, it shall take appropriate disciplinary and corrective action.

4. **Records of proceedings.** The minutes of the board and all committees with board authority shall contain:

(a) the names of the persons who disclosed or otherwise were found to have a financial interest in connection with a transaction or arrangement, and the nature of the financial interest; and

(b) the names of the persons who were present for discussions and votes relating to the transaction or arrangement, the content of the discussion, including any alternatives to the proposed transaction or arrangement, and a record of any votes taken in connection therewith.

5. **Compensation committees.** A voting member of the board of directors, or of any committee whose jurisdiction includes compensation matters, and who receives compensation, directly or indirectly, from the Corporation for services is precluded from discussing and voting on matters pertaining to that member's compensation. However, such a person is not prohibited from providing information to the board of directors or any committee regarding compensation of similarly situated persons.

6. **Annual statements.** Each director, principal officer and member of a committee with board delegated powers shall annually sign a statement which affirms that such person:

(a) has received a copy of this conflicts of interest policy;

(b) has read and understands the policy;

(c) has agreed to comply with the policy; and

APPENDIX A | Sample Conflicts-of-Interest Policy

(d) understands that the Corporation is a charitable organization and that in order to maintain its federal tax exemption it must engage primarily in activities which accomplish one or more of its tax-exempt purposes.

7. **Periodic reviews.** To ensure that the Corporation operates in a manner consistent with its charitable purposes and that it does not engage in activities that could jeopardize its status as an organization exempt from federal income tax, periodic reviews shall be conducted. The periodic reviews shall, at a minimum, include the following subjects:

(a) whether compensation arrangements and benefits are reasonable and are consistent with the results of arm's-length bargaining;

(b) whether acquisitions of goods or services result in inurement or impermissible private benefit;

(c) whether partnership and joint venture arrangements conform to written policies, are properly recorded, reflect reasonable payments for goods and services, further the Corporation's charitable purposes and do not result in inurement or impermissible private benefit; and

(d) whether agreements to provide goods or services further the Corporation's charitable purposes and do not result in inurement or impermissible private benefit.

8. **Use of outside experts.** In conducting the periodic reviews provided for in Section 7, the Corporation may, but need not, use outside advisors. If outside experts are used, their use shall not relieve the board of its responsibility for ensuring that periodic reviews are conducted.

APPENDIX B

Sample Executive Compensation-Setting Policy

Section 1.01

Setting and approval of key executive employee compensation arrangements. Compensation arrangements of key executive employees of the Corporation shall be approved in advance by an authorized body (as defined in Section 1.03) of the Corporation who shall have obtained and relied upon appropriate data as to comparability (as defined in Section 1.05) prior to making its determination. The authorized body shall adequately document (as defined in Section 1.06) the basis for its determination concurrently with making that determination.

Section 1.02

Key executive employee. For purposes of this policy, the term "key executive employee" includes the officers and directors of the Corporation and any individual who has powers and responsibilities similar to officers and directors of the Corporation. The term includes any person who, regardless of title, has ultimate responsibility for implementing the decisions of the Board, for supervising the management, administration, or operation of the Corporation as a whole, or for managing the finances of the Corporation as a whole.

Section 1.03

Authorized body. The term "authorized body" shall, with respect to the CEO or top management official of the Corporation, include the Board of Directors of the Corporation or a committee of the Board of Directors, which may be composed of any individuals permitted under state law or the Corporation's Bylaws to serve on such a committee, to the extent that the committee is permitted by state law to act on behalf of the Board of Directors. However, such authorized body shall be composed solely of individuals who do not have a conflict of interest (as defined in Section 1.04) with respect to such compensation arrangement.

With respect to key executive employees other than the CEO or top management official, the authorized body consists solely of the CEO, who is authorized by the Board of Directors to establish such compensation, provided that the CEO does not have a conflict of interest (as defined in Section 1.04) with respect to such compensation arrangement. In the event that the CEO has a conflict of interest with respect to any key executive employee, the authorized body with respect to that employee shall be the authorized body described in the preceding paragraph.

Section 1.04
Absence of conflict of interest. A member of the governing body authorized to approve key executive employee compensation arrangements does not have a conflict of interest with respect to a compensation arrangement only if the member:

(a) Is not a disqualified person (within the meaning of Treas. Reg. §53.4958-3) participating in or economically benefiting from the compensation arrangement, and is not a member of the family (as defined in Treas. Reg. §53.4958-3(b)(1)) of any such disqualified person;

(b) Is not in an employment relationship subject to the direction or control of any disqualified person participating in or economically benefiting from the compensation arrangement;

(c) Does not receive compensation or other payments subject to approval by any disqualified person participating in or economically benefiting from the compensation arrangement;

(d) Has no material financial interest affected by the compensation arrangement; and

(e) Does not approve a transaction providing economic benefits to any disqualified person participating in the compensation arrangement, who in turn has approved or will approve a transaction providing economic benefits to the member.

Section 1.05
Appropriate data as to comparability. The authorized body has appropriate data as to comparability if, given the knowledge and expertise of its members, it has information sufficient to determine whether the compensation arrangement in its entirety is reasonable. Relevant information shall include, but is not limited to, compensation levels paid by similarly situated organizations, both taxable and tax-exempt, for functionally comparable positions; the availability of similar services in the geographic area of the Corpora-

tion; current compensation surveys compiled by independent firms; and actual written offers from similar institutions competing for the services of the individual for whom the compensation arrangement is being set. Updated comparability data should be obtained by the authorized body on a periodic basis, generally at least every three years. However, more frequent updates of comparability data should be obtained if annual compensation increases exceed a modest percentage in keeping with increases generally applicable to all employees.

Section 1.06

Adequate documentation. The written or electronic records of the authorized body shall note:

(a) The terms of the compensation arrangement that was approved and the date it was approved;

(b) The members of the authorized body who were present during debate on the compensation arrangement that was approved and those who voted on it;

(c) The comparability data obtained and relied upon by the authorized body and how the data was obtained; and

(d) Any actions taken with respect to consideration of the compensation arrangement by anyone who is otherwise a member of the authorized body but who had a conflict of interest with respect to the compensation arrangement.

If the authorized body determines that reasonable compensation for a specific arrangement is higher than the range of comparability data obtained, the authorized body must record the basis for its determination.

The documentation outlined in this section shall be duly recorded in the minutes of the authorized body before the later of the next meeting of the authorized body or 60 days after the final action or actions of the authorized body are taken. Such records shall be reviewed and approved by the authorized body as reasonable, accurate and complete within a reasonable time period thereafter.

APPENDIX C

Sample Policy on Dishonesty, Fraud, and Whistleblower Protection

Ethical and Legal Standards for Conduct
[Insert Organization name here] ("**the Organization**") requires all of its directors, officers and employees to observe high standards of business and personal ethics in the conduct of their duties and responsibilities. As employees and representatives of **the Organization**, we must practice honesty and integrity in fulfilling our responsibilities and comply with applicable laws and regulations.

Reporting responsibility
It is the responsibility of all directors, officers and employees to report actual or suspected acts of dishonesty, fraud, or illegal activity in accordance with this policy.

No retaliation
No director, officer or employee who in good faith reports a matter described in the preceding paragraph shall suffer harassment, retaliation or adverse employment consequence. An employee who retaliates against someone who has reported a matter in good faith is subject to discipline up to and including termination of employment. This policy is intended to encourage and enable employees and others to raise serious concerns within **the Organization** prior to seeking resolution outside **the Organization**.

Reporting violations
The Organization maintains an open-door policy and suggests that employees share their questions, concerns, suggestions or complaints with someone who can address them properly. In most cases, an employee's supervisor is in the best position to address an area of concern. However, if you are not comfortable speaking with your supervisor or you are not satisfied with your supervisor's response, you are encouraged to speak with someone in the Human Resources Department or anyone in management whom you are comfortable in approaching. Supervisors and managers are required to report actual or suspected acts of

dishonesty, fraud, or illegal activity to **the Organization**'s Compliance Officer, who has specific and exclusive responsibility to investigate all reported violations. For suspected fraud, or when you are not satisfied or uncomfortable with following **the Organization**'s open-door policy, individuals should contact **the Organization**'s Compliance Officer directly.

Compliance Officer

The Organization's Compliance Officer is responsible for investigating and resolving all reported complaints and allegations concerning actual or suspected acts of dishonesty, fraud, or illegal activity and, at his discretion, shall advise the Executive Director and/or the audit committee. The Compliance Officer has direct access to the audit committee of the board of directors and is required to report to the audit committee at least annually on compliance activity. **The Organization**'s Compliance Officer is **[Insert title of designated Compliance Officer. For example, the chair of the audit committee]. [Note: If the Organization does not have an audit committee or its equivalent, change the reference to the finance committee or the board of directors itself.]**

Accounting and auditing matters

The audit committee of the board of directors shall address all reported concerns or complaints regarding corporate accounting practices, internal controls or auditing. The Compliance Officer shall immediately notify the audit committee of any such complaint and work with the committee until the matter is resolved. **[Note: If the Organization does not have an audit committee or its equivalent, change the reference to the finance committee or the board of directors itself.]**

Acting in good faith

Anyone filing a complaint concerning actual or suspected acts of dishonesty, fraud, or illegal activity must be acting in good faith and have reasonable grounds for believing the information disclosed indicates a violation of **the Organization's** policy. Any allegations that prove not to be substantiated and which prove to have been made maliciously or knowingly to be false will be viewed as a serious offense subject to disciplinary action.

Confidentiality

Violations or suspected violations may be submitted on a confidential basis by the complainant or may be submitted anonymously. Reports of violations or suspected violations will be kept confidential to the extent possible, consistent with the need to conduct an adequate investigation.

Handling of reported violations

The Compliance Officer will notify the sender and acknowledge receipt of the reported violation or suspected violation within five business days. All reports will be promptly investigated and appropriate corrective action will be taken if warranted by the investigation.